THE EPOCHS OF PHILOSOPHY

Edited by JOHN GRIER HIBBEN, Princeton University

The aim of the series on *The Epochs of Philosophy* is to present the significant features of philosophical thought in the chief periods of its development. There is no attempt to give a complete account in every case of the men or their works which these various periods have produced; but rather to estimate and interpret the characteristic contributions which each age may have made to the permanent store of philosophical knowledge. Such a process of interpretation, therefore, must be necessarily selective. And in the light of the specific purposes of this series the principle of selection suggests itself, namely, to emphasise especially those doctrines which have appeared as effective factors in the evolution of philosophical thought as a whole. Moreover, these various periods are intimately connected; the history is a continuous one. While there are several distinct epochs of philosophy, there is but one movement of philosophical thought, and it is hoped that the present series will serve, in some slight measure at least, to deepen the impression of that fundamental unity which characterises the progress of philosophy through the many phases of its development.

VOLUMES AND AUTHORS

THE BEGINNINGS OF GREEK PHILOSOPHY
  By F. J. E. WOODBRIDGE, Professor in Columbia University.

THE PLATONIC PHILOSOPHY
  By A. E. TAYLOR, Professor of Moral Philosophy, St. Andrew's University.

THE ARISTOTELIAN PHILOSOPHY
  By PAUL SHOREY, Professor of Greek, University of Chicago.

THE EPOCHS OF PHILOSOPHY

STOIC AND EPICUREAN
 By R. D. Hicks, Fellow and late Lecturer Trinity College, Cambridge. (Now ready.)

NEO-PLATONISM AND CHRISTIANITY
 By F. W. Bussell, Vice-Principal of Brasenose College, Oxford.

THE MEDIÆVAL PHILOSOPHY
 (Author to be announced later.)

THE PHILOSOPHY OF THE RENAISSANCE
 By Charles M. Bakewell, Professor of Philosophy, Yale University.

THE RISE OF THE HISTORICAL METHOD IN PHILOSOPHY
 By J. E. Creighton, Professor of Logic and Metaphysics, Cornell University.

THE PHILOSOPHY OF RATIONALISM
 By Frank Thilly, Professor of Ethics, Cornell University.

THE PHILOSOPHY OF THE ENLIGHTENMENT
 By John Grier Hibben, Professor of Logic, Princeton University. (Now ready.)

THE CRITICAL PHILOSOPHY
 By Josiah Royce, Professor of the History of Philosophy, Harvard University.

THE IDEALISTIC MOVEMENT OF THOUGHT IN THE NINETEENTH CENTURY
 By J. B. Baillie, Professor of Moral Philosophy, Aberdeen University.

An additional volume (title to be announced later) is expected from A. S. Pringle-Pattison, Professor of Logic and Metaphysics in the University of Edinburgh.

THE PHILOSOPHY
OF THE ENLIGHTENMENT

'Αλλ', ὦ φίλε, ἦν δ' ἐγώ, μέτρον τῶν τοιούτων ἀπολεῖπον καὶ ὁτιοῦν τοῦ ὄντος οὐ πάνυ μετρίως γίγνεται· ἀτελὲς γὰρ οὐδὲν οὐδενὸς μέτρον.—PLATO, *Republic*, VI, 504, C.

EPOCHS OF PHILOSOPHY

THE PHILOSOPHY OF THE ENLIGHTENMENT

BY

JOHN GRIER HIBBEN, Ph.D., LL.D.
STUART PROFESSOR OF LOGIC, PRINCETON UNIVERSITY

NEW YORK
CHARLES SCRIBNER'S SONS
1910

Copyright, 1910, by
CHARLES SCRIBNER'S SONS

Published February, 1910

TO
MY DAUGHTER

PREFACE

THE age of the *Enlightenment* has a peculiar interest and value for the student of the history of philosophy. The philosophical output of this period is unusually rich and significant, embracing as it does the classical writings of Locke, Berkeley, Hume, Leibniz, Rousseau and Kant, and therefore may well be studied for the material which these separate contributions severally contain. But, more than this, the eighteenth-century philosophy is a period in which a great movement of thought is exhibited, and that, too, on a large and conspicuous stage. England, France, Germany form its settings. It begins with Locke and is completed in Kant. And whatever significance Kant may possess for the philosophical world to-day attaches also to this period, for this period served to open the way for the critical philosophy of the great master which is its appropriate culmination.

Moreover, the practical influences of the philosophical discussions of this age are of such extent and importance as to engage the attention of the ordinary reader of history, as well as that of the more special worker in the field of philosophy. In England religious controversy, political theory, and moral standards were profoundly affected by the philosophical tendencies of the day; in France the social and political doctrines became involved with the philosophical, and they were not without a dominating influence upon the popular mind, not only throughout the period preceding the French Revolution, but also during the years of its progress as well; in Germany the same tendencies manifested themselves in theological controversy on the one hand, and in the quickening of poetical insight and interpretation on the other, so that poets became philosophers, and philosophers became poets. The movement of philosophical thought in this age, moreover, is typical of great movements of thought generally, and in this aspect is both illuminating and suggestive as a representative historical study. The tendencies which here prevail, the characteristic differences in point of view, as well as the complementary relation of opposed opinions, are all repeated again and again in the various political, social, religious, moral, and philosophical controversies which emerge through every significant period in the history of thought.

I wish to take this opportunity of expressing my indebtedness to my friend and colleague, Professor Norman Smith, whose suggestions and criticism have proved invaluable to me in the preparation of this book.

J. G. H.

PRINCETON, *January* 30, 1910.

CONTENTS

CHAPTER I

PAGE

THE AGE OF THE ENLIGHTENMENT . . . 3

The period from Locke's *Essay* to Kant's *Critique*, 3; characteristic features of the eighteenth-century philosophy, 3; the *Essay Concerning Human Understanding*, 6; the three stages of the movement of thought in this century, 7; idealism of Berkeley, 9; materialistic movement in England and France, 10; scepticism of Hume, 11; the function of scepticism in the development of thought, 12; the rationalism of Leibniz, 13; Kant's work of reconstruction, 15; influence of Rousseau, 16; offices of the practical reason, 16; practical influences of the *Enlightenment*, 18; deism, 19; utilitarianism, 19; individualism in politics, 20; Kant's contribution to the practical problems of this age, 21; references, 24.

CHAPTER II

LOCKE'S INNER AND OUTER WORLD . . . 25

Locke's love of truth, 25; origin of the *Essay*, 26; an appeal for intellectual freedom, 27; his method, psychological, 27; Locke's inner world, sensation and reflection, 29; mind, regarded as passive in receiving the sensory materials of knowledge, 31; its later activity, mechanical, 34; the mind's organising function, 38; Leibniz's criticism of Locke, 38; intellectualism of Locke, 39; canon of philosophical criticism, 40; the idea of self, 42; Locke's outer world, 44; reality of knowledge, 44; primary and secondary qualities of matter, 46; nature of substance, 48; idea of God, 51; concept of causation, 53; influence of Locke, 55; references, 56.

CONTENTS

CHAPTER III
BERKELEY'S IDEALISM . . . . **PAGE 57**

Relation to Locke, 57; no material substance, 59; no abstract ideas, 60; no distinction between primary and secondary qualities of matter, 60; theory of vision, 61; Berkeley's idealism explained, 62; idea of God, 66; doctrine of spiritual substance, 68; causation, 69; universal language of nature, 71; criticism of Berkeley, 72; notion and idea, 73; idealism of the *Siris*, 75; anticipations of Kant, 80; Berkeley in America, 81; references, 84.

CHAPTER IV
HUME'S SCEPTICISM **85**

Relation to Locke and Berkeley, 85; his argument a *reductio ad absurdum* of Locke's position, 87; Huxley on Hume, 87; impressions and ideas, 88; Hume's fundamental canon of criticism, 89; doctrine of causation, 90; doctrine of substance, 93; idea of self, 95; criticism of Hume, 97; abstract ideas, 99; function of imagination in thought, 100; Hume, sceptical of his own scepticism, 102; relation to Kant, 104; effect upon Thomas Reid, 108; references, 110.

CHAPTER V
THE MATERIALISTIC MOVEMENT IN ENGLAND AND FRANCE **111**

Relation to Locke, 111; David Hartley, 112; Joseph Priestley, 116; Voltaire's *Lettres sur les Anglais*, 119; Condillac, 120; Helvetius, 122; Lamettrie, 123; Diderot, 124; Holbach, 131; Cabanis, 134.

CHAPTER VI
ROUSSEAU'S PHILOSOPHY OF FEELING . . . **136**

Relation to the *Encyclopædists*, 136; his early materialism, 136; his protest on behalf of feeling, 138; *Profession of faith of the Savoyard Vicar*, 141; man regarded as a machine, 144; Rousseau's *Discourses*, 145; *Contrat Social*, 148; reason and feeling, 150; individualism, 152;

CONTENTS xi

Confessions, 153; feeling and conduct, 154; Rousseau's pragmatism, 157; influence upon Kant, 158; references, 160.

CHAPTER VII

THE PHILOSOPHY OF LEIBNIZ 161

Relation to Locke, 161; the *Nouveaux Essais*, 162; Leibniz's rationalism, 163; the *Characteristica Universalis*, 164; symbolic logic, 165; doctrine of substance, 166; substance as entelechy, 169; doctrine of the monads, 170; the identity of indiscernibles, 171; appetition, 172; representative function of the monads, 173; perception, 174; theory of causation, 176; relation of monads to God, 177; pre-established harmony, 178; relation of mind to body, 181; parallelism, 183; efficient and final causes, 183; world of nature and world of divine purpose, 184; Leibniz's theory of knowledge, 185; Kant's task, 188; substance as a centre of force, 188; doctrine of evolution, 190; summary, 193; references, 193.

CHAPTER VIII

THE CONFLICT OF TYPICAL PHILOSOPHICAL INFLUENCES IN GERMANY 194

Kant's characterisation of the *Aufklärung*, 194; influence of Leibniz and Wolff, 194; influence of Locke, 195; pietism, 195; the poet-philosophers, 196; Wolff's philosophy and influence, 197; Lessing and his philosophy, 200; *Wolfenbüttler Fragmente*, 203; Herder, 206; influence of Spinoza, 208; Thomasius, 210; popular philosophers, 210; Mendelssohn, 211; Nicolai, 212; empirical philosophy of Tetens, 212; summary, 213; references, 214.

CHAPTER IX

THE CRITICAL PHILOSOPHY OF KANT . . . 215

Kant's relation to the *Aufklärung*, 215; the mediating tendency of his mind, 216; periods in his philosophical thinking, 217; the *Dissertation*, 219; letter to Marcus Herz,

220; the *Critique of Pure Reason*, a logic of limits, 222; transcendental method, 223; meaning of *a priori*, 224; synthetic and analytic judgments, 225; synthetic judgments *a priori*, 226; metaphysic of induction, 227; nature of causation, 228; nature of thought, 229; divisions of the *Critique*, 231; forms of sensibility, 233; *categories* of the understanding, 235; phenomena and noumena, 238; *Ideas* of the reason, 240; the *antinomies*, 244; *Kritik der praktischen Vernunft*, 247; *Kritik der Urtheilskraft*, 249; summary, 251; references, 252.

CHAPTER X

THE PRACTICAL INFLUENCES OF ENLIGHTENMENT 253

Three lines of influence, 253; Locke's ethical position, 254; Hume's treatment of Locke's premises, 259; Hume's idea of sympathy, 261; Adam Smith, 262; David Hartley and associationism, 264; Mandeville, 267; Shaftesbury, 268; philosophy of deism, 272; Locke's influence, 273; the English deists, 275; Hume on religion, 276; deism in France and Germany, 279; political tendencies, 280; Locke's *Treatises of Government*, 280; influence in England and France, 281; Rousseau's *Contrat Social*, 282; Kant's contribution to the ethical influences of this age, 284; to the religious, 286; to the political, 290; references, 292.

LIST OF LITERARY WORKS OF THIS PERIOD 293

INDEX 307

THE PHILOSOPHY OF THE ENLIGHTENMENT

THE PHILOSOPHY OF THE ENLIGHTENMENT

CHAPTER I

THE AGE OF THE ENLIGHTENMENT

The significant movement of thought known as the *Enlightenment*, or *Aufklärung*, falls in the main within the period of the eighteenth century. It is seldom, however, that the turn of a century happens to coincide exactly with the beginning or the end of a great epoch, either political, religious or philosophical. The period in philosophy which is referred to in a general way as the eighteenth century begins virtually in the year 1690 with the publication of Locke's famous *Essay Concerning Human Understanding*, and is brought to its close in the year 1781 with the appearance of Kant's *Critique of Pure Reason*. They are the natural boundaries of this "philosophical century."

It was an age characterised by a restless spirit of inquiry—a century of challenge. A new life was awake and stirred in the minds of men. Traditions which had been long venerated became the objects of searching investigation and criticism. The authority of the church, of the state and of the school was no longer regarded as the court of last appeal. The old beliefs which failed to justify themselves at the bar of reason were discarded. The foundations of time-honoured systems seemed shifting and uncertain. There was an insistent demand for the free play of the individual judgment. There was, also, a constant reference to the light of reason, the inner illumination shining bright and clear in contrast to the shadows of mysticism, or to the false and flickering light of dogmatism. Hence the name of the age of illumination, or enlightenment,—the name, also, of the age of reason.

In this period there was more particularly a spirit of protest against metaphysical speculation, that is, against all attempts to explain the phenomena of human existence in any manner which transcends the ordinary processes of reason, and consequently possesses no firm foundation of reality. And reality, in turn, was conceived as that which is akin to nature and to the general course of natural phenomena as perceived through the channels of the various senses. There was an attempt to reduce the problems of thought to the basis of extreme simplicity, and to make a common-sense view of things everywhere prevail.

The spirit of the age might find characteristic expression in some such words as these: Let us not concern ourselves with idle speculation in reference to things which the mind of man can never compass and understand. Why busy ourselves concerning the deeper significance and purpose of nature which our thought is utterly incapable of penetrating? While we may observe and classify the phenomena of nature, and formulate the laws of their behaviour, we can never hope to comprehend their inner meaning, forever veiled and obscure. Nature, which seems so near—of which, indeed, we ourselves are a part—

THE AGE OF THE ENLIGHTENMENT 5

nevertheless lies far beyond our ken. And the being and nature of God, who must be regarded as dwelling in a sphere far out and beyond the outermost bounds of nature, must remain still more incomprehensible. If we cannot understand the inscrutable mysteries of the world which we have seen, much less the mystery of God whom we have not seen. From the contemplation, therefore, of the world and of God, we must turn our eyes to the more rewarding study of the inner self. Let every man examine the phenomena of life as they unfold themselves within this inner world of his own consciousness. Here at least is the light in which he can see light. To every one who thus mines the treasures of his own nature there must come the quiet satisfaction of being able to insist, I know myself. Such is the spirit of this age. It is reflected in Pope's line,

"The proper study of mankind is man."

In this search after knowledge, while inquiry was introspective, it was not by any means reflective. It lacked penetration, and while moving freely and thoroughly in a careful surface investigation, it was never able to fathom and explore the lower depths of thought.

It was a restricted area of inquiry, therefore, which the philosophy of the *Enlightenment* set for itself. If in this region, it was urged, there can be found no evidence for the existence of God, then faith must not hold what reason cannot prove; if there are no immutable principles of morality clearly attested, then man must be content with a working ethic of prudence and expediency; if there are no intimations of immortality, one can at least live in the fulness of the present; if the foundations of the state are shaken, then let the state itself fall with them; but in spite of what may be lost or of what may be saved, let no one's convictions transcend the actual and indisputable facts upon which they are observed to rest. Let man once for all penetrate "the mist and veil of words," and get at the truth of things. If there is no appeal to "the god of things as they are," there is, at least, the appeal direct to things as they are themselves.

With all of its obvious limitations and defects, this method of inquiry was nevertheless frank, open-minded and ingenuous. The right of individual opinion was respected; a spirit of tolerance prevailed; and philosophy was afforded a free forum.

The key-note of the age was set by John Locke scholar of Christ Church, Oxford, trained in the diplomatic service, widely travelled, secretary of the first Earl of Shaftesbury, a profound student of the theory of government, champion of toleration, a man of affairs, and withal a philosopher, whose habit of mind fitted him in an eminent degree to deal with speculative problems from a practical point of view. In his *Essay Concerning Human Understanding*, Locke insists that all knowledge comes to us from two sources only—from sensation and reflection. Therefore we ought scrupulously to eliminate from our philosophy everything which it is not possible to trace to this elemental origin. Aught else of speculation, of sentiment or of opinion rests upon a basis of fancy and not of fact. All inquiry, consequently, must be limited to the problems which arise in this field. Beyond these lies not only the undiscovered country, but the undiscoverable as well.

The world of knowledge from this point of view shows a variety of manifold forms, but is of one and the same substance throughout, namely, that which is constantly supplied by the ceaseless activity of the senses. Thus we find the problem of knowledge reduced to its lowest terms. By restricting the area of knowledge, the area of difficulty is likewise diminished; for many perplexing problems are thus eliminated, and a common-sense method of interpreting actually observed facts of experience commends itself as involving only clear ideas which all mankind can understand and appreciate. It was, indeed, a characteristic feature of this age, the demand that all ideas should be clear and self-illuminating. It was a part of the heritage which had come to that generation from Descartes, who had emphatically insisted that clear and distinct ideas are to be regarded as the sole test of truth. Locke placed before his own mind the same standard, and sought to realise it by a simplification of the sources of knowledge. It is here that the development of thought in the age of the *Enlightenment* had its beginning.

The history of this development illustrates certain fundamental principles concerning the progress of thought which are not only of interest in themselves, but will serve also to stimulate the critical insight and appreciation of any one who undertakes the serious study of this period of philosophy. We find in the eighteenth century a great movement of thought, which furnishes us a basis for an historical study of the theory of knowledge. But this is not all. It may be regarded also as the type of great thought movements in general. It has in this respect peculiarly a representative value; for if we interpret aright the controlling forces which underlie this development, and the various phases of their manifestation, there will be disclosed, in rough outline at least, the programme which every progressive movement of thought tends to follow. There are three stages of such a development. The first is that in which some significant idea finds expression, and, because not yet fully developed, it is necessarily partial, one-sided or extreme. The second stage is that of controversy. The idea must be subjected to a running fire of criticism. Whatever it may conceal as contradictory, incoherent or absurd, will thus be brought to light. The third stage is always a period of reconstruction, wherein contradictions are resolved, limitations are removed, and whatever may have been inadequate is completed by supplying the complementary elements which were wanting in the original doctrine or theory. This Hegelian procedure is illustrated in the progress of philosophical thought which the eighteenth century produced. And such a method of thought development is by no means a fanciful conceit of Hegel's. It is a process which is familiar to every one who, in his own thinking, has become conscious of the expanding and transforming stages through which his various opinions have passed, from the initial assertion, through the testing of criticism and controversy, until the final reconstruction and restatement of the original belief is reached.

At the beginning of such a development as that which the eighteenth century exhibits, the content of philosophical thought is reduced to a minimum. Its simplicity, however, is that of a germ possessing in a high degree the potential of an exceedingly complex growth. Any idea which starts a great movement of thought must be subjected to the practical test of its power to adapt itself to all possible varieties of mental environment. It must be received into many and various types of minds; it must adjust itself to many different temperaments, and be regarded from many points of view. It is only in this manner that its full significance can be revealed, and its true worth adequately appreciated. In this period of trying out, whatever is potential in the initial idea will be rendered actual; its logical implications will be made explicit, and their necessary consequences set forth in a rigorous and complete manner; whatever is partial will be revealed, and all latent error will be eliminated.

This is exactly what occurred in reference to Locke's fundamental contention that we know only that which comes through the avenues of the senses, and what may follow from reflection upon the material which is thus furnished. An exceedingly simple statement of the sources of knowledge. But there is no statement, however simple, which is not beset with difficulties and which may not become the subject of radical differences of opinion, and possibly of heated controversy. This simple statement of the Lockian theory of knowledge experienced two diametrically opposite phases of development, which in itself indicates its indefiniteness and incompleteness. One of these phases was essentially idealistic and the other materialistic, and each in turn grounded in the original premisses of Locke concerning the sources of knowledge.

The idealistic interpretation is represented by Bishop Berkeley. Starting from Locke's stand-point that the elemental springs of knowledge are to be traced to the sensations, Berkeley insists that inasmuch as every sensation is an experience occurring in the individual consciousness, it must be composed, therefore, at the last analysis, of that which is mental and not physical. Whatever appears in consciousness must partake of the character of the very element in which it appears. As to the physical object of sensation which is supposed to be outside of us and is regarded crudely as its cause, we know absolutely nothing. We know only the passing phenomena of consciousness whose parts are fashioned of mental elements or thought entities. To say, as Locke does, that we know only sensations originally, means, therefore, according to Berkeley's interpretation, that we know merely the objects of knowledge as they appear to us in consciousness, wrought of the elements of the mind only. Ideas, therefore, are the stuff out of which our experience is formed. While Locke had said that there was some external object corresponding to every perception, although its true nature could never be known to the observing mind, Berkeley insists that there is no external object to know other than the idea in the mind. Our ideas which come to us through sense perception do not represent a world lying beyond them; they are that world itself.

At the same time and, strangely enough, under the same influence, there developed a sensationalistic philosophy, which in its extreme form drifted inevitably into materialism. It flourished not only on British soil, but survived its transplanting into France, and with the changed environment gained in vigour and extent. In England this phase of the movement is represented by Hartley, Priestley, Erasmus Darwin and others; in France by that brilliant coterie of writers who gave to the world the French Encyclopædia and the revolutionary philosophy. Of this group the most pronounced in the creed of materialism were Diderot, Helvetius and Holbach.

Here surely is an anomaly. How can the same premisses yield so widely different conclusions? How

THE AGE OF THE ENLIGHTENMENT 11

can Locke's empirical beginnings develop on the one hand into Berkeley's idealism, and on the other into Holbach's materialistic and atheistic *Le Système de la nature?* The situation, however, is not an impossible one. Upon a closer consideration, it will be seen to be both logical and natural. For we may lay it down as a general principle characteristic of every great movement of thought that, starting from a statement which is merely a partial expression of the complete truth, it must necessarily give rise to opposed results according to radical differences in the point of view and the method of interpretation. Moreover, every movement of thought must find its beginnings in some partial and indefinite expression of truth; for if it should start with a complete statement of truth, it would then be absurd to expect any possible development of it.

This, therefore, may be regarded as the first characteristic of every significant movement of thought, an initial doctrine, regarded from a single and circumscribed point of view, developing diametrically opposed conclusions. The simplicity of the original statement thus at once breaks up in the process of interpretation and elaboration into a complexity of contradictory opinions, and these contradictions clearly prove the original incompleteness.

The inadequacy of the beginnings of thought may also be illustrated more directly and particularly by showing that the conclusions which logically follow from them are unsatisfactory as a final explanation, and that the seemingly firm foundations upon which they rest are shifting and uncertain. In reference to the philosophical position of Locke, we find the task of exposing its fundamental weakness falling to the lot of David Hume. The philosophy of Hume is a natural reaction from the extreme position of Berkeley, and at the same time its logical outcome. Because of the unsatisfactory results which Hume reaches in the logical unfolding of Locke's theory of knowledge, his attitude becomes one of radical scepticism. If Berkeley's position is tenable that Locke's doctrine leaves us only ideas as the material of our knowledge, then, Hume insists, we may, it is true, construct these elemental ideas into a world in which we can live and move and have our being; but we have no assurance whatsoever that the component elements are held together by any bonds of necessary connection, or that they possess any inherent substantiality. We think that there are real substances, individually separate and distinct, and we think there is some underlying relation of cause and effect which is the cohesive tie uniting them all into a system of interdependent parts. But such a way of looking at things is only a convenient mental habit which we take for granted as a matter of course, because we have never paused seriously to question it. We must remember that our thinking it true does not make it true, and that the most obvious assumption which the mind may entertain does not of itself guarantee its trustworthiness. Berkeley was correct in denying the existence of matter, Hume would say, but he should have gone further and have denied also the reality of ideas themselves as regards their substantial essence, and their necessary connection in any system of knowledge.

This negative criticism, which in itself marks no real progress of thought, is nevertheless an exceedingly important factor in any such progress. It shows the inadequacy of half truths, and sweeps the board of all inconsistencies and confusions of thought. If noth-

THE AGE OF THE ENLIGHTENMENT 13

ing remains, that very fact of itself is of advantage in inciting to renewed effort along lines which will swing clear of initial misconceptions, unwarrantable assumptions and partial premises. As Descartes has very wisely said: "Those who travel very slowly may yet make far greater progress, provided they keep always to the straight road, than those who, however well they run, forsake it."[1]

Thus, if an initial idea leads through the various phases of its logical unfolding to an untenable position, then by this process of a *reductio ad absurdum*, the original idea itself must be challenged at its source. This is Hume's peculiar contribution—that of enlightening the thought of the eighteenth century as to the inadequacy of Locke's foundations of knowledge as interpreted by Berkeley. Inasmuch, therefore, as Locke's position, that we know only sensations as the beginning of all knowledge, seems to lead on one hand to an extreme idealism, and on the other to extreme materialism, or else to a point of view of radical scepticism, we are naturally forced to the conclusion that Locke must have overlooked an essential and significant factor in his account of the sources of knowledge. Is there any trace of such a factor in the midst of the eighteenth century philosophy? There undoubtedly is. For when the influence of Locke's *Essay* began to be felt in Germany, and his empirical philosophy had gained a hearing and a following as well, there came into conflict with it an opposite stream of tendency in philosophical thinking which may be traced through Leibniz to Spinoza and Descartes, and which in the eighteenth century was represented most conspicuously in the philosophy of Wolff, namely, that of rationalism.

[1] *Discourse on Method*, Part I.

14 THE ENLIGHTENMENT

The point of view of rationalism has regard particularly to the nature of reason itself. It insists that there are certain clear and distinct ideas native to the very character of thought which serve as a body of primary truths from which it is possible to develop by logical procedure an entire system of philosophical dogma. Moreover, such a system is supposed to sketch, in broad outline at least, the general field of knowledge. During the latter half of the eighteenth century this method of philosophical thought had developed an extreme philosophical position, and under the dominance of Wolff's mechanical and artificial habit of mind had become a system of dry-as-dust scholastic formulæ. It was a body of knowledge, but lacked the breath of life.

Through these opposed tendencies of empiricism and rationalism, each forced by the momentum of thought to an extreme expression, the way was prepared for a complete reconstruction of philosophical doctrine which was achieved by the genius of Immanuel Kant. His masterly insight discovered in the empiricism of Locke the germs of rationalism, and in the rationalism of Liebniz the potential elements of empiricism.

It was Hume whose scepticism first impressed Kant with the unsatisfactory results of the traditional methods of philosophical thinking, and opened before him the new way. The office of a sceptic in philosophy is most perfectly illustrated in the influence which Hume exerted upon the mind of Kant, leading him in the first place to a destructive analysis of the philosophical dogma in which he had been schooled, and then beyond that to the more serious task of constructive interpretation. Scepticism as an essential moment in the philosophy of the *Enlighten-*

ment expresses not a final goal, but merely a transition stage in the progress of reflective thought.

Kant's problem was that of marking the precise limits of empiricism and rationalism, and of demonstrating thereby their complementary rather than contradictory nature. He examines the extreme positions of empiricism and rationalism, and then proceeds to build into a single system whatever elements of truth these seemingly opposed doctrines contain.

This marks the third stage of the movement of thought, the construction of a fully rounded body of truth by filling out the half truth which marks its initial expression. The antithesis of a rationalistic and an empirical philosophy was reconciled in the Kantian synthesis, according to which the material of our ideas is furnished by the senses in its crude state, but the form which this material is constrained to take in consciousness is the labour of the reason. As Kant succinctly puts it, "ideas without any perception by the senses are empty, but mere sensations without ideas are blind."[1] Upon the raw material of sensation the mind brings to bear its organising and constructing activity, ordering all things according to the compulsion of its own nature. We are in error when we say that we receive impressions through the avenues of the senses. The mind is never passive, but actively creative in every sense perception, however simple and elemental it may appear. A merely receptive experience, therefore, may not be regarded as the sole beginning of knowledge, for the experience is nothing without the thought which renders the elements of experience intelligible. Mere sensations in themselves, or any combination which may be made of them, can never

[1] *Kritik der reinen Vernunft*, Adickes p. 100.

produce a body of knowledge any more than crude ore can fashion itself into a curiously chased jewel. The simple sensation as the primal element of knowledge is a philosophical fiction. The simplest possible sensation at its first appearance in consciousness is already indefinitely complex, shot through and through with the threads of necessary connections and relations determined by the very nature of the thought processes in whose medium it necessarily comes into being. This, accordingly, is Kant's peculiar office, that of uniting these two opposed points of view, the empirical and the rational, upon a higher plane, wherein the elements of truth in each may be harmoniously conserved and ordered according to their mutual relations and functions.

Moreover, Kant also insisted most emphatically that such a position as that of Locke's was too circumscribed, and therefore could not represent in any adequate manner the full wealth of our conscious life. The tendency of the following of Locke in France, and in Germany as well, had been to emphasise unduly the function of reason as they conceived it. It is true, Kant confesses, that by the pure reason we can come to know only the phenomena of experience, the world of appearance; and no activity of the speculative reason is able to transcend this surface show of things, and reveal the substantial nature and significance of things as they are in themselves, the world of reality. But it must not be overlooked that there is also the practical reason, that quality of reason which feels and wills and acts, yet, nevertheless, maintains its essential character as reason. In this view Kant was influenced to no small extent by the insistence of Rousseau, who protested most vehemently against the methods of the age of reason, and insisted that man must be regarded as something more than a mere logical machine. Under the stimulus of Rousseau, Kant was not slow to see that the world of experience is not a world of knowledge exclusively. It is a world, also, of values; a world of purpose and of achievement. We feel an instinctive need of certain fundamental concepts which will make such a world intelligible, and which, at the same time, will offer an adequate and worthy end for human endeavour. These concepts, or postulates, of the practical reason compose that Kantian trinity of ideas, namely, God, freedom and immortality.

This is the last phase in the development of thought which proceeded from Locke's sensational basis of knowledge as its starting-point. And in the light of this development, there emerge certain general conclusions which indicate the fundamental characteristics of the necessities of thought. They are as follows:

It is impossible to solve a philosophical problem satisfactorily by reducing the area of difficulty. We may cut the knot, but we fail to disentangle it. It seems, at the first glance, to simplify philosophical difficulties incalculably, by drawing the line so as to exclude rigorously all metaphysical considerations; by endeavouring to beat out all perplexities in the sphere of the particular facts of experience; and by a method of common-sense interpretation of such facts for what they are worth in themselves and in accordance with their obvious face value. While such a procedure seems to be eminently fair, and is most attractive, appealing as it does to man's instinctive predisposition to regard favourably any method which is simple and straightforward, nevertheless the post-Lockian development of philosophical thought demonstrates that the simple phenomena of experience are not self-explanatory. It is better to profess some principles of metaphysics rather than to repudiate them, and yet, at the same time, in the course of one's thinking, unwittingly to assume them when under the pressure of logical necessity itself. Nothing leads to such confusion and obscurity of thought as the assumption of a crude metaphysic, the presence of which in one's thinking is not recognised, and whose significance, therefore, as an essential and determining factor is not appreciated. Reduction to simplest terms is not necessarily explanation. This is the lesson of the *Aufklärung* on its speculative side.

Every philosophical movement, moreover, which possesses vitality should affect the life of an age on its practical side also. Otherwise it cannot be considered a great movement of thought. Philosophy is not of the school merely, although many seem to think that it is; it exercises a profound influence also upon the thought, and therefore upon the life, of a people, both directly and indirectly. This is illustrated in a marked degree by the philosophy of the *Enlightenment*. In France and Germany especially, philosophical questions were discussed generally by the people as well as by the scholarly class. There was everywhere during the latter half of the eighteenth century a popular demand for a "philosophy for the masses." With the principles of Locke widely disseminated and discussed in the café and salon and even among the rank and file of the people generally, the empirical philosophy exerted a remarkable influence upon the religious, the moral and the political life of that age.

THE AGE OF THE ENLIGHTENMENT 19

In religion there was an evident tendency toward deism, which, particularly in France, gradually drifted toward atheism.

In ethics the principles of utilitarianism prevailed, and became the dominant moral creed.

In politics there was a tendency toward extreme individualism, accompanied by an urgent plea for a return of man to the state of nature, and a protest against all existing institutions, social as well as political.

This practical development, it is evident, was the inevitable outcome of Locke's position. The process is a logical one, from the premise that we know only that which is given to us by the activity of the senses, to the conclusion that, if God exists, it must be in a region quite beyond the world as we know it through experience. For God surely cannot be discovered in the sensory sources of knowledge, and therefore, if He exists at all, it must be in a sphere transcending a world which is composed wholly of original elements given in sensation. This is deism, and the way is not far from deism to atheism, and many there were in that age who found it. In France the logical outcome of the deistical trend of thought was the endeavour to substitute for the worship of a God, a religion of nature and a worship of reason.

The utilitarian basis of ethics also is related to the position of Locke; for starting with sensations as the sole source of knowledge, one comes instinctively to value sensations according to the pleasure or the pain which may accompany them. Consequently the pleasure or pain accompaniments of our sensations will be regarded naturally as the standards of conduct, and this is essentially the psychological ground of the ethic of utilitarianism. It is the practical working out in conduct of Locke's theory of knowledge.

As regards the political phase of the philosophy of the *Enlightenment*, we find that the emphasis which that age placed upon the individual as the supreme tribunal of last appeal, turned the attention of all minds to the rights of the individual as against the traditional rights of the classes and the divine right of kings. The insistence upon a return to the fundamental basis of human nature as the primary source of knowledge was transferred to the sphere of politics by Rousseau, who urged a return, in a modified sense, to the natural state of man as the ideal of the communal as well as the individual life. Locke had likened the beginnings of all consciousness in the experience of the individual to a *tabula rasa*, a clean sheet, containing no record of the past, no hereditary tracings of predisposition, no potentiality of constructive and organising powers. Such a doctrine was peculiarly adaptable to the political disposition of that age, and met with a natural response in the general spirit of discontent with the old, and a yearning after a new order of things. The new order was to begin with a *tabula rasa*, a clean page, upon which to write the history of regenerate days.

As with the speculative ideas of this age, so also these more practical results were felt to be one-sided in their development. They, too, needed the correcting and supplementing influence of some larger comprehensive idea which should serve to unify them, a fundamental principle of truth whose office might prove constructive rather than destructive, capable of clearing the vision and of grounding conviction upon a surer foundation. Again, it was necessary to show that these most complex phenomena cannot be explained by reducing them to their lowest terms, and also that the final phase in the course of a progressive development is not to be explained merely by tracing it back to its elemental beginnings, but that these beginnings, the rather, are to be understood and interpreted in the light of the more complex results which grow out of them.

Here, again, Kant rendered an inestimable service. He found God not outside of the world but in it. He could not be conceived as dwelling apart from the world of thought and activity, but must be discovered in His central place, as author and governor of the moral order which constitutes our world of purpose and desire, a God immanent as well as transcendent. So, also, in protest against the utilitarian trend of his day, Kant insisted upon the recognition of the law of moral obligation, and upon a reverence of that law as the supreme standard of conduct. Such a principle cannot be reduced to the canons of prudence and expediency; it is a principle which it is impossible to trace to any naturalistic basis as its ground. It takes its rise in our moral consciousness. It becomes a constant and controlling power in our lives, subduing the wayward and whimsical sway of the senses. In the sphere of the body politic, moreover, Kant's voice was raised in vehement protest against the prevalent doctrine which regarded man as essentially a creature whose desires are to receive fullest gratification, and whose maximum of happiness it is the office of government to secure. He, on the contrary, laid peculiar stress upon the dignity and worth of man regarded as a person, and upon the duties as well as the rights which grow out of this idea of personality. Man is not merely a bundle of sensory reactions, a child of nature impelled by the full flood of animal life, a thing, a means to an end; <u>he is to be regarded always as an end in himself</u>, and thereby responding to his vocation as a person in the deepest significance of that designation. Moreover, the individual is constrained, by his very nature as a rational being, to regard every other person as an end in himself, and never as a means to an end. It is a common inheritance such as this, and the appreciation of the responsibilities which it entails, that tend to bind mankind together in a society so strongly knit that it will prove capable of withstanding the shock of revolution as well as the ordinary disintegrating forces which sap a nation's strength and vitality.

The tendencies which appear on a large scale in a great movement of thought are to be met with, also, on a smaller scale in the experience of every individual as he may endeavour to think himself out of the manifold difficulties which attend the formulation of a philosophy of life. These tendencies may be briefly summarised as the desire to reduce the area of perplexity in philosophical thinking to its minimum dimensions, the exclusion of metaphysical explanation, the tendency to develop an extreme position which reveals its own weakness, and, finally, the tendency to drift into an attitude of scepticism concerning all philosophical theories whatsoever. Then, if happily a reaction occurs, which indicates health and vigour of mind, there comes an inner compulsion to seek some comprehensive constructive principle by which the scattered fragments of a destructive criticism may be built anew upon solid foundations.

Kant himself passed through these several phases of thought in the development of his philosophical system. <u>In his own experience he exhibits a recapitu-</u>

lation of the philosophical movement of his century. Early in his career he came under the influence of the traditional rationalism; later on he experienced a reaction due to the principles of the Lockian empiricism; and, finally, the influence of Hume helped to bring about a transition stage of scepticism, from which he eventually emerged upon that higher plane in which his constructive genius found free play and scope.

Every one who feels upon him the burden and mystery of life must pass through some such process of thought as this. For truth does not appear to us full formed, nor is she always clothed in the garb of simplicity, nor does she speak a language easy to understand. She must be wooed and won, in the face of difficulties and in spite of doubts, by the patient labour of the mind.

There is, moreover, in our day and generation as strong if not a stronger tendency to reduce all the experiences of our intellectual life to the simple basis of natural phenomena. It is the popular demand for a philosophy of naturalism. There is much talk at present of the science of ethics and of the science of religion; of a philosophy without a metaphysic, of a psychology without a soul. At the beginning of the twentieth century it would be well to reflect that the eighteenth century was confronted with certain problems in the process of the historical development of philosophical thought which were solved once for all. Chief among these historical conclusions is this, that, in addition to the phenomena of human nature, we are compelled to recognise some fundamental principle of reason which can give them unity, and present some worthy purpose as the end of their activity. Whatever that principle may be, whether the "synthetic unity of apperception," according to Kant, or one of the "moments of the eternal spirit," according to Hegel, or simply the ordering and organising power of the mind as we, in the habit of an old-fashioned view of things, have been wont to consider it, we are nevertheless constrained to recognise it as the supreme principle of reason, of feeling and of conduct.

REFERENCES.—J. Mackintosh: *On the Progress of Ethical Philosophy During the Seventeenth and Eighteenth Centuries.* Edinburgh, 1872.

H. Hettner: *Litteraturgeschichte des Achtzehntenjahrhunderts.* Brunswick, 1862.

L. Stephen: *History of English Thought in the Eighteenth Century.* London, 1876.

Immanuel Kant: *Beantwortung der Frage: was ist Aufklärung.* Werke, Vol. IV. Hartenstein.

Kuno Fischer: *Francis Bacon und Seine Schule.* Heidelberg, 1904.

A. Riehl: *Der Philosophische Kritizismus: Zweite Auflage.* Leipzig, 1908.

W. Windelband: *A History of Philosophy.* Part V. Translation. London–New York, 1893.

R. Eucken: *Die Lebensanschauungen der Grossen Denker.* Leipzig, 1897.

CHAPTER II

LOCKE'S INNER AND OUTER WORLD

The beginnings of the philosophical movement which is to be the subject of our study we find in Locke (1632–1704). In the *Essay Concerning Human Understanding* Locke proposes to construct the world of knowledge by exhibiting its natural evolution from the original elements of experience as they appear in their simplest expression, to the most complex and abstruse ideas which the mind is capable of entertaining. He regards the process throughout as a continuous one, and also as self-explanatory. Upon this undertaking Locke enters with a most admirable spirit, being led to his inquiry through a sincere and impartial love of the truth; and actuated, moreover, by the desire to discover that truth by his own reason, freed from the trammels of authority and tradition. Some idea of the peculiar importance of Locke's contribution to the history of philosophical thought may be gathered from a remark of A. Riehl's: "The *Essay Concerning Human Understanding* marks not merely a new epoch in philosophy, but rather a new philosophy itself."[1] In the midst of a busy life, with its exacting demands and increasing burdens of responsibility, Locke found some quiet moments in which to question the workings of his own mind, and thereby discover, to some extent at least, the true nature of its mysterious functions.

[1] A. Riehl, *Der Philosophische Kritizismus*, vol. I, p. 2.

The idea of this excursion into the undiscovered regions of the inner life of thought was suggested to him, in the first instance, by a chance discussion which arose among a group of his friends. The account which he himself gives of the origin of the *Essay* is of such interest that I venture to quote it at length: "Were it fit to trouble thee with the history of this *Essay*, I should tell thee that five or six friends meeting at my chamber (at the home of Lord Ashley (Shaftesbury), in Exeter House, London), and discoursing on a subject very remote from this, found themselves quickly at a stand by the difficulties that rose on every side. After we had awhile puzzled ourselves, without coming any nearer a resolution of those doubts which perplexed us, it came into my thoughts that we took a wrong course; and that before we set ourselves upon inquiries of that nature it was necessary to examine our own abilities, and see what *objects* our understandings were or were not fitted to deal with. This I proposed to the company, who all readily assented; and thereupon it was agreed that this should be our first inquiry. Some hasty and undigested thoughts on a subject I had never before considered, which I set down against our next meeting, gave the first entrance in this discourse; which, having been thus begun by chance, was continued by entreaty; written by incoherent parcels; and after long intervals of neglect, resumed again, as my humour or occasions permitted; and at last, in a retirement (in Holland) where an attendance on my health gave me leisure, it was brought into that order thou now seest it." [1]

"To examine our own abilities, and see what ob-

---

[1] *The Epistle to the Reader.* Fraser's edition of the *Essay*, vol. I. p, 9*f*. All subsequent references are to this edition.

jects our understandings were or were not fitted to deal with," is a task similar to that which Kant set for himself in the *Critique of Pure Reason*. In this respect Locke is the forerunner of Kant, but only in the sense that it was vouchsafed to him merely to behold the land from afar which, however, he was not able himself to possess. The *Essay* is a plea for the recognition of intellectual freedom, in much the same manner as his *Epistola de Tolerentia* is a plea for religious liberty, and his *Treatises on Government*, for political liberty. In the attempt, however, to free the mind from the domination of innate ideas, and to provide a clean page upon which to write the record of its own activity, he overlooked the significant truth that the mind cannot be made independent of itself, but must be determined by the necessities of its own nature. This is the point which Locke failed to grasp, and which, therefore, marks the fundamental defect of his otherwise masterly inquiry. For intellectual freedom can never be a freedom from the inner constraint of the processes of thought themselves, which like the pressure of the atmosphere are after all no obstacle to free movement, but the rather make such free movement possible. But criticism must not precede exposition. Therefore let us turn our attention to a more particular examination of the method and point of view of the *Essay*.

Locke's method is essentially psychological; it is an attempt to trace the natural history of our ideas to their simplest beginnings in consciousness. And all speculations which reach beyond the scope of this method of inquiry Locke rigorously excludes. As to the purpose, and the corresponding limitations of the field of his investigations, Locke clearly states his position as follows: "It shall suffice to my present purpose to consider the discerning faculties of a man, as they are employed about the objects which they have to do with. And I shall imagine I have not wholly misemployed myself in the thoughts I shall have on this occasion if, in this historical plain method, I can give any account of the ways whereby our understandings come to attain those notions of things we have, and can set down any measures of the certainty of our knowledge. . . . If, by this inquiry into the nature of the understanding, I can discover the powers thereof; how far they reach; to what things they are in any degree proportionate; and where they fail us, I suppose it may be of use to prevail with the busy mind of man to be more cautious in meddling with things exceeding its comprehension; to stop when it is at the utmost extent of its tether; and to sit down in a quiet ignorance of those things which, upon examination, are found to be beyond the reach of our capacities. We should not then, perhaps, be so forward, out of an affectation of an universal knowledge, to raise questions, and perplex ourselves and others with disputes about things to which our understandings are not suited, and of which we cannot frame in our minds any clear or distinct impressions, or whereof (as it has perhaps too often happened) we have not any notions at all. . . . How far short soever men's knowledge may come of an universal or perfect comprehension of whatsoever is, it yet secures their great concernments, that they have light enough to lead them to the knowledge of their Maker, and the sight of their own duties." [1]

I have quoted these passages in order to show in Locke's own words his general conception of the undertaking before him, and as an illustration also

[1] The *Essay*, Introduction, § 2, 4, 5.

of certain characteristic features of the philosophy of the *Enlightenment* in its empirical phase, namely, the insistence upon inquiry within the range of concrete facts, the demand that the various ideas corresponding to these facts must be distinct and clear, the silencing of all questions concerning matters too deep or too obscure for the human mind to comprehend, and the complete satisfaction in being able to frame at least a practical philosophy of life. The pragmatic point of view is evident throughout the *Essay*, as when Locke, for instance, insists later in the Introduction that "our business here is not to know all things, but those which concern our conduct. If we can find out those measures whereby a rational creature, put in that state in which man is in this world, may and ought to govern his opinions, and actions depending thereon, we need not be troubled that some other things escape our knowledge." [1]

The sources of all knowledge Locke finds in sensation and reflection. The first book of the *Essay* is devoted to his preliminary and fundamental contention that there are no innate ideas either speculative or practical. He then proceeds to show that the mind is like a dark room, wholly shut off from the light save through a single opening. Through this the light streams from a central source resident in the senses. Through this process of illumination there is a complete representation of things as they lie without the mind. They thus picture themselves upon the screen of consciousness. There is, therefore, an inner world of ideas, and an outer world of things which correspond to them. The inner world of consciousness is illumined by the light which enters from without. Locke's figure of a dark cabinet with an

[1] Introduction, § 6.

opening to admit the light from the external world reminds one of Plato's illustration of the cave, wherein the various forms outlined on the wall of the cavern are merely the shadow symbols of the real substances which they all too inadequately portray.

The one inlet through which the light enters from the outer world, according to Locke, is that of sensation. The senses furnish the elemental materials of all our knowledge, so that a man begins to have ideas when he first has any sensation.[1]

In addition to sensation, which constitutes the external sense, there is an internal sense, that of reflection, which is to be regarded as the source of ideas also. By reflection Locke means "the perception of the operations of our own mind within us as it is employed about the ideas it has got; which operations, when the soul comes to reflect on, and consider, do furnish the understanding with another set of ideas which could not be had from things without. And such are perception, thinking, doubting, believing, reasoning, knowing, willing and all the different actings of our own mind."[2]

Reflection, therefore, is a term which is used by Locke to signify our consciousness of the nature of the active machinery of the mind. It is a consciousness, however, of processes merely, and not of their content. The actual content of knowledge is furnished by the senses, to which all of our ideas can be eventually traced. The operations of the mind, of which reflection makes us conscious, and the ideas which they furnish, are phrases sufficiently comprehensive in themselves, as well as sufficiently indefinite, to embrace any conceivable theory of knowledge whatsoever. Their meaning must be more specifi-

[1] Book II, chap. I, § 23. [2] Book II, chap. I, § 4.

cally determined. The essential point, therefore, in reference to the system which we are to examine is this: What is the peculiar significance which Locke attaches to such phrases; and in what sense does he use them in his account of the process by which the higher and more complex forms of thought are developed out of the material presented to the mind through the simple experiences of sense perception? While it must be allowed that in addition to the primary sensations, as the source whence the materials of knowledge are constantly supplied, Locke also recognises the active powers of the mind as operative in constructing this material into an ordered body of knowledge; nevertheless, he fails to appreciate in any due sense the proper function of this activity, and the full significance of the rôle which it plays in the life of the intellect. It is in this respect that his theory of knowledge has proved inadequate, and has opened the way to misunderstandings and contradictions on the part of the many who have built upon his foundations.

Locke's initial error, I think, is to be found in the assertion, oft repeated, that the mind is passive in the process of receiving the sensory materials of knowledge. He says, for instance: "Thus the first capacity of human intellect is, that the mind is fitted to receive the impressions made on it. . . . In this part the understanding is merely passive; and whether or no it will have these beginnings, and as it were, materials of knowledge, is not in its own power. . . . These simple ideas, when offered to the mind, the understanding can no more refuse to have, nor alter when they are imprinted, nor blot them out and make new ones itself, than a mirror can refuse, alter or obliterate the images or ideas which the objects set before it do therein produce. As the bodies that surround us do diversely affect our organs, the mind is forced to receive the impressions, and cannot avoid the perception of those ideas that are annexed to them." [1]

This conception, that the mind is like a mirror, that it receives its impressions, that its original ideas are imprinted upon it by the activity of the senses, clearly indicates Locke's fundamental point of view in regarding the mind as passive in the early beginnings of the growth of knowledge. He does not allow the possibility of any mental reaction, which in the very process of receiving nevertheless modifies the material received. Moreover, in explaining the function of reflection, he calls it "the perception of the operations of our own mind within us, as it is employed about the ideas it has got." [2]

According to this statement, Locke takes the position that the process of reflection starts as an active function after a certain body of ideas are given to the mind and received by it in a purely passive manner. In another passage Locke draws a similar distinction between the process of perception and that of thinking. He says: "Perception, as it is the first faculty of the mind exercised about our ideas; so it is the first and simplest idea we have from reflection, and is by some called thinking in general. Though thinking, in the propriety of the English tongue, signifies that sort of operation in the mind about its ideas, wherein the mind is active; where it, with some degree of voluntary attention, considers anything. For in bare, naked perception the mind is, for the most part, only passive; and what it perceives, it cannot avoid perceiving." [3]

[1] *Essay*, Book II, chap. I, § 24, 25. [2] *Ib.*, Book II, chap. I, § 4.
[3] *Ib.*, Book II, chap. IX, § 1.

To conceive the mind as passively receiving the various impressions conveyed to it by the senses does not represent adequately its true function. The mind, even in the simplest process of perception, is never passive, but on the contrary ceaselessly active. Whatever is furnished by the senses is presented in the form of crude sensory material which the mind immediately seizes upon, and by its own activity fashions into forms whose essential nature is their intelligibility. The process of perception, therefore, is not merely a process of transmission of sensory stimulation, but rather a process of transmutation, whereby the resulting idea in consciousness appears as the product of an exceedingly subtle alchemy of the mind. It is not given fully formed to the receiving consciousness, but takes its shape along the lines of the mind's constructive energy itself. Otherwise, if the idea were the mere copy of the sensory stimulus we might naturally expect that it would be a picture of the accompanying brain modification, for that is the stage in the sensory series which immediately precedes the resulting perception. It is needless to state that no idea which appears in the mind ever possesses such a content.

The mind's activity in every process of perception serves to render the resulting product even in its simplest forms an idea which is indefinitely complex. Locke's supposition that the mind has furnished to it through "naked perception" a number of sensational units of ultimate simplicity is a psychological fiction. There is no such thing as a "naked perception," or a simple sensation, appearing in consciousness completely detached and isolated. The term idea, as used by Locke, has a certain ambiguity attaching to it in this respect, that, while regarding it as the psychological unit of sensory experience, it expands under the very act of contemplation into an idea whose essential nature is its intelligibility,—that is, an idea which is thought related and thought constituted. The original elements out of which our body of knowledge is built up are infused with thought significance and implication. They do not appear as distinct and separate, but variously related. They are bound up with ideas of existence, power, unity, succession and the like—ideas which Locke assumes as a matter of course, but which are wholly inconsistent with the doctrine of the simplicity of the sensory elements which he alleges are capable of forming the basis of all our knowledge. In Locke's diatribe against innate ideas he overlooks the native constructive powers of the mind which perform the necessary function of rendering the crude data of experience intelligible at the very beginnings of our nascent knowledge.

But not only does Locke start the activity of the mind at too advanced a stage in the processes of our thinking, but also he conceives of that activity as operating upon the elemental ideas conveyed to the mind by the senses in a purely mechanical and artificial manner. As regards the nature of this activity Locke says: "We have hitherto considered those ideas in the reception whereof the mind is only passive, which are those simple ones received from sensation and reflection before mentioned, whereof the mind cannot make one to itself, nor have any idea which does not wholly consist of them. But as the mind is wholly passive in the reception of all its simple ideas, so it exerts several acts of its own, whereby out of its simple ideas, as the materials and foundations of the rest, the others are framed. The acts of the mind, wherein it exerts its power over its simple ideas, are chiefly these three: (1) Combining several simple ideas into one compound one; and thus all *complex ideas* are made. (2) The second is bringing two ideas, whether simple or complex, together, and setting them by one another, so as to take a view of them at once, without uniting them into one; by which way it gets all its *ideas of relations*. (3) The third is separating them from all other ideas that accompany them in their real existence; this is called abstraction and thus all its *general ideas* are made. This shows man's power and its way of operation to be much the same in the material and intellectual world. For the materials in both being such as he has no power over, either to make or destroy, all that man can do is either to unite them together, or set them by one another, or wholly separate them. . . . In this faculty of repeating and joining together its ideas, the mind has great power in varying and multiplying the objects of its thoughts, infinitely beyond what sensation or reflection furnished it with; but all this still confined to those simple ideas which it received from those two sources, and which are the ultimate materials of all its compositions."[1]

This passage has been quoted at length in order to indicate clearly the mechanical manner in which the activity of the mind, according to our author, operates upon the given elements of knowledge from without, compounding part with part, relating parts to one another, or separating the parts which appear originally together. That Locke regards this activity as working *ab extra* upon the elementary material which the mind receives, is proved by the analogy which he

[1] *Essay*, Book II, chap. XII, § 1, 2.

draws between the mind's activity as it works upon its given material, and that mechanical activity which man exercises upon the materials furnished to his hand; for these materials he can modify and manipulate only by working upon them from without. But the analogy of the sculptor or the craftsman is a very inadequate figure to convey the true function of the mind in ordering and transforming its material. The activity of the mind even in the simplest processes of perception is far more than the "faculty of repeating and joining together its ideas." The mind does not work upon the elements of thought in this mechanical way from without, but within the material which it organises. Voltaire once said of Locke that he "traced the development of the human reason as a good anatomist explains the machinery of the human body." [1]

A physiologist of the mind and not an anatomist is needed, however, in order to give a satisfactory account of thought as a living process. For the activity of the mind is like the vital principle which works within the fibre and tissue of an organism—that architectonic principle of a plant or animal which builds its parts by organisation and not by composition. After the manner of every living process, its method of operation is concealed and lies beyond the range of obvious explanations. In every account which Locke gives, however, of the formation of our complex ideas, he fails to appreciate their organic nature. This is true of his simple or mixed "modes," that is, those modifications which the mind makes of the original elements presented to it; also as regards his theory of the nature of "substances," wherein a number of these original sensory elements form a

[1] Voltaire, *Lettres sur les Anglais*, Lettre XIII, *sur M. Locke*.

group whose several qualities seem knit together to constitute a definite thing; so also concerning all "relations," wherein these elements, while appearing separately, show some underlying connection. Whatever may be the particular form which the mind fashions out of the given material, it is always regarded by Locke as the result of some mechanical composition. For instance, he derives the idea of infinity by a process of adding space to space which knows no limit, and in a similar manner the idea of eternity is produced by adding stretches of time to time, also without limit.[1]

In these instances Locke's idea of the infinite is what Hegel characterises as *Die schlechte oder negative Unendlichkeit*, that is, a tedious multiplication of finite terms in a never-ending process. Such an endless progression can only bring weariness to the mind which attempts to follow it.[2]

Locke is vaguely conscious of this defect in his account of this evolution of the idea of the infinite in our thought by the process of continuous addition. For he acknowledges that only "those ideas that consist of parts are capable of being augmented by every addition of the least part; but if you take the idea of white, which one parcel of snow yielded yesterday to our sight, and another idea of white from another parcel of snow you see to-day, and put them together in your mind, they embody, as it were, and run into one, and the idea of whiteness is not at all increased; and if we add a less degree of whiteness to a greater, we are so far from increasing that we diminish it."[3]

[1] *Essay*, vol. I, Book II, chap. XVII, § 3, 4, 5.
[2] Hibben, *Hegel's Logic*, p. 97.
[3] *Essay*, vol. I, Book II, chap. XVII, § 6.

If Locke had appreciated the full significance of this limitation of the mind's compounding activity, it would have led him to a more profound philosophical view concerning the function of thought in the process of constructing our world of knowledge.

Again, the combinations which Locke insists are brought about by the activities of the mind working upon the original sensory elements possess a unity which cannot be accounted for by a mere juxtaposition of parts. The unity which underlies our complex ideas is essentially a unity of organisation. In such an idea as that of the relation of cause and effect, or that of substance, the underlying bond is not discoverable in the attempt, even though it should prove successful, of separating the complex idea into a number of original elements which are detached and isolated. The whole in such a case is not equal to the mere sum of its parts. The simple process of the putting together of part to part mechanically can never form a relation between the parts which has any other than an artificial significance and therefore can never transform the combination of its parts into an organic whole. What is wanting is a central unifying principle which is capable of organising the various parts into a complete whole. And such a principle it is possible to discover in the reason, working not *upon* but *within* the elemental materials given in consciousness, informing them according to its constructive power, which power is simply the expression of the inherent necessities of the mind's essential nature itself. It is Leibniz who first notes the inadequacy of Locke's view concerning the origin of our body of knowledge, and its mode of development. Leibniz significantly remarks in reference to this point: "You oppose to me this axiom received by the philosophers, *that* there is nothing in the soul which does not come from the senses. But you must except the soul and its affections. *Nihil est in intellectu, quod non fuerit in sensu,* excipe: nisi ipse intellectus."[1]

It is, indeed, in the intellect itself that we may discover a function which Locke himself never fully appreciated. While the aim of the *Essay Concerning Human Understanding* was the vindication of the sufficiency of reason in constructing a world of knowledge without the adventitious aid of "innate ideas and infused principles" mysteriously possessed, nevertheless, strange to say, Locke's weakness lay not in magnifying the offices of reason, but the rather in his failure to comprehend its proper function and scope as a vital force in organising the crude materials of knowledge. And it was just this defect which characterised the development of the empirical philosophy among the followers of Locke in the eighteenth century. In that *age of reason* there was no appreciation of the constraint of reason in determining the lines according to which the world of thought, the world of values, the world of purpose and of conduct, is to be constructed.

Certain commentators of Locke insist, however, that he fully appreciated the part which the active powers of the mind must needs play in organising the crude data of experience, and even go so far as to urge, as Webb, in his *Intellectualism of Locke*, that the author of the *Essay Concerning Human Understanding* should not be classified at all as an empiricist, but as an intellectualist. It is true that there are certain detached statements, which may be gleaned from various portions of the *Essay* and which upon

[1] Leibniz, *Nouveaux Essais*, Book II, chap. I, § 2.

their face value may be interpreted in the spirit of a philosophy of rationalism; this applies particularly to Locke's account of the possibility of an abstract system, both of pure mathematics and of formal ethics. Nevertheless, this in itself does not by any means make Locke's general system of philosophy a form of intellectualism. His habit of mind and the spirit which pervades his work are of a different order. His philosophical attitude and point of view are to be judged by the line of general direction which his thought pursues, and not by the chance excursions it may take here and there from the clearly defined path which his main purpose has determined. Particular sentences or detached paragraphs, which occur now and again in the general treatment of a subject, do not necessarily reflect a writer's fundamental philosophical bent. In this regard it may be said of Locke, as indeed of any other author, that his expressed views on various subjects in the course of the development of his main thesis, must measure up to a certain standard which a judicious philosophical criticism naturally demands. And the canon of such a critical estimate may be expressed somewhat as follows: An author's general philosophical position is not to be assessed according to the face value merely of any passing observation which he may chance to make; but all such observations are to be properly discounted under certain circumstances, namely: (1) when an author is not aware of the full significance of his statements in respect to their bearing upon the general body of doctrine which it is his avowed purpose to maintain; (2) or, when he does not appreciate the fact that the introduction of a given statement into the argument which he is unfolding tends logically to contradict the truth of his original presuppositions; (3) or, when he introduces the material under question at the circumference and not at the centre of his exposition, so that it becomes an episode rather than an integral part of his system as a whole.

I am persuaded that Locke's alleged intellectualistic principles of knowledge show all of these defects, and therefore they must be judged accordingly. They are at variance with his main contention; they contradict his presuppositions; and they are incidental and not central to the elaboration of the fundamental principles of his theory of knowledge. The *Essay* must be interpreted according to the explicit theory which the author advances, and not according to the implications which certain portions of his development of that theory may convey, particularly when such implications are read into his general system in the light shed upon it by the post-Lockian movement of thought in the eighteenth century. It would be well to have in mind in this connection Locke's own commentary upon the proper method of interpreting the *Essay*. He writes a few months before his death to his friend Anthony Collins: "You have done me and my book a great honour for having bestowed so much of your thought upon it. You have a comprehensive knowledge of it, and do not stick in the incidents, which I find many people do; which, whether true or false, make nothing to the main design of the *Essay;* that lies in a little compass." [1]

This observation of Locke must be heeded most assiduously if one is to reach an appreciative understanding of the significance of the *Essay*, and its influence upon subsequent philosophical thought. There is a temptation to "stick in the incidents," and,

[1] Fraser's Introduction to the *Essay*, vol. I, p. liv.

in consequence, a failure to grasp comprehensively Locke's system as a whole.

Moreover there is a most important portion of our body of knowledge, and a significant factor in the processes of thought as well, which Locke finds in his inner world, and yet which is not given solely through the immediate deliverances of sensation or reflection, that is, the knowledge of self. This knowledge, according to his view, rests upon "an internal infallible perception that we are. In every act of sensation, reasoning or thinking we are conscious to ourselves of our own being, and in this matter come not short of the highest degree of certainty." [1]

Now, while it is obvious that the inner self is revealed in the act of sensation, it nevertheless transcends the process which reveals it. According to Locke's interpretation of the nature and function of the self, it is far more than a simple by-product of sensation or even of reflection. This is very clearly indicated in one of Locke's letters to Stillingfleet, Bishop of Worcester, with whom he carried on the famous controversy concerning the alleged sceptical tendencies of the *Essay*. One of the charges in Stillingfleet's indictment was that Locke's idea of the sameness of person was indifferent to the idea of sameness of body, and that such a position was inimical to the Christian doctrine of the resurrection of the body. Locke replies to this: "My idea of personal identity makes the same body not to be necessary to making the same person, either here or after death; and even in this life, the particles of the bodies of the same persons change every moment, and there is no such identity in the *body* as in the *person*." [2]

[1] *Essay*, Book IV, chap. IX, § 3.
[2] *Ib.*, Book II, chap. XXVII, § 15, n. 2.

The idea of a self, therefore, as a person transcending its bodily setting and the source of its sensations, is a conception which, by a rigorous logic, Locke's philosophy is not entitled to assume. It is a bit of knowledge the fundamental nature of which cannot be translated, even according to Locke's own account of it, in terms of any purely sensory elements. Although it is true that the idea of self is intimately associated with the stream of sensory experiences, and with the reflective consciousness of our mental machinery, it cannot be reduced, however, to a mere sensation, or to reflection, as Locke understands and explicitly defines these terms. The idea of self as a personality must therefore be regarded as an unexplored remainder which the premises of the *Essay* are incapable of reaching.

Locke, moreover, acknowledges that personal identity is essentially identity of consciousness,[1] and it is this identity of consciousness which is the unifying bond of the manifold experiences of life. It is impossible for Locke to construct his world of knowledge as a self-consistent whole without this assumption of a central self. And this is certainly an assumption involving a definite metaphysic which wholly transcends the original presuppositions of Locke, and the general programme of methodological inquiry which from the beginning he set himself to pursue. Later, Hume, by a more consistent logical analysis, clearly proved that the Lockian premises could never reach a distinct central self, and that the idea of such a self is a wholly gratuitous assumption.

We find, therefore, that Locke's inner world develops at the expense of his logic, and according to

[1] *Essay*, Book II, chap. XXVII, § 23.

processes whose mechanical mode of operation are not capable of giving life to knowledge.

This inner world, moreover, is made up of ideas which represent the objects of an outer world. We pass, therefore, to a consideration of the nature and scope of this other world as it is conceived by Locke.

If the presuppositions of the *Essay* are to be strictly interpeted, the author is not entitled to any outer world whatsoever. Such a world, however, he assumes as a matter of course. And yet in making such an assumption he goes beyond the original simplicity which characterises the ideas as they are given through our sensations. For these ideas are regarded by him solely as facts of consciousness, and, strictly speaking, do not refer to anything beyond themselves. Locke says that "whatsoever the mind perceives *in itself*, or is the immediate object of perception, thought or understanding, that I call *idea*." [1]

The task which Locke sets for himself is to build up the entire body of knowledge out of elements which are thus simply facts of the mind. The consistent interpretation, however, of the significance of these elemental ideas from this point of view proves to be inadequate. The world which they by themselves constitute is unsatisfactory and unreal. Locke himself is deeply sensible of the impotency of his simple ideas in this respect, and, accordingly, of the misleading character of his definition of knowledge as the "perception of the agreement or disagreement of our ideas." [2]

In speaking of the reality of knowledge, he makes the following significant remark: "I doubt not but my reader, by this time, may be apt to think that I

---

[1] *Essay*, Book II, chap. VIII, § 8.
[2] *Ib.*, Book IV, chap. I, § 1, 2.

have been all this while only building a castle in the air; and be ready to say to me: 'To what purpose all this stir? Knowledge,' say you, 'is only the perception of the agreement or disagreement of our own ideas; but who knows what those ideas may be? Is there anything so extravagant as the imaginations of men's brains? Where is the head that has no chimeras in it? Or, if there be a sober and a wise man, what difference will there be, by your rules, between his knowledge and that of the most extravagant fancy in the world? They both have their ideas, and perceive their agreement and disagreement one with another. . . . But of what use is all this fine knowledge of *men's own imaginations*, to a man that inquires after the reality of things? It matters not what men's fancies are, it is a knowledge of things that is only to be prized; it is this alone gives a value to our reasonings and preference to one man's knowledge over another's, that it is of things as they really are, and not of dreams and fancies.'

"To which I answer: That if our knowledge of our ideas terminate in them and reach no further, where there is something further intended, our most serious thoughts will be of little more use than the reveries of a crazy brain; and the truths built thereon of no more weight than the discourses of a man who sees things clearly in a dream, and with great assurance utters them. . . . It is evident that the mind knows not things immediately, but only by the intervention of the ideas it has of them. Our knowledge, therefore, is real only so far as there is a *conformity* between our ideas and the reality of things. . . .

"There are simple ideas which, since the mind, as has been showed, can by no means make to itself, must necessarily be the product of things operating on the mind, in a natural way, and producing therein those perceptions which, by the wisdom and will of our Maker, they are ordained and adapted to. From whence it follows, that simple ideas are not fictions of our fancies, but the natural and regular productions of things without us, really operating upon us; and so carry with them all the conformity which is intended or which our state requires." [1]

This position, however, is taken by Locke at the expense of consistency. The alleged conformity between our ideas and the reality of things is certainly an assumption which is not warranted by the most liberal interpretation of his original premises. An idea which, as it appears in consciousness, refers to something beyond its bare content, is itself no longer a simple idea, but is indefinitely complicated by an implied metaphysic which is supposed to find no place in Locke's system of knowledge. That our perceptions are "ordained and adapted to" the external world according to "the wisdom and will of our Maker," is a doctrine which certainly runs far beyond the limits marked by the empirical beginnings of knowledge in sensation and reflection.

Starting with this unwarrantable assumption of an external world, Locke undertakes an inquiry concerning the detailed information which our ideas are capable of conveying to the mind as to the nature of its various objects of knowledge.

In reference to the character of the information which we gain, he discriminates most carefully between what he is pleased to call the primary and the secondary qualities of matter. He says: "To discover the nature of our *ideas* the better, and to discourse of them intelligibly, it will be convenient to

---

[1] *Essay*, Book IV, chap. IV, § 1, 2, 3, 4.

distinguish them *as they are ideas or perceptions in our minds;* and *as they are modifications of matter in the bodies that cause such perceptions in us:* that so we may not think (as perhaps usually is done) that they are exactly the images and resemblances of something inherent in the subject (*i. e.*, the substance perceived). . . . Whatsoever the mind perceives *in itself*, or is the immediate object of perception, thought or understanding, that I call *idea;* and the power to produce any idea in our mind, I call quality of the subject wherein that power is. . . . Qualities thus considered in bodies are:

"*First*, such as are utterly inseparable from the body, in what state soever it be; and such as in all the alterations and changes it suffers, all the force can be used upon it, it constantly keeps; and such as sense constantly finds in every particle of matter, which has bulk enough to be perceived; and the mind finds inseparable from every particle of matter though less than to make itself singly perceived by our senses. . . . These I call *original* or *primary qualities* of body, which I think we may observe to produce simple ideas in us, viz., solidity, extension, figure, motion or rest, number. *Secondly*, such qualities which, in truth, are nothing in the objects themselves but powers to produce various sensations in us by their primary qualities, *i. e.*, by the bulk, figure, texture and motion of their insensible parts, as colours, sounds, tastes, etc. These I call *secondary qualities*." [1]

The primary qualities, inasmuch as they do fairly represent the nature of things external to us, may be regarded as constants; they are always the same, whether in the thing perceived or in the perception of

[1] *Essay*, Book II, chap. VIII, § 7, 8, 9, 10.

it. On the other hand, the secondary qualities are variable to an indefinite degree. As causes they do not resemble the effects which appear in our consciousness in the various forms of sense-perception. Whatever the cause may be specifically, it is always, according to Locke, some kind of modification of the primary qualities of matter. However, the object which produces the sensation red or blue is not itself red or blue. No more do we expect to find sweetness in sugar or harmony in sound, but only in our sensory reactions as we are variously affected by the external stimulus acting upon us. We might as well conclude that there is some quality of pain resident in the knife itself which resembles the pain which we feel when the knife cuts into our flesh. The world of colour, of sound, of taste, takes its character from the nature of the organism which is played upon by the different forces of nature. A slight alteration or modification of the retina, and the many-hued variety of the sky, of land and of sea will be transformed into a dull, uniform gray. In this sense, we may truly say that the kingdom of the world is in us.

But while the tone and tint of nature may be reflected from within; nevertheless, according to Locke, the definite forms and shapes which nature assumes are in themselves what they appear to be in our perception of them. The idea of extension, for instance, fairly and adequately represents the true nature of the several objects presented to the mind in the field of perception. So also the idea of solidity, or of movement through space, or of rest, or of duration and position in time.

But when Locke comes to the question of the nature of substance, he is compelled to acknowledge that his idea of substance is not such a perfect representation of things as they are. In reference to his conception of substance as a complex group of simple qualities which are always united together in consciousness, Locke confesses that "because, not imagining how these simple ideas *can* subsist, we accustom ourselves to suppose some *substratum* wherein they do subsist, and from which they do result, which therefore we call *substance*."[1]

In this statement Locke does not relieve the difficulties attending the nature of substance. On the contrary, he begs the question. For what the nature of this substance may be at the last analysis, the complex idea does not reveal. Moreover, our complex ideas of substances are largely made up of secondary qualities; and the secondary qualities, in turn, are regarded as the result of certain modifications and dispositions of the primary qualities. The connection between the activity of the primary qualities and the resulting effects which constitute the secondary qualities remains unknown. Therefore with any given qualities there is no necessary implication concerning any others. It is impossible to discover why some always unite together in a particular manner and by inseparable bonds, and others are wholly incompatible.

Substance, therefore, according to Locke, possesses a nominal and not a real essence. It is merely a verbal convenience by which we can readily designate something whose real significance is concealed. Locke's idea of substance, therefore, is thus reduced to that of the "unknown support and cause of the union of several distinct, simple ideas."[2]

The Bishop of Worcester, in his controversy with

---

[1] *Essay*, Book II, chap. XXIII, § 1.
[2] *Ib.*, Book III, chap. VI, § 21.

Locke, was particularly concerned about this indefinite characterisation of substance, for he was convinced that in denying that we have a clear idea of substance, Locke had "excluded the notion out of rational discourse," and that also, in defining substance to be "something we know not what," there was serious danger of opening the way to a general attitude of scepticism, and that indeed of a most radical nature.

However, Locke's idea of substance is not quite as indefinite as Stillingfleet supposes, for it is evident that he feels a compulsion to refer a group of simple qualities always appearing together to something as their support and the cause of their constant coherence which is far more than the mere sum of these qualities themselves. Locke distinguishes between ideas which are to be regarded as *archetypes*, and those which are to be regarded as *ectypes*. The idea as *archetype* is one which the mind frames of itself, and having no reference to anything in an external world, does not fall short of a completely adequate expression of that which the mind intends; such are the abstract concepts of mathematics and of ethics. The idea as *ectype*, on the other hand, is always an idea which represents something in the world without, of which it is a more or less adequate copy.[1]

The habit of thought to interpret certain ideas of this *ectype* order in a manner which necessitates a reference to something beyond themselves, transcends the simple processes of sensation and reflection. It implies a latent metaphysic which Locke would be loath to acknowledge, and which it would be impossible to reconcile with his original assumptions.

In addition, moreover, to the external world of

[1] *Essay*, Book II, chap. XXXI, § 12, 13, 14.

substantial persons and things which, even though never adequately known, must nevertheless possess some kind of reality, Locke claims that there must be also a Supreme Being of whose existence we have clear and abundant evidence. The proof which he offers is in the form of a deduction from the certain conviction, as a direct intuition of consciousness, that there is an inner self. He says: "Though God has given us no innate ideas of himself; though he has stamped no original characters on our minds wherein we may read his being; yet, having furnished us with those faculties our minds are endowed with, he hath not left himself without witness, since we have sense, perception and reason and cannot want a clear proof of him, as long as we carry *ourselves* about us. . . .

"I think it is beyond question that man has a clear idea of his own being; he knows certainly he exists, and that he is something. . . . In the next place, man knows by an intuitive certainty that bare *nothing can no more produce any real being than it can be equal to two right angles.* . . . If, therefore, we know there is some real being, and that nonentity cannot produce any real being, it is an evident demonstration, that from eternity there has been something; since what was not from eternity had a beginning; and what had a beginning must be produced by something else. Next, it is evident that what had its being and beginning from another, must also have all that which is in and belongs to its being from another too. All the powers it has must be owing to and received from the same source. This eternal source, then, of all being must also be the source and original of all power; and so *this* eternal *Being* must be also the most powerful.

"Again, a man finds in *himself* perception and knowledge. We have then got one step further; and we are certain now that there is not only some being, but some knowing, intelligent being in the world. There was a time, then, when there was no knowing being and when knowledge began to be; or else there has been also *a knowing being from eternity.* If it be said, there was a time when no being had any knowledge, when that eternal being was void of all understanding; I reply, that then it was impossible there should ever have been any knowledge, it being as impossible that things wholly void of knowledge, and operating blindly and without any perception, should produce a knowing being, as it is impossible that a triangle should make itself three angles bigger than two right ones.

"Thus, from the consideration of ourselves, and what we infallibly find in our own constitutions, our reason leads us to the knowledge of this certain and evident truth,—*That there is an eternal, most powerful and most knowing* Being; which, whether any one will please to call God, it matters not." [1]

In this proof we recognise the old cosmological argument, *a contingentia mundi*. It not only indicates that Locke has a theology as well as a metaphysic, but also that his theological position rests upon a foundation whose security, in turn, depends solely upon the validity of certain metaphysical assumptions. The principles, that everything that has a beginning must have a cause, and that every given effect must have a sufficient cause, are regarded by Locke as axiomatic, and as such they certainly cannot be traced to any sensory source as their origin.

[1] *Essay*, Book IV, chap. X, § 1 *ff.*

The chief point to emphasise for the purpose of our interpretation and criticism of this argument of Locke's is, that the idea of God is deduced by a process of reasoning which rests wholly upon certain assumptions concerning the nature of the causal relation. Locke assumes as axiomatic that the relation of cause and effect is that of an underlying necessary connection between events, a conception which Hume later vigorously attacked. In commenting upon Locke's argument, Hume insists that Locke falls into the fallacy of begging the question, for " 'tis sufficient only to observe, that when we exclude all causes we really do exclude them, and neither suppose nothing nor the object itself to be the causes of the existence; and consequently can draw no argument from the absurdity of these suppositions to prove the absurdity of that exclusion. If everything must have a cause, it follows, that upon the exclusion of other causes we must accept of the object itself or of nothing as causes. But 'tis the very point in question, whether everything must have a cause or not; and therefore, according to all just reasoning, it ought never to be taken for granted." [1]

Locke, however, not only indulges in a gratuitous assumption inconsistent with his empirical point of view in general, but he adopts a conception of the causal relation which is not at all in keeping with his specific account of the nature of causation presented in an earlier part of the *Essay*. In his explanation of the origin of our idea of causation, he says: "In the notice that our senses take of the constant vicissitude of things, we cannot but observe that several particular, both qualities and substances, begin to exist." [2]

[1] Hume, *A Treatise of Human Nature*, vol. I, Part III, § 3.
[2] *Essay*, Book II, chap. XXVI, § 1.

A mere observation of the "vicissitude of things" can never give the idea of causation as a necessary connection. Stillingfleet drew Locke's attention to this, and in Locke's reply, in his first *Letter* to the Bishop, he allows that the idea of causation implies a necessary principle of reason, and clearly states that "everything that has a beginning must have a cause is a true principle of reason, which we come to know by perceiving that *the idea of a beginning to be* is *necessarily connected* with *the idea of some operation;* and the idea of *operation* with *something operating, which we call a cause*.[1]

This, however, is essentially a metaphysical principle which no simple observation of the "vicissitude of things," by itself, however exact or protracted it may be, can ever discover. The reference to a fundamental principle of reasoning is certainly a departure from the strict adherence to a purely empirical interpretation of the beginnings of knowledge, which consistency surely demands. Without a metaphysical basis for the doctrine of causation, Locke's argument for the being of God wants a sufficient ground to establish its validity.

It is a matter of considerable interest to note that Locke's idea of God is that of a being external both to the world and to self. He emphasises the transcendency, but has no conception whatsoever of the immanency of God. In his chapter on the "Existence of God" there is in this connection a significant sentence: "From what has been said, it is plain to me we have a more certain knowledge of the existence of a God than of anything our senses have not immediately discovered to us. Nay, I presume I may

---

[1] Locke's *First Letter*, p. 1..

say, that we more certainly know that there is a God than that there is anything else without us." [1]

This conception of a God without, outside of self, outside of the world, is, of course, the central idea of deism. It is an idea which naturally fits into Locke's conception of the function of reason in thought; for as reason is regarded as operating mechanically upon the elemental materials of consciousness from without, so also the divine reason may be readily conceived in a like manner as operating upon the elements of the universe, fashioning and ordering them from without, rather than operating as a power of life within.

We are now to examine the development of Locke's philosophy as it affected the various writers who came under his influence. Inasmuch as Locke had frankly acknowledged that the idea of substance carried with it merely an intimation of some unknown support of the phenomena of experience, this left the way naturally open for a various interpretation of the nature of this unknown something. Locke's position in this respect, because it was indefinite and vague, admitted both of the idealistic and the materialistic conclusions which were drawn from it. The idealistic interpretation finds its most complete expression in the writings of Bishop Berkeley, who was in a sense a follower of Locke, yet differing radically from him in many essential particulars, and developing his philosophical thought along independent and original lines.

REFERENCES.—Lord King: *Life of John Locke*. London, 1829.
Henry Richard Fox Bourne: *Life of John Locke*. London, 1876.
R. Adamson: *The Development of Modern Philosophy*. Vol. I. Edinburgh, 1903.

[1] *Essay*, Book IV, chap. X, § 6.

S. Alexander: *Locke.* (*Philosophies, Ancient and Modern.*) London, 1908.
Cousin: *La Philosophie de Locke.* Sixth edition. Paris, 1863.
T. Fowler: *Locke.* (*English Men of Letters.*) London, 1880.
A. C. Fraser: *Locke.* (*Philosophical Classics for English Readers.*) Edinburgh, 1890.
A. C. Fraser: *Edition of Locke's Essay.* Clarendon Press, 1894.
T. H. Green: *Introduction to Hume's Treatise of Human Nature. Green's Works*, vol. I, London, 1885, or *Green & Grose Edition of Hume's Treatise*, vol. I, London, 1874.
Leibniz: *Nouveaux Essais.* Translation. London, 1896.
James McCosh: *Locke's Theory of Knowledge, with a Notice of Berkeley.* New York, 1884.
A. W. Moore: *Existence, Meaning and Reality in Locke's Essay.* Vol. III, Part II, of *Chicago University Decennial Publications.* Chicago, 1903.
Thomas Reid: *An Inquiry into the Human Mind on the Principles of Common Sense.* Edinburgh, 1764.
Dugald Stewart: *Locke's Account of the Sources of Human Knowledge. Works*, vol. V, pp. 55–86. Edinburgh, 1854.
T. E. Webb: *The Intellectualism of Locke.* Dublin, 1857.

CHAPTER III

BERKELEY'S IDEALISM

George Berkeley (1685–1753) was by natural endowment a philosopher. In his *Commonplace Book*, written while a student in Trinity College, Dublin, there is a characteristic record which indicates the native trend of his mind: "I was distrustful at eight years old, and consequently by nature disposed for these new doctrines." [1]

The early precocity developed steadily in his student days, and before he had left Trinity College he had outlined in the scattered fragments of his journal all of the central ideas which later found definite form and expression in his philosophical works.

While still at Trinity College, he came under the influence of Locke, whose *Essay* had been introduced into Dublin with the enthusiastic commendation of William Molyneux, Locke's ardent admirer and intimate friend, and a prominent member of the Irish Parliament. Berkeley's philosophy is based upon the presuppositions of Locke, subjected, however, to a more rigorous logic. He represents, therefore, an advanced phase in that dialectic movement of thought whose beginnings we first discover in the *Essay Concerning Human Understanding*. There are many statements throughout his *Commonplace Book* which show his early sympathy with a strictly empirical point of view, and the general method

---

[1] *Commonplace Book*, Fraser's edition of *Berkeley's Works*, vol. I, p. 79.

of the *Essay*. The following may serve as a typical example of the many references of this nature: "Mind is a congeries of perceptions. Take away perceptions, and you take away the mind. Put the perceptions and you put the mind. . . . We must with the mob place certainty in the senses. . . .

"I approve of this axiom of the Schoolmen, '*Nihil est in intellectu, quod non prius fuit in sensu.*' I wish they had stuck to it. It had never taught them the doctrine of abstract ideas."[1]

The first paragraph of Berkeley's *Principles of Human Knowledge* is substantially a restatement of the fundamental position of the *Essay*. This also forms the foundation upon which Berkeley endeavours to raise the entire superstructure of knowledge. He says: "It is evident to any one who takes a survey of the *objects of human knowledge*, that they are either *ideas* actually imprinted on the senses; or else such as are perceived by attending to the passions and operations of the mind; or, lastly, *ideas* formed by help of memory and imagination— either compounding, dividing or barely representing those originally perceived in the aforesaid ways. By sight, I have the ideas of light and colours, with their several degrees and variations. By touch, I perceive hard and soft, heat and cold, motion and resistance; and of all these more or less either as to quantity or degree. Smelling furnishes me with odours; the palate with tastes; and hearing conveys sounds to the mind in all their variety of tone and composition. And as several of these are observed to accompany each other, they come to be marked by one name, and so to be reputed as one *thing*. Thus, for example, a

---

[1] Frazer's *Berkeley*, vol. I, pp. 27, 44, 48. (All subsequent references to Berkeley will be to Frazer's edition.)

certain colour, taste, smell, figure and consistence having been observed to go together, are accounted one distinct thing, signified by the name apple; other collections of ideas constitute a stone, a tree, a book and the like sensible things; which, as they are pleasing or disagreeable, excite the passions of love, hatred, joy, grief and so forth." [1]

Berkeley thus starts with Locke's assumption that the elemental unit of all knowledge is the concrete particular experience of sense. He insists, however, that what is presented to our minds through the process of sense-perception, namely, the particular idea, is in every case an exhaustive expression of all that we can possibly know of the actual experience which appears in consciousness as the object of knowledge. Locke had endeavoured to go behind the idea in the mind, and had declared most emphatically that there is some substance in the form of an external object corresponding to the idea in the mind; and that while we do not know *what* this object is, we undoubtedly know that *it is*.

Berkeley contends, on the contrary, that the assumption of the existence of any material substance outside and independent of the observing mind is wholly gratuitous and unwarrantable upon a strict interpretation of the original premises of Locke. The mind is to be regarded, therefore, as having no function of reference beyond itself. The fundamental error in Locke's reasoning Berkeley traces to his failure to appreciate the illusory nature of all abstract ideas. An abstract idea, he maintains, is a pure fiction of the mind, and becomes a fatal source of confusion in thought, for abstraction is essentially a process of separating ideas indissolubly bound to-

[1] *Principles of Human Knowledge*, vol. I, p. 257 *f*.

gether. This was the ground principle of Berkeley's polemic position. And it grew out of the impossible conception which, in his judgment, Locke had entertained concerning the nature of substance. He held that Locke had taken a wholly unwarrantable course in his reasoning when he had abstracted the idea of an underlying something which was the unknown *substratum* of a group of various qualities always appearing together in consciousness, and had regarded it as an external independent thing. If Locke had strictly excluded any such abstract conception as this, and had consistently held together in his thought the qualities of a thing as coextensive with the thing itself, and if he had never allowed the object of knowledge to be regarded as distinct from the group of qualities constituting the idea of it in consciousness, then he never would have made the lamentable mistake of separating the world of appearance from the world of reality. Berkeley's position as regards abstract ideas was most highly commended by David Hume, who said of it: "I look upon this to be one of the greatest and most valuable discoveries that has been made of late years in the republic of letters." [1]

The doctrine of abstract ideas we may regard, therefore, as the first point of departure of Berkeley's thought from that of Locke. The second is his position concerning Locke's distinction between the primary and secondary qualities of matter. Locke, it will be remembered, had held that while the secondary qualities of matter—colours, sounds, odours, flavours and the like—do not represent the actual properties of the object perceived, but rather the manner in which our peculiar kind of organism may

[1] Hume, *A Treatise of Human Nature*, Part I, § 7.

be affected, the primary qualities of form, figure, extension and solidity, nevertheless, do fairly represent the nature of the object as it really is.

Berkeley, on the contrary, completely wipes out all distinctions whatsoever between the supposed primary and secondary qualities of matter, and considers the ideas of extension, figure, motion, rest, solidity and number quite as subjective as taste, colour or sound. The primary and secondary qualities shade off so imperceptibly the one into the other that it is impossible to draw a consistent line of demarcation between them. Here, again, is the fallacy and the folly of abstract ideas. If the colour is subjective, so also is the extended surface, because you cannot have a surface which is not at the same time coloured as well. Mere extension void of colour is a highly abstract idea which represents a *tour de force* of our mental activity without any correspondence whatsoever with our actual experiences. In an early essay, which was the result of his philosophical thinking while still in Dublin, and published when he was only twenty-four years of age, entitled *Essay Towards a New Theory of Vision*, Berkeley had already laid the foundation for this veiw as to the indirect and subjective character of our perception of the so-called primary qualities of matter; and consequently it became the foundation also of his theory of idealism. In this *Essay* he attempts to show in detail that we have no immediate intuition of distance by sight, but that our perception of it is indirect, composed of a group of suggestions and inferences connected with the elemental sensations attending the process of vision, and further complicated by the intimate associations with the materials of knowledge furnished by the sense of touch. It follows, therefore, that the idea of distance and of position, with the consequent ideas of form and figure, are quite as dependent upon the interpreting mind as the ideas of colour and taste. The same may be shown also of the ideas of solidity, motion and rest, number and the like. We find, therefore, Berkeley's world of ideas assuming shape and determining its own bounds, so as to comprise within itself the entire body of our knowledge. For him the world of ideas is the world of reality.

To appreciate Berkeley's contribution to the general movement of thought which we are studying, as well as to estimate critically the value of his philosophical position in itself, it will be necessary to gain a sympathetic understanding of his idealistic point of view, and to enter with some degree of discernment into the spirit of his interpretation of the world as it lies before him, in its infinite variety of beauty and power, as a world of ideas only. By a sympathetic appreciation of Berkeley's position, I mean the honest endeavour on our part to see things as he saw them, without the prejudice due to our habitual mode of viewing the world of experience. In this way we can certainly come to a clearer understanding of his theory, without committing ourselves in the least to his cause. Let us inquire then more particularly as to the manner in which Berkeley interpreted the simple elements of his own experience and out of them built his world of ideas. He discovers, in the first place, obviously enough that all objects of perception reveal themselves as to their existence and characteristic qualities within the all-embracing element of consciousness. They fall wholly within this element, and never can appear outside of it. As they pass beyond the bounds of consciousness, they at once fade out into nothingness. While in the focus of our attentive and perceiving mind, they appear with an indefinable atmosphere of reality about them. As they disappear from the field of perception, the idea of them as a memory can never compete with the original impression in vividness, in distinctness of detail or in the actual warmth of reality. When I speak of the external world, that world is never external to my thought, although I may properly conceive of it as external to me. My thought, so far as it perceives the world, completely embraces and possesses it.

Moreover, these objects of my perception, these objects which make up the world for me as I know it, take on a certain character from the very nature of the consciousness itself wherein they stand revealed. There is no object of perception which is not tinged by this consciousness colouring. We perceive all things through the many-hued glass of our sense-furnished minds. There is no other machinery of perception possible; for every quality, whether primary or secondary, of what we are pleased to call material objects without us, is mediated by one or more of the organs of sensation.

Sound, colour, size and shape all vary with the senses through whose channels they become objects of perception to the mind. The object, therefore, in its entirety, as it appears in consciousness, is a composite of sense-received and mind-interpreted qualities. Whatever we imagine to be present in such an object as a supposed property, and yet with no capacity whatever of disclosing its nature to the observing mind, must remain forever unknown, and therefore must be regarded as wholly unreal; it is a fancy, and not a fact of the mind. Every property of every object, therefore, is in reality what it appears to be in the consciousness of the mind which observes it. An idea, Berkeley insists, must be like an idea, and cannot be conceived as representing some external thing composed of elemental parts wholly unlike itself, such as is the popular conception of matter—"an inert, senseless substance, in which extension, figure and motion do actually subsist." [1]

As all perceived properties of the objects of experience are in terms of sense elements according to the capacity of the mind to interpret them, they are not only mentally discerned, but they are also, in a certain sense, mentally constituted. The world, therefore, exists for the observing mind. Its nature, its characteristic features, whatever it possesses of significance for us, are due wholly to this transforming function of perception. If there are concealed properties in the world which are incapable of expressing themselves through the ordinary channels of sense-perception, then these supposed qualities, as far as we are concerned, do not exist. Whatever the world may be in itself, we know it, and we are so constituted that it is possible for us to know it, only when all its various elements are translated in terms of thought and appear as ideas in the mind. The nature of the world, therefore, is capable essentially of just that kind of self-expression which possesses this peculiar significance for the observing mind, and as such exercises a function which must needs represent the very core of its reality. This is Berkeley's thought, which he compresses into the characteristic formula, *esse* is *percipi*. It would be well perhaps for us to have before us his own commentary upon it:

[1] *Principles*, Part I, § 8, 9.

"That neither our thoughts nor passions nor ideas formed by the imagination exist without the mind is what everybody will allow. And to me it seems no less evident that the various sensations, or ideas imprinted on the Sense, however blended or combined together (that is, whatever objects they compose), cannot exist otherwise than in a mind perceiving them. I think an intuitive knowledge may be obtained of this, by any one that shall attend to what is meant by the term *exist* when applied to sensible things. The table I write on I say exists; that is, I see and feel it; and if I were out of my study, I should say it existed; meaning thereby that if I was in my study, I might perceive it, or that some other spirit actually does perceive it. There was an odour, that is, it was smelt; there was a sound, that is, it was heard; a colour or figure, and it was perceived by sight or touch. This is all that I can understand by these and the like expressions. For as to what is said of the *absolute* existence of unthinking things, without any relation to their being perceived, that is to me perfectly unintelligible. Their *esse* is *percipi;* nor is it possible that they should have any existence out of the minds or thinking things which perceive them." [1]

Existence with Berkeley must be evidenced by appearance, that is, by the manner in which an object of our knowledge manifests itself to the observing mind. If it is incapable of revealing itself in the guise of any appearance whatsoever, the reality of its existence is reduced to the vanishing point. Moreover as we conceive of any variation occurring in the nature of the observing mind, we must also allow that the world, as interpreted by such a mind, would

[1] *Principles*, Part I, § 3.

undergo a corresponding variation in the general aspect which it presents.

For the sake of a clearer understanding of Berkeley's contention, let us suppose that two observers of the world in which they live are so constituted that, as regards their several perceptions, there is a complete reciprocal reversal of sensory reaction; that is, whatever appears hard to the one is soft to the other; what seems heavy to one is light to the other; bitter, sweet; and sweet, bitter; and all colours as observed by one, appear as the complementary colours to the other. Then the reality which the world in each case would seem to exhibit in these various observed qualities would be so oppositely interpreted as to constitute two worlds and not one. In other words, our world is, in its essential nature, adapted to that peculiar type of sense-furnished minds such as we possess. Reality, therefore, according to Berkeley, is that which is able to reveal itself to the observing mind in such a way that its various qualities can be expressed in terms of ideas which are received through the senses.

The question at once suggests itself as to whether an object of knowledge which thus evidences its reality in the field of sense-perception, ceases to exist as soon as the attention of the observing mind is withdrawn. Berkeley meets such an objection by the theory which he dogmatically advances, that every existing thing, if not disclosing itself to an actual observing mind at some particular time or place, must be regarded at least as possibly under the inspection of some mind somewhere; and always, in general, under the continuous and sustaining observation of the Eternal Mind. Berkeley deduces the idea of God from the necessities of his idealistic position. He says: "Whence I conclude, not that sensible things have no real existence, but that, seeing they depend not on my thought, and have an existence distinct from being perceived by me, *there must be some other Mind wherein they exist.* As sure, therefore, as the sensible world really exists, so sure is there an infinite omnipresent Spirit who contains and supports it.

"Men commonly believe that all things are known or perceived by God, because they believe the being of a God; whereas I, on the other side, immediately and necessarily conclude the being of a God, because all sensible things must be perceived by him. For philosophers, though they acknowledge all corporeal beings to be perceived by God, yet they attribute to them an absolute subsistence distinct from their being perceived by any mind whatever; which I do not. Besides, is there no difference between saying: *There is a God, therefore he perceives all things;* and saying: *Sensible things do really exist, and if they really exist, they are necessarily perceived by an infinite Mind; therefore there is an infinite Mind or God*"? [1]

The world, therefore, must be regarded as so constituted, in respect to its essential nature, that its fundamental reality finds expression solely in terms of sense-determined thought. All colour and sound, light and shade, day and night, the glory of summer and the storms of winter, all the labours of man, "the furniture of earth and the choir of heaven," exist only for the mind which is able to penetrate their mysteries, interpret their significance and express the nature of their reality in those terms which none but the nature of mind can devise. The mind's reaction

---

[1] "The Second Dialogue between Hylas and Philonous," Fraser's *Berkeley*, vol. I, p. 424.

upon the objects of perception as they variously appear in consciousness reveals, in that very process, the nature also of the reality in which these objects are essentially grounded. What is matter? We can only describe it in terms which are known to us; and as known to us the object of knowledge presents itself in the field of observation already saturated with thought.

Now this capacity of revealing its inner nature to mind which every object possesses, and which is of the very essence of its reality, can belong only to that kind of substance which also partakes of the nature of mind, that is, a spiritual substance. Berkeley insists that only mind can act upon mind in such a way as to produce ideas in it; and that it is impossible to conceive of a so-called material substance producing ideas. This is the function of spiritual substance alone. Berkeley finds in the control over our own ideas, which we as spiritual substances exert, an intimation that the ideas which seem to be given to us from a world without are, in reality, the result of a like spiritual substance in nature acting directly upon our minds. As to his conception of a spiritual substance and its peculiar function in the economy of nature and the mind of man, the following passage will furnish a very clear and satisfactory exposition:

"A Spirit is one simple, undivided, active being. As it perceives ideas it is called the *understanding*, and as it produces or otherwise operates about them it is called the *will*. Hence there can be no *idea* formed of a soul or spirit; for all ideas whatever being passive and inert (*vid.* § 25), they cannot represent into us, by way of image or likeness, that which acts. A little attention will make it plain to any one that to have an idea which shall be *like* that active

Principle of motion and change of ideas is absolutely impossible. Such is the nature of spirit, or that which acts, that it cannot be of itself perceived, but only by the effects which it produceth. . . . I find I can excite ideas in my mind at pleasure, and vary and shift the scene as oft as I think fit. It is no more than *willing*, and straightway this or that idea arises in my fancy; and by the same power it is obliterated and makes way for another. This making and unmaking of ideas doth very properly denominate the mind active. Thus much is certain, and grounded on experience: but when we talk of unthinking agents, or of exciting ideas exclusive of volition, we only amuse ourselves with words.

"But, whatever power I may have over my own thoughts, I find the ideas actually perceived by sense have not a like dependence on *my* will. When in broad daylight I open my eyes, it is not in my power to choose whether I shall see or no, or to determine what particular objects shall present themselves to my view; and so likewise as to the hearing and other senses; the ideas imprinted on them are not creatures of *my* will. There is, therefore, some other Will or Spirit that produces them." [1]

In Locke's doctrine of causation, it will be remembered, ideas of sensation are connected as cause and effect with one another and with things. With Berkeley, however, the causal stimulus resides wholly in the mind which produces the panorama of sense impressions on the screen of our consciousness and determines their natural order of sequence and coexistence, rendering them "strong, orderly and coherent," [2] thus serving to differentiate them distinctly from the fancies of the imagination.

[1] *Principles*, Part I, § 27, 28, 29.   [2] *Ib.*, Part I, § 30, 33.

The laws of nature according to Berkeley are merely the "set rules or established methods, wherein the mind we depend on excites in us the ideas of sense."[1]

Any observed connection of ideas in our thought does not, therefore, imply any relation of cause and effect existing between them. They all issue at a common source. Our groups of ideas and their seeming coherence must be regarded merely as certain marks or signs of the things they signify.[2]

An illustration perhaps will make this quite subtle conception clearer. We speak of a book which we have just finished reading. Its reality for us is what it contains and is able to supply to our thought. Eliminate wholly its significance for thought, and nothing remains. Moreover the elements by which its thought becomes known to us, the lettered page, are merely the sign language into which the thought significance has been originally stored by an intelligence, a spiritual substance, like ourselves. In precisely a similar manner the sense impressions which we receive from the world about us are symbolic expressions, conveying to us ideas concerning the things they signify. The phenomena of nature, therefore, form among themselves a kind of sign language, a symbolical representation of the thought which the all-controlling Mind of the universe would impart to us. If we were less ignorant of its art, we could penetrate more deeply into the secrets of nature and the mystery of the world. As Berkeley says: "It is the searching after and endeavouring to understand this language (if I may so call it) of the Author of Nature that ought to be the employment of the natural philosopher; and not the pretending to

---

[1] *Principles*, Part I, § 30.   [2] *Ib.*, Part I, § 32, 33.

explain things by *corporeal* causes, which doctrine seems to have too much estranged the minds of men from that Active Principle, that supreme and wise Spirit, in whom we live and move and have our being." [1]

Berkeley's ideal was the humanisation of science. This conception had been explicitly expressed in his previous essay on *A New Theory of Vision*, where he elaborates more fully the salient features of this doctrine: "Upon the whole I think we may fairly conclude that the proper objects of Vision constitute the Universal Language of Nature; whereby we are instructed how to regulate our actions, in order to attain those things that are necessary to the preservation and well-being of our bodies, as also to avoid whatever may be hurtful and destructive of them. It is by their information that we are principally guided in all the transactions and concerns of life. And the manner wherein they signify and mark out unto us the objects which are at a distance is the same with that of languages and signs of human appointment; which do not suggest the things signified by any likeness or identity of nature, but only by an habitual connection that experience has made us observe between them." [2]

Such is Berkeley's idealism, as I have attempted to sketch it, with its naïve and daring assumptions, its protest against scholastic speculation obscured in the haze of words, its evident theological bias, its over-weighted argument, and its strong underlying *motif*, namely, the purpose to undermine the materialistic foundations of the current philosophical tendencies toward scepticism and infidelity.

[1] *Principles*, Part I, § 66.
[2] *An Essay towards a New Theory of Vision*, § 147.

This conception may appear fanciful and strained, and it may provoke our judgment to react against it with an emphatic protest. And yet, notwithstanding its essential contradiction of the common mode of viewing things, it appeals, nevertheless, to the critical and even hostile reader with a strange fascination. We feel that it is an idea which at least challenges consideration, though it may not produce conviction. In spite of ourselves we follow the lead of this special pleader with a growing interest in the subtlety of his thought, and in the skill with which he orders his argument. He commands our admiration by his freedom from all suggestion of the usual or ordinary, and by his evident determination to see things in their own light and with his own eyes.

Through a wide range of his speculation, Berkeley possessed the courage of his logic, and yet he faltered at certain crucial points. He feels instinctively that there are certain weak places structurally in his system which he proceeds to strengthen by additional assumptions, without being clearly aware of the logical inconsistency involved. For instance, he denies the possibility of material substance, upon the ground that such a conception is an abstract idea unwarrantably separated from the group of perceived properties which constitute the essential setting of the object itself. And yet, not wishing to be forced by his own logic to a position of purely subjective idealism, he finds himself constrained to assert that there must needs be some spiritual substance operating as the cause of the various phenomena whose appearance in the field of consciousness, independent of our volition, can be explained only upon such a supposition. His argument proves too much. If a material substance is a gratuitous assumption, then also a spiritual substance; for a spiritual substance is quite as abstract a conception as a material substance.

Again, he finds in consciousness at the initial stages of our knowledge merely a sensory affection of the organism, the crude impression of sensation; and yet in the development of his theory of knowledge he insensibly transforms this elemental *datum* of sense into the consciousness of a perceived object. There is a distinct difference between a feeling and the knowledge of a thing which is felt, and which is a determined object of knowledge sustaining relations to other objects as well as to the mind capable of observing it. When the object of knowledge is no longer a mere element of sensuous experience, but has become an element in an intelligible system, then such a transformation demands some explanation of the nature of the process which underlies it. This Berkeley does not attempt to give. However, he is in a vague way conscious of a change of significance in his interpretation of the original ideas of sensation. It is a matter of considerable interest to note how Berkeley at times draws an evident distinction between the term *idea* as a quality of sense, and *notion* as a product of thought quite free of any sense mediation. This distinction is not one of explicit definition so much as of usage. In the second edition of his *Principles of Knowledge* he adds the word *notion* to the original text in the following paragraph, the added phrase being marked by brackets: "In a large sense, indeed, we may be said to have an idea [or rather a notion] of *spirit*. That is, we understand the meaning of the word, otherwise we could not affirm or deny anything of it. Moreover, as we conceive the ideas that are in the minds of other spirits by means of our own, which we suppose to be resemblances of them, so we know other spirits by means of our own soul, which in that sense is the image or idea of them; it having a like respect to other spirits that blueness or heat by me perceived has to those ideas perceived by another." [1]

Both the *notion* of spirit and the accompanying argument certainly are not by any means the result of sensory ideas or any combination of them. There is another passage which Berkeley adds in the second edition as though to qualify a certain recognised incompleteness of the earlier exposition: "We comprehend our own existence by inward feeling or reflection, and that of other spirits by reason. We may be said to have some knowledge or *notion* of our own minds, of spirits and active beings whereof in a strict sense we have not *ideas*. In like manner we know and have a *notion* of relations between things or ideas; which relations are distinct from the ideas or things related, inasmuch as the latter may be perceived by us without our perceiving the former. To me it seems that *ideas*, *spirits* and *relations* are all in their respective kinds the object of human knowledge and subject of discourse; and that the term *idea* would be improperly extended to signify everything we know or have any notion of." [2]

This reference to a knowledge of self, of spirit and of relations, which cannot be traced to sensory ideas as its source, indicates an appreciation of the inadequacy of the strictly empirical origin of our knowledge. It may be regarded, however, in the light of a vague intimation on Berkeley's part of the necessity of assuming certain intelligible relations in order to explain the organisation of the world of knowledge,

[1] *Principles*, Part I, § 140.   [2] *Ib.*, Part I, § 89.

rather than any explicit formulation of the same as an essential and significant part of his doctrine.

If our general point of view is correct that the movement of thought in this period is a process of evolution, then it is only natural to expect that, in a given stage of its development, we should be able to find certain ideas in a germinal or potential state which are destined to appear in full flower and fruit at a later stage of the unfolding process. And in an eminent degree Berkeley's idealism furnishes an excellent illustration of this very thing. Vaguely, and even inconsistently with his original position, he occasionally speaks, in the spirit at least if not in the letter, of the Kantian philosophy.

This is particularly noticeable in the later form of his idealism as seen in his essay entitled *Siris: A Chain of Philosophical Reflexions and Inquiries.* The *Siris* shows a tendency throughout to rise above a point of view which regards the world solely as a congeries of sense-determined ideas, and to move also toward a recognition and restoration of the constructive and informing powers of the intellect. Berkeley calls his essay "a chain of philosophical reflexions and inquiries," and adds, as a commentary upon this title, that "there are many links in the Chain which connects the two extremes of what is grossly sensible and purely intelligible, and it seems a tedious work, by the slow helps of memory, imagination and reason, oppressed and overwhelmed as we are by the senses, through erroneous principles, and long ambages of words and notions, to struggle upward into the light of truth; yet, as this gradually dawns, farther discoveries still correct the style and clear up the notions." [1]

[1] Fraser's Edition, vol. III. *Siris*, § 296.

Starting in this essay with a preliminary discussion of the therapeutic virtue of tar-water as a panacea for all ills that the flesh is heir to, Berkeley proceeds, by natural stages, to a consideration of the assumed volatile substance which constitutes the essential principle of this healing potion and is also the secret of its efficacy. Thence his thought is led by obvious suggestion to the vital fire or spirit which he believes must animate all things, and which, in turn, he is constrained to think must be itself kindled and sustained by the all-controlling Spirit or Mind of the universe. In the earlier idealism, the supreme Mind was regarded as acting directly upon other minds, producing by the resulting reaction the world of ideas in consciousness; in this later form there is the introduction of a series of secondary causes acted upon by the supreme Mind, and in turn capable of affecting the mind of man through the various processes of sense perception.

This feature of Berkeley's later idealism is evident in the following passages, which are typical of the general trend of his thought in this essay: "The order and course of things, and the experiments we daily make, show there is a Mind that governs and actuates this mundane system, as the proper real agent and cause; and that the inferior instrumental cause is pure æther, fire, or the substance of light (§ 29, 37, 136, 149), which is applied and determined by an Infinite Mind in the macrocosm or universe, with unlimited power, and according to stated rules, as it is in the microcosm with limited power and skill by the human mind. We have no proof, either from experiment or reason, of any other Agent, or efficient cause, than Mind or Spirit. When, therefore, we speak of corporeal agents or corporeal causes; this is to be understood in a different, subordinate and improper sense.

"The *calidum innatum*, the vital flame or animal spirit in man, is supposed the *cause* of all motions in the several parts of his body, whether voluntary or natural. That is, it is accounted the instrument, by means whereof the *mind* exerts and manifests herself in the motions of the body. In the same sense, may not *fire* be said to have force, to operate and agitate the whole system of the world; which is held together and informed by one presiding Mind; and animated throughout by one and the same fiery substance, as an instrumental and mechanical agent, not as a primary real efficient?

"No eye could ever hitherto discern, and no sense perceive, the animal spirit in a human body otherwise than from its effects. The same may be said of pure fire, or the spirit of the universe, which is perceived only by means of some other bodies, on which it operates or with which it is joined. What the chemists say of pure acids being never found alone might as well be said of pure fire.

"In the human body the mind orders and moves the limbs; but the animal spirit is supposed the immediate physical cause of their motion. So likewise, in the mundane system, a mind presides; but the immediate, mechanical or instrumental cause, that moves or animates all its parts, is the pure elementary fire or spirit of the world. The more fine or subtle part is supposed to receive the impressions of the First Mover, and communicate them to the grosser sensible parts of this world. Motion, though in metaphysical rigour and truth a passion or mere effect, yet in physics passeth for an action. And by this action all effects are supposed to be produced.

Hence the various communications, determinations, accelerations of motion, constitute the laws of nature. The pure æther or invisible fire contains parts of different kinds, that are impressed with different forces or subjected to different laws of motion, attraction, repulsion and expansion, and endued with divers distinct habitudes toward other bodies. These seem to constitute the many various qualities (§ 37, 40, 44), virtues, flavours, odours and colours which distinguish natural productions." [1]

In these passages the recurrent ideas of vital fire, the interposition of secondary causes, the analogy between the vital energy of the body and the driving power of the world, all are ideas quite foreign to the idealism of the *Principles of Knowledge* and the *Dialogues*. The ideas have grown to be something more than sensible signs whose interpretation discovers to us the order, unity and harmony of nature. In the later thought of Berkeley there is an evident touch of the Platonic idealism. His world of ideas appears no longer inert and incapable of operating as efficient causes, but, on the contrary, as a centre of active power.

This view is not only expressed in the *Siris*, but is also explicitly illustrated and established by references to the Platonic idealism, as may be seen in the following passage: "It may seem, perhaps, to those who have been taught to discourse about substratums, more reasonable and pious, to attribute to the Deity a more substantial being than the notional entities of wisdom, order, law, virtue or goodness; which being only complex ideas framed and put together by the understanding, are its own creatures, and have noth-

[1] *Siris*, § 154, 156, 159, 161, 162.

ing substantial, real or independent in them.¹ But it must be considered that, in the Platonic system, order, virtue, law, goodness and wisdom are not creatures of the soul of man, but innate, and originally existent therein, not as an accident in a substance, but as light to enlighten, and as a guide to govern. In Plato's style, the term *idea* doth not merely signify an inert, inactive object of the understanding, but is used as synonymous with αἴτιον and αρχή, cause and principle. ² According to that philosopher, goodness, beauty, virtue and such like are not figments of the mind, nor mere mixed modes, nor yet abstract ideas in the modern sense, but the most real beings, intellectual and unchangeable; and therefore more real than the fleeting, transient objects of sense (§ 306), which wanting stability cannot be subjects of science (§ 264, 266, 297), much less of intellectual knowledge.

" By Parmenides, Timæus and Plato a distinction was made, as hath been observed already, between *genitum* and *ens*. The former sort is always generating or *in fieri* (§ 304, 306), but never exists; because it never continues the same, being in a constant change, ever perishing and producing. By *entia* they understand things remote from sense, invisible and intellectual, which never changing are still the same, and may therefore be said truly to exist. Οὐσία, which is generally translated substance, but more

¹ A reference to Locke's view that our complex ideas which he calls mixed modes possess no substantial reality. See *Essay Concerning Human Understanding*, Book IV, chap. IV, § 12.
² See Berkeley's earlier account of the nature of *idea* where he insists that " all our ideas, sensations, notions, or the things which we perceive, by whatsoever names they may be distinguished are visibly inactive; there is nothing of power or agency included in them." *Principles of Knowledge*, Part I, § 25.

properly essence, was not thought to belong to things sensible and corporeal which have no stability; but rather to intellectual ideas, though discerned with more difficulty, and making less impression on a mind stupefied and immersed in animal life, than gross objects that continually beset and solicit our senses. The most refined human intellect, exerted to its utmost reach, can only seize some imperfect glimpses of the Divine Ideas (§ 313, 330), abstracted from all things corporeal, sensible and imaginable.[1]

It will be seen that mind has come to occupy a more central place in Berkeley's theory of knowledge. His starting-point in the ideas received through sensation has been left far afield. He recognises a process of rationalising our knowledge which transcends the professed empirical basis of the *Principles*. This distinction between sense and intellect and their several offices and functions is one which emerges in this later phase of his idealism, and is characteristic of a growing appreciation of the inadequacy of his earlier position. The idea of the *Siris* as a chain of philosophical reflections is an endeavour on Berkeley's part to rise above the things of sense and give them an intelligible interpretation according to the clearer light of reason. This distinction has already been noted in the paragraph which has been quoted above from the *Siris*. It is still more explicitly stated and emphasised in the following comparison which Berkeley draws between the nature of sense and of intellect: "Sense, at first, besets and overbears the mind. The sensible appearances are all in all; our reasonings are employed about them; our desires terminate in them; we look no farther for realities or causes; till intellect begins to dawn, and cast a ray on this

[1] *Siris*, § 335, 336, 337.

shadowy scene. We then perceive the true principle of unity, identity and existence. Those things that before seemed to constitute the whole of Being, upon taking an intellectual view of things, prove to be but fleeting phantoms. From the outward form of gross masses which occupy the vulgar, a curious inquirer proceeds to examine the inward structure and minute parts, and from observing the motions in nature to discover the laws of those motions. By the way he frames his hypothesis and suits his language to this natural philosophy, and these fit the occasion and answer the end of a maker of experiments or mechanic; who means only to apply the powers of nature and reduce the phenomena to rules. But if, proceeding still in his analysis and inquiry, he ascends from the sensible into the intellectual world, and beholds things in a new light and a new order, he will then change his system and perceive that what he took for substances and causes are but fleeting shadows; that the Mind contains all, and acts all, and is to all created beings the source of unity and identity, harmony and order, existence and stability." [1]

This seems to approach very nearly the Kantian point of view. Indeed, there are some sentences in the *Siris* which might very properly find a place in the text of the *Critique of Pure Reason* itself, particularly the following: "As understanding perceiveth not, that is, doth not hear, or see, or feel, so sense knoweth not: and although the mind may use both sense and fancy, as means whereby to arrive at knowledge, yet sense or soul, so far forth as sensitive, knoweth nothing." [2]

We must not, however, hastily conclude that

[1] *Siris*, § 294, 295.   [2] *Ib.*, § 305.

Berkeley anticipated the Kantian theory of knowledge. This cannot be allowed for the simple reason that Berkeley never appreciated the full significance of his later views and their obvious inconsistency with the fundamental position which characterises his earlier idealism. Had he appreciated the full force of his argument in the *Siris* he would have been keenly sensible of the evident modification which his initial presuppositions had undergone through the maturing process of his later thought, and he would have felt it incumbent upon him to state explicitly the relation of the one to the other. It is a long road from the expressed conviction of the *Commonplace Book* that "mind is a congeries of perceptions," [1] to the last word of his philosophy, that "sense or soul, so far forth as sensitive, knoweth nothing."

Again, as in the criticism of Locke, it must be kept well in mind that an author's views which do not square with his fundamental position and the essential features of its systematic development cannot possibly receive that consideration which otherwise they would naturally command. A position which is reached by logical inconsistency, however advanced and important it may be, cannot be held except through an honest effort at retrenchment and reconstruction. This Berkeley, unfortunately, did not attempt.

His idealism as the outcome of the Lockian principles of empiricism became the subject of Hume's keen logical analysis. While this critical inquiry resulted in a philosophy of scepticism, nevertheless the very inconsistencies themselves of Berkeley's wealth of knowledge are highly suggestive, and may be regarded in a way as a prophecy of the more care-

---

[1] *Commonplace Book*, p. 27.

fully guarded and logically defensible principles of the philosophy of Kant.

Before passing to a consideration of the development of philosophical thought in this period as it takes its course in the writings of Hume, it will be of interest, particularly to American scholars, to note the rather romantic relation of this Irish Bishop to the cause of philosophy in the American colonies. An idealist in his visions as well as in his more sober exercises of thought, Berkeley conceived the project of establishing a college in the Bermuda or Summer Islands where both the English youth of the plantations and the young American savages might be educated together to the end of effecting "the reformation of manners among the English in our Western plantations and the propagation of the Gospel among the American savages." [1]

This vision of an academic Utopia in the Summer Islands, with its noble missionary impulse, was never realised. Through many vicissitudes of fortune Berkeley resolutely bent his activities to further this scheme. This necessitated a journey to America and a consequent residence there of some three years. His temporary home was chosen in Rhode Island just outside of Newport, and along the coast at a place which Berkeley called Whitehall. Here he was visited by Samuel Johnson, the Episcopal missionary at Stratford, afterward president of Kings College in New York, now Columbia University.

Through intercourse and correspondence with Berkeley, Johnson became a convert to "the new way of ideas," and later illustrated the doctrines of idealism in a work entitled *Elementa Philosophica*.

Jonathan Edwards, who was a pupil of Johnson's

[1] Fraser's *Berkeley*, p. 120.

at Yale College, and grounded in the principles of idealism, shows, especially in his earlier writings, the marks of his training. As regards the idealistic nature of the objects of sense perception and the ultimate cause which produces them, and the function which the phenomena of nature play as signs of divine power and will, all this bears the stamp of Berkeley's idealism in high relief. Thus the two most important contributors in those early days to philosophical thought in America—and pioneers as well in exploring the things of the mind—were profoundly influenced by the personality and teachings of one who, while he failed to establish a university for the youth of our country, nevertheless created a body of doctrine for its scholars.[1]

REFERENCES.—R. Adamson: *The Development of Modern Philosophy*, vol. I. Edinburgh, 1903.
James F. Ferrier: *Berkeley and Idealism*. Works, vol. III, pp. 289-377. Edinburgh and London, 1866.
A. Campbell Fraser: *Berkeley*. (*Philosophical Classics for English Readers*.) Edinburgh, 1899.
A. Campbell Fraser: *Berkeley's Complete Works*. Clarendon Press, 1901.
T. H. Green: *Introduction to Hume's Treatise of Human Nature*. Green's Works, vol. I. London, 1885.
Professor Huxley: *Critiques and Addresses*, pp. 320 ff. New York, 1873.
James McCosh: *Locke's Theory of Knowledge, with a Notice of Berkeley*. New York, 1884.
J. S. Mill: *Dissertations*, vols. II and IV. New York, 1874-5.
Dugald Stewart: *Idealism of Berkeley*. Works, vol. V, pp. 87-119. Edinburgh, 1854-8.
M. H. Calkins: *Persistent Problems in Philosophy*. N. Y., 1907.

[1] See Fraser, *Berkeley's Works*, vol. III, Appendix C., Samuel Johnson and Jonathan Edwards.

CHAPTER IV

HUME'S SCEPTICISM

Taking up again the main lines of the development of thought in this period, we find the philosophy both of Locke and Berkeley subjected to the critical analysis of Hume.

David Hume (1711-76) contributes a Scotch strain to the British philosophy of the eighteenth century; which may be regarded as a natural complement to the contributions of Locke and Berkeley, as representatives of England and Ireland. This Scotch thinker is an iconoclast in philosophy. His is a naked intellect, free from superstition and prejudice, progressing in its own dry light. He had an inveterate hatred of any unwarrantable assumption. His moral nature as well as his intellectual revolted from the idea of taking more than was strictly one's logical due, as though it were an overt act of theft itself. Whatever might be the results of his thinking, he demanded a complete intellectual emancipation in the processes of it. His mind was by nature pre-eminently fitted for the signal task of philosophical criticism. While his analysis may not reach any positive conclusion, nevertheless its negative and sceptical outcome has been of no small service in disclosing the insufficiency of the fundamental premises of a purely empirical view of things.

Proceeding from the initial stand-point of Locke and accepting Berkeley's criticism of certain of

Locke's conclusions, particularly concerning his conception of substance and causation, Hume pushes his unswerving logic to its final and inevitable consequences. His is a "sifting humour," as he himself styles it, and after this manner the masterly power of his analytic discrimination endeavours to separate the various complex phenomena of mind into their elemental parts and so discover for each its proper place and significance.

Exposed to Hume's subtle criticism, the world of knowledge which Locke had laboriously constructed by adding part to part is found to disappear altogether. It disintegrates into separate and disconnected elements, among which there is no bond of union or principle of organisation. As Berkeley had sought to destroy all material substance, so now Hume, in turn, attempts to undermine the reality of any spiritual substance. He uses Berkeley's criticism of Locke as a vantage ground in turn for his repudiation of Berkeley. The idea of a world of order and system, spiritually attested, Hume would not allow, because it could not be rationally defended. He did not believe in a world of knowledge, but in a world as a series of sense impressions detached and unrelated. He was convinced that there cannot be any fundamental principles of thought intellectually grounded and justified; but that there is merely an habitual experience traceable to its ultimate source in a certain psychological disposition.

From this point of view Hume develops the argument of his *Treatise of Human Nature*. His proof logically is a *reductio ad absurdum* of Locke's position. We might very properly say in the spirit of Hume: Given Locke's premises, there remains in the final assessment nothing substantial, systematic or necessary, but merely the fleeting impressions of the moment, an instinctive habit of the mind in grouping these impressions in sequence and coexistence through the aid of a convenient imagination, and a central personality purely factitious and ever vanishing. Hume never turned again to a re-examination of the integrity of Locke's presuppositions, as every *reductio ad absurdum* procedure imperatively suggests. On the contrary, he accepted frankly the negative results of his criticism. What is Hume's philosophy but a "splendid failure," as Green admirably characterises it? And yet withal as an essential moment in the progress of philosophical thought, it serves a most valuable purpose in exhibiting by the bold strokes of his genius the significant inadequacy of the empirical philosophy.

Hume's scepticism, however, is not flippant, nor is it arrogant, nor yet cynical. It is touched throughout with awe and reverence at the mystery both of nature and of mind. It is the unfathomableness of their depths which made all labour of the human understanding seem to him so pitiably futile, and he was unreservedly convinced that it is impossible for man to enter into the way of their secrets. While the spirit in which Hume accepted the negative results of his acute argument compels our admiration, nevertheless his final attitude of scepticism is to be regarded merely as a transition stage of thought in the progressive movement of which his writings are an essential factor. That movement proceeds to more positive and satisfying results, and yet not without illuminating glimpses which may be gained from a study of Hume by the way.

Professor Huxley, in his volume on Hume, takes the untenable position that Hume's philosophy forms the fundamental basis for a true scientific method and attitude of mind, and therefore, in this sense, is not sceptical and negative merely, but positive and constructive.

Huxley goes so far as to identify in essential particulars the work of Hume and that of Kant. He says: "The aim of the *Kritik der reinen Vernunft* is essentially the same as that of the *Treatise of Human Nature*, by which, indeed, Kant was led to develop that 'critical philosophy' with which his name and fame are indissolubly bound up, and if the details of Kant's criticism differ from those of Hume, they coincide with them in their main result, which is the limitation of all knowledge of reality to the world of phenomena revealed to us by experience." [1]

Kant's work of interpreting the phenomena of experience, however, begins where the labours of Hume end; moreover, Kant introduces into the heart of his critical philosophy the ideas of necessity and universality as essential factors in the process of constructing the elements of experience into a coherent body of knowledge. And it is against the possibility of these very ideas that the whole force of Hume's argument is directed.

A more detailed examination of Hume's position will show that he assumes, as the two elemental units of thought, impressions and ideas; the impression is the actually experienced sense perception, the idea is the memory image of it. This twofold source of knowledge is reducible at the last analysis to one simply, inasmuch as every idea may be traced to some original sense impression. This is substantially the presupposition which marks the beginning of the Lockian theory of knowledge. The origin of

[1] Huxley, *David Hume*, p. 58.

all thought, therefore, is narrowed in its scope to a bare appearance—that particular object of knowledge as it shows itself in consciousness. Hume is most emphatic in his opinion that while the thought ranges within these limits, it will avoid confusion and error. The phenomenal world is his sole concern. "As long as we confine our speculations to *the appearances* of objects to our senses without entering into disquisitions concerning their real nature and operations, we are safe from all difficulties, and can never be embarrass'd by any question. . . . The appearances of objects to our senses are all consistent; and no difficulties can ever arise, but from the obscurity of the terms we make use of. If we carry our inquiry beyond the appearances of objects to the senses I am afraid that most of our conclusions will be full of scepticism and uncertainty." [1]

To this restricted area Hume would confine all excursions of the intellect with an unvarying logical consistency. And in this respect his argument is conspicuously free from all the naïve assumptions and unwitting inconsequence which emerge in the course both of Locke's and Berkeley's attempts to construct a systematic body of knowledge out of the elemental units of sense perception.

Hume insists that every idea which lays claim to recognition in our thinking must be assessed according to a certain fundamental standard of criticism. Moreover, the general principle of criticism to which all his ideas must be submitted is the direct outcome of his central doctrine concerning the ultimate source of all knowledge. This principle is that no simple idea can be allowed in thought which cannot show at

[1] *A Treatise of Human Nature*, vol. I, p. 368, footnote. (References to Hume's works are to the edition of Green and Grose.)

its face value some original impression. This is the single standard according to which every idea entertained by the mind must be eventually redeemable.[1]

If it is not, the idea in question must rank merely as a fancy of the imagination, or as some deposit in the mind of traditional superstition or inherited prejudice. Any complex idea, being reducible to its lowest terms in a number of simple ideas, must be subjected at the last analysis to a similar test. Hume's analytical method of criticism, therefore, is a process of reduction to elemental parts, and these in turn are to be traced to their original source in the various sense impressions. Moreover, inasmuch as each simple impression represents a separate particular element of experience, it can have no reference beyond itself. Therefore there can be no such thing as any connecting bond of cause and effect relation among our several impressions, or any underlying substance other than the bare impression itself. These are the two points of incidence upon which the force of Hume's negative criticism is concentrated—the ideas of causation and of substance. As to the relation of cause and effect, Hume insists that our various perceptions are all distinct existences, entirely "loose and separate," and that the mind experiences them as detached elements and therefore can never discover any real connection among such distinct existences.[2]

"Tho' certain sensations," Hume maintains, "may at one time be united, we quickly find they admit of a separation, and may be presented apart."[3]

He declares, moreover, that reason is powerless to justify the conception of power or efficiency such as that which is contained in the popular notion of

[1] *A Treatise of Human Nature*, vol. I, p. 313 *ff*.
[2] *Ib.*, vol. I, p. 559.   [3] *Ib.*, vol. I, p. 370.

causation. For reason is never creative; it cannot give birth to any idea which is not first supplied to it as an original sense impression, and no sense impression gives any idea of power. If the idea of power or efficiency is not in the original impression, it cannot be reached through any process of abstraction which may be applied to a group of impressions often repeated. Hume in this respect shares Berkeley's deeply rooted antipathy to abstract ideas.[1]

"From the mere repetition of any past impression, even to infinity, there never will arise any new original idea, such as that of a necessary connexion; and the number of impressions has in this case no more effect than if we confined ourselves to one only."[2]

Naturally the question will suggest itself, *Whence* comes this idea of "necessary connexion" which the common mind seems constrained to assume in all relations of cause and effect? Hume would reply, This is not an idea logically grounded at all. Its warrant is solely psychological; that is, the result of an inveterate habit, or custom, of passing in thought from one of two correlatives to the other. We bind together the related experiences in our minds, but the tie is one of convenience and not of necessity. This manner of seeing things together is due to an essentially unreasoning and unreasonable habit of mind. "We have already taken notice of certain relations," says Hume, "which make us pass from one object to another, even tho' there be no reason to determine us to that transition;[3] and this we may establish for a general rule, that wherever the mind constantly

---

[1] *A Treatise of Human Nature*, vol. I, p. 325*f*.
[2] *Ib.*, vol. I, p. 389.
[3] The relations referred to are those which arise through association of ideas.

and uniformly makes a transition without any reason, it is influenc'd by these relations. Now this is exactly the present case. Reason can never show us the connection of one object with another, tho' aided by experience, and the observation of their constant conjunction in all past instances. When the mind, therefore, passes from the idea or impression of one object to the idea or belief of another, it is not determin'd by reason but by certain principles, which associate together the ideas of these objects and unite them in the imagination." [1]

In Hume's doctrine concerning the relation of cause and effect, there is thus a complete transference of the source of the causal idea from the sphere of the reason to that of the imagination. He regards the relation of cause and effect as so mysterious that it is wholly beyond the capacity of the human intellect to discover the secret of its hidden meaning. Inasmuch as thought is capable of observing only the superficial phenomena of a constant conjunction it is not warranted in inferring an inner and necessary connection. "Perhaps 'twill appear in the end," Hume very shrewdly suggests, "that the necessary connexion depends on the inference, instead of the inference's depending on the necessary connexion." [2]

However this may be, Hume would have us appreciate this at least, that our minds play only upon the surface of the causal problem. We never "bottom" it, to use a phrase of Locke. What causes the stone to fall to the earth? or the tides to ebb and flow? or what holds the planet to its orbit? Reason may describe the phenomena to the last degree of scientific exactitude, and may determine the proximate antecedent in each specific case, but it can discover no

[1] *A Treatise of Human Nature*, vol. I, p. 392 *f.* [2] *Ib.*, p. 389.

adequate explanation of the ultimate nature of the phenomena themselves. The mind expects in a blind unreasoning way that things will happen in the future as in the past. The imagination quickens this feeling of expectancy; but the attempt of reason to justify it is wholly futile. It cannot exhibit the *modus operandi* of the action of a cause in producing its effect, even though in its simplest form of manifestation. The habit of mind which relates experiences as cause and effect is a customary mode of viewing things which is fostered by the imagination. Customary things do not seem to need explanation. Their very commonplace nature tends to conceal their mystery. We accept them as a matter of course, but when we are challenged by a more exacting demand to furnish some adequate explanation of them in reason, we then begin to appreciate how superficial is our ordinary attitude of mind, and what meagre results seem to satisfy our inquiring disposition.

The concept of substance receives a similar treatment at Hume's hands. Not only is there no necessary bond of connection between the various objects which from time to time appear in the field of consciousness; but there is none also between the different qualities which coinhere in one and the same object. They are likewise separate and distinct appearances. No cohesive bond really holds them together. The proof of this is the simple application of Hume's general principle of interpretation, namely, that we are not entitled in reason to assume the reality of any idea of which there is not an original impression corresponding to it. This is the touchstone of all critical inquiry. Applying it to the idea of substance, it at once vanishes. "I wou'd fain ask those philosophers," says Hume, "who found so much of their reasonings on the distinction of substance and accident (that is, the property of a substance) and imagine we have clear ideas of each, whether the idea of *substance* be deriv'd from the impressions of sensation, or of reflection? If it be convey'd to us by our senses, I ask which of them; and after what manner? If it be perceiv'd by the eyes, it must be a colour; if by the ears, a sound; if by the palate, a taste; and so of the other senses. But I believe none will assert that substance is either a colour, or sound, or taste. The idea of substance must therefore be deriv'd from an impression of reflection, if it really exists. But the impressions of reflection resolve themselves into our passions and emotions; none of which can possibly represent a substance. We have therefore no idea of substance distinct from that of a collection of particular qualities, nor have we any other meaning when we either talk or reason concerning it. The idea of substance as well as that of a mode (*i. e.*, a complex idea composed of a number of simple qualities variously modified) is nothing but a collection of simple ideas, that are united by the imagination, and have a particular name assigned them, by which we are able to recall, either to ourselves or others that collection." [1] According to such an extremely nominalistic view as this, the substantial bond uniting together the various separate qualities of any object, and constituting a single distinct thing, exists alone in the imagination. The idea of substance furnishes a convenient way of regarding the different objects of consciousness; but the substantial as well as the causal connections are both alike of subjective origin and import.

[1] *A Treatise of Human Nature*, p. 324.

So far, Hume is in accord with Berkeley. But Hume carries his argument a step further. He would likewise do away with the idea of spiritual substance. Berkeley's belief in the existence of a spiritual substance behind the world of phenomenal appearance was based upon his conviction as to the substantial reality of an abiding self amidst the ever-varying changes of one's conscious life. As there is the direct evidence of consciousness as to the reality of a spiritual self underlying the activities and phenomena of our mental life, so also the idea of a spiritual self in turn affords us an intimation of the reality of a spiritual substance underlying the phenomena of nature, and making them known to us through the varied operations of the senses. Hume declares that all suppositions such as these of Berkeley must be regarded as wholly gratuitous. He strikes at the very heart of Berkeley's belief in a spiritual substance, by repudiating most vehemently all evidence adduced for the existence of any central self, separate and distinct from the constantly accompanying impressions, of which the ever-moving stream of consciousness is completely and exclusively composed. Among the phenomena of the mind, therefore, there is no occasion or place for anything but the transient play of shifting impressions. Hume's doctrine of the self is so characteristic of the extreme and radical nature of his negative criticism that I venture to quote from it in this connection somewhat at length:

"There are some philosophers who imagine we are every moment intimately conscious of what we call our SELF; that we feel its existence and its continuance in existence; and are certain, beyond the evidence of a demonstration, both of its perfect identity and simplicity. The strongest sensation, the most violent passion say they, instead of distracting us from this view, only fix it the more intensely, and make us consider their influence on *self* either by their pain or pleasure. To attempt a farther proof of this were to weaken its evidence; since no proof can be deriv'd from any fact of which we are so intimately conscious; nor is there anything of which we can be certain, if we doubt of this.

"Unluckily all these positive assertions are contrary to that very experience, which is pleaded for them, nor have we any idea of *self*, after the manner it is here explain'd. For from what impression cou'd this idea be deriv'd? This question 'tis impossible to answer without a manifest contradiction and absurdity; and yet 'tis a question, which must necessarily be answer'd, if we wou'd have the idea of self pass for clear and intelligible. It must be some one impression that gives rise to every real idea. But self or person is not any one impression, but that to which our several impressions and ideas are suppos'd to have a reference. If any impression gives rise to the idea of self, that impression must continue invariably the same, thro' the whole course of our lives; since self is suppos'd to exist after that manner. But there is no impression constant and invariable. Pain and pleasure, grief and joy, passions and sensations succeed each other, and never all exist at the same time. It cannot, therefore, be from any of these impressions, or from any other, that the idea of self is deriv'd; and consequently there is no such idea.

"But, farther, what must become of all our particular perceptions upon this hypothesis? All these are different, and distinguishable, and separable from each other, and may be separately consider'd, and may exist separately, and have no need of anything to support their existence. After what manner, therefore, do they belong to self; and how are they connected with it? For my part, when I enter most intimately into what I call *myself*, I always stumble on some particular perception or other, of heat or cold, light or shade, love or hatred, pain or pleasure. I never catch *myself* at any time without a perception, and never can observe anything but the perception. When my perceptions are remov'd for any time, as by sound sleep, so long am I insensible of *myself*, and may truly be said not to exist. And were all my perceptions remov'd by death, and cou'd I neither think, nor feel, nor see, nor love, nor hate after the dissolution of my body, I shou'd be entirely annihilated, nor do I conceive what is farther requisite to make me a perfect non-entity. If any one, upon serious and unprejudic'd reflection, thinks he has a different notion of *himself*, I must confess I can reason no longer with him. All I can allow him is, that he may be in the right as well as I, and that we are essentially different in this particular. He may, perhaps, perceive something simple and continu'd, which he calls *himself;* tho' I am certain there is no such principle in me." [1]

This then is the conclusion of the whole matter—no causation, no substance, no self; our world of knowledge not a world at all, only a collection of separate and distinct phenomena, and not a body of interrelated parts; a group, but not a system; many elements, but not a totality; many organs, but not an organism; ordered throughout by the compulsion of fancy, but not by the constraint of reason.

[1] *A Treatise of Human Nature*, p. 533 *f.*

Exposed to this searching analysis, Berkeley's world fades away as well as Locke's. Nothing which can claim any substantial reality remains.

The question naturally suggests itself, Do results of so negative a character prove merely the futility of philosophy? They do most certainly, if we are content to rest philosophy's case at this point. However, by the very nature of their sweeping negations, the result of Hume's argument suggests to the inquiring mind the possibility that the premises of which they are the logical conclusion may be subjected with profit to a more thorough re-examination. If the outcome of Hume's criticism does not direct our thought forward, it at least will serve to point it backward. This regressive process of criticism Hume himself never attempted. It is possible, however, and it may prove profitable as well, to intimate, in broad outline at least, this return of thought to the beginnings of Hume's argument.

Starting with impressions, naked and isolated, each complete and sufficient in its own separate existence, with no reference to anything beyond itself, unconnected and unrelated, with no implication of objective reality or subjective certitude—from such dead and barren premises is it possible to expect in the conclusion a full and living content? And this is pre-eminently the service of Hume, that by the subtle processes of keen analysis he demonstrated the wholly inadequate nature of these detached units of knowledge. If that which is wanting cannot be supplied, then Hume's scepticism must ever remain the last word of philosophy.

The reason that Hume did not discern the inadequacy of his own premises was that he did not appreciate the complete significance of his fundamental principle of interpretation; and therefore failed to see that it might be significantly applied to his own argument. I refer to the doctrine which he had received with such enthusiasm from Berkeley, namely, the repudiation of all abstract ideas in the processes of reasoning. His own philosophical procedure, however, is not above reproach in this particular. For it is based on the most abstract of abstractions, namely, the existence of detached, unconnected, unrelated impressions. In other words, he regards each impression apart from its concrete setting. Hume's simple impression, which plays such an important and conspicuous rôle in his discussion, is abstract in the extreme; and as such ranks as a psychological fiction of the first order. No such simple impression, unrelated and unconnected, ever appears in the field of consciousness. Hume in this respect falls into the same error that Locke did. The truth is that every impression, however simple it may seem, is exceedingly complex. It does not present itself to us in any way and at any place which chance or fancy may direct, but it finds its proper place and proclaims its peculiar significance amidst the co-ordinate elements of that great body of knowledge which is constantly sustained and ordered by the constructive activity of the mind. Hume's doctrine that all abstract ideas possess a radically misleading character is, in fact, a two-edged sword of criticism. With him it cuts but the one way; however we may quite as well turn its other edge against his own argument. He cuts away the idea of a self separate from and underlying our several impressions. He insists that he can never find himself without an accompanying impression as a necessary setting. On the other hand, we may with equal cogency insist that there is never a consciousness of any impression whatsoever without the idea of self implicit in it. It is the constant and persistent element in every experience. Again, Hume urges that we never experience a simple impression of power or of efficacy itself; on the other hand, it may be argued also that the relation which we commonly call causal never appears apart from some idea of power or of efficacy suggested by it and indissolubly connected with it. So also, while the impression of substance is never given in consciousness as a separate experience apart from the accompanying qualities characteristic of the observed object, likewise the constant group of co-ordinated qualities appearing together cannot be observed apart from the single substantial object in which these collective qualities seem to inhere.

Considerations such as these lead us to conclude that Hume is not entitled to his bare abstraction of a simple unrelated impression as the unit of knowledge. No psychological analysis, however subtle, can ever reveal it. Therefore with a fiction for its foundation, the superstructure which is built upon it must fall of its own weight.

Again, there is an unwarrantable abstraction in Hume's separation of the function of the imagination from that of the intellect. The compulsion of thought which we feel in passing from an observed antecedent to a lively expectation of a definite result which we think will inevitably follow from it, Hume refers to the offices of the imagination, and not of the reason. "When the mind, therefore, passes from the idea or impression of one object to the idea or belief of another, it is not determin'd by reason, but by certain principles, which associate together the ideas of these objects, and unite them in the imagination. Had ideas no more union in the fancy than objects seem to have to the understanding, we cou'd never draw any inference from causes to effects, nor repose belief in any matter of fact. The influence, therefore, depends solely on the union of ideas."[1]

The imagination and reason, however, cannot be properly separated. To do so is an unwarrantable abstraction. Not only is there no natural antithesis between the logical processes of thought and the imagination, but the logical processes of thought are themselves dependent upon the imagination as a necessary auxiliary to their proper functioning. Inference is essentially a process of ideal construction. The mind supplies, through ideas which necessity suggests, what is not explicit in observation or the literal content of the given premises, but what nevertheless is present implicitly. It is peculiarly the function of the imagination to expand what is actually given, and in this manner create for thought what is not present to the senses. The imagination in its working function is essentially a logical faculty; the imagination at play, however, may swing clear of logic altogether and wander unrestrained in the boundless fields of fancy. The distinction between the imagination at play and the imagination in the work of thought is this, that the former is free of all control save that of whim or chance suggestion; the latter, however, owns to a feeling of constraint that commands the thought, whether we will or not.

When Hume refers the feeling of compulsion which the memory of customary relations of cause and effect

[1] *A Treatise of Human Nature*, p. 392 *f.*

engenders, to the imagination, it is to the imagination in its working capacity, and as an ally in co-operating with the activities of the intellect. In other words, there is a thought coefficient in such a function of the imagination which possesses a deep significance in the theory of knowledge, but which Hume, however, wholly fails to appreciate. It is not merely that the mind passes easily from one idea to another associated with it, by the aid of the imagination, but that the mind is conscious that in certain situations and under certain conditions it *must* so pass. And this necessity is something more than the suggestion of fancy or the quickening of the memory; also the laws of nature are something more than "an unqualified habit of expectancy." While Hume shows no disposition to re-examine the foundations of his sceptical conclusions, on the other hand, he is not wholly satisfied with the negative results of his argument. True to his temperament and habit of thought, we find him, at the end of the discussion in the *Treatise*, finally sceptical of his scepticism. In a most significant passage in the Appendix to this work, Hume expresses his own dissatisfaction with the results of his inquiry. He says: "Philosophers begin to be reconcil'd to the principle, *that we have no idea of external substance, distinct from the ideas of particular qualities.* This must pave the way for a like principle with regard to the mind, *that we have no notion of it, distinct from the particular perceptions.* So far I seem to be attended with sufficient evidence. But having thus loosen'd all our particular perceptions, when I proceed to explain the principle of connexion, which binds them together, and makes us attribute to them a real simplicity and identity; I am sensible that my account is very defective, and that nothing but the seeming evidence of the precedent reasonings cou'd have induc'd me to receive it. If perceptions are distinct existences, they form a whole only by being connected together. But no connexions among distinct existences are ever discoverable by human understanding. We only *feel* a connexion, or determination of thought, to pass from one object to another. It follows, therefore, that the thought alone finds personal identity, when reflecting on the train of past perceptions that compose a mind, the ideas of them are felt to be connected together, and naturally introduce each other. However extraordinary this conclusion may seem, it need not surprise us. Most philosophers seem inclin'd to think that personal identity *arises* from consciousness; and consciousness is nothing but a reflected thought or perception. The present philosophy, therefore, has so far a promising aspect. But all my hopes vanish when I come to explain the principles that unite our successive perceptions in our thought or consciousness. I cannot discover any theory which gives me satisfaction on this head.

"In short, there are two principles, which I cannot render consistent; nor is it in my power to renounce either of them, viz.: *that all our distinct perceptions are distinct existences,* and *that the mind never perceives any real connexion among distinct existences.* Did our perceptions either inhere in something simple and individual, or did the mind perceive some real connexion among them, there wou'd be no difficulty in the case. For my part, I must plead the privilege of a sceptic, and confess that this difficulty is too hard for my understanding. I pretend not, however, to pronounce it absolutely insuperable. Others, perhaps, or myself, upon more mature reflections, may discover some hypothesis that will reconcile those contradictions." [1]

In this frank confession Hume evidently appreciates the unsatisfactory character of the results which his reasoning had reached. His view of the field of consciousness is that of a screen upon which a continuous series of pictures is thrown. In spite of the ordered arrangement of the scenes which are presented, and their seemingly logical sequence, the fact remains that each is separate and distinct, and the relations which they sustain one to another for the time being represent no real connection whatsoever. This stereopticon view of our sense-perceptions, figured on the screen of consciousness, is a very fair description of Hume's doctrine of the particularity of the several simple impressions as units of knowledge. But such a view is not satisfactory, and Hume himself felt it. The discrete nature of the particular elements of consciousness does not appeal to the ordinary observer as a true account of the intricately woven web of perceptions. Hume himself concedes this indirectly and by implication at least.

As we discovered in Berkeley a potential element which was to appear in its fully developed form in the later philosophy of Kant, so also in Hume there are, here and there, significant intimations which suggest a solution of his scepticism and show that it is properly to be regarded as a transition stage in a larger movement of thought. In reference to the origin of the idea of necessary connexion which seems to be so indissolubly associated in our minds with the relation of cause and effect, and which is the crux of the perplexing and insoluble problem, as it

[1] *A Treatise of Human Nature*, vol. I, p. 559 *f.*

presented itself to Hume, it is exceedingly interesting to note that Hume himself seems vaguely to recognise the necessity of assuming a definite function of thought in constructing our various impressions into an intelligible system. A conspicuous illustration of his appreciation of this synthetic factor in knowledge is contained in the following passage: "Tho' the several resembling instances, which give rise to the idea of power, have no influence on each other, and can never produce any new quality *in the object* which can be the model of that idea, yet the *observation* of this resemblance produces a new impression *in the mind*, which is its real model. For after we have observ'd the resemblance in a sufficient number of instances, we immediately feel a determination of the mind to pass from one object to its usual attendant, and to conceive it in a stronger light upon account of that relation. This determination is the only effect of the resemblance; and therefore must be the same with power or efficacy, whose idea is deriv'd from the resemblance. The several instances of resembling conjunctions lead us into the notion of power and necessity. These instances are in themselves totally distinct from each other, and have no union but in the mind, which observes them, and collects their ideas. Necessity, then, is the effect of this observation, and is nothing but an internal impression of the mind, or a determination to carry our thoughts from one object to another." [1]

This element of necessity as a thought determination was never developed by Hume, and evidently he failed to appreciate, in any adequate manner, its significance for the theory of knowledge. Its latent possibilities, therefore, remained undiscovered until

[1] *A Treatise of Human Nature*, p. 459.

they developed under the more profound criticism of Kant, and became the foundation of his system of knowledge.

In the paragraph just quoted it is obvious that Hume's natural tendency is to refer thought, and the object of thought, to two distinct and separate spheres. And this again is the result of his habit of mind to force his ideas to an undue degree of abstraction. This separating, particularising process influences all of his thinking. But the object of thought cannot be thus isolated. It can appear in consciousness only as thought related in a setting of thought, and rendered significant by its thought determinations. To separate thought and its object by an artificial process of abstraction is simply to drive out the inner spirit by destroying the outer body. Surely there must be some fundamental basis of co-ordination between the world of observation and the observing mind, so that whatever is a necessity of thought is an implication of the nature of reality as well.

There is another significant passage which in a way is an unconscious prophecy of that Copernican revolution in philosophy which Kant was shortly to effect, and that, indeed, not wholly without the influence which Hume himself exerted upon this new order of thinking: "But tho' this be the only reasonable account we can give of necessity, the contrary notion is so riveted in the mind from the principles above mention'd, that I doubt not but my sentiments will be treated by many as extravagant and ridiculous. What! the efficacy of causes lie in the determination of the mind! As if causes did not operate entirely independent of the mind, and wou'd not continue their operation, even tho' there was no mind existent to contemplate them, or reason concerning them.

Thought may well depend on causes for its operation, but not causes on thought. This is to reverse the order of nature, and make that secondary which is really primary. To every operation there is a power proportion'd; and this power must be plac'd on the body, that operates. If we remove the power from one cause, we must ascribe it to another. But to remove it from all causes, and bestow it on a being that is no ways related to the cause or effect, but by perceiving them, is a gross absurdity, and contrary to the most certain principles of human reason.

"I can only reply to all these arguments, that the case is here much the same, as if a blind man shou'd pretend to find a great many absurdities in the supposition, that the colour of scarlet is not the same with the sound of a trumpet, nor light the same with solidity." [1]

Hume was evidently far on the way toward a readjustment of his earlier empirical principles to the logical requirements of his later insight. The illumination, however, which his thought experienced in this particular was due to certain fitful flashes and not to any steady glow of light. Had Hume sufficiently appreciated the significance of this "determination of the mind" in all of its bearings—and he would have appreciated it fully, if he had brought his keen analysis to play upon it—not only would he have prepared the way for the philosophy of Kant, but he would have anticipated it as well. The faculty of reason which he employed so brilliantly as an instrument of thought, he failed to appreciate adequately as regards its essentially constructive capacity. Before Hume's perplexities could be cleared and his scepticism resolved, it was necessary that

[1] *A Treatise of Human Nature*, p. 461 *f.*

another should undertake the difficult but rewarding task of the critique of the pure reason. Hume's method of destructive analysis proves too much. His very mental prowess refutes him. Green cleverly gives his estimate of Hume and his work in this particular: "Unless man had consciously detached himself from nature, no *Treatise on Human Nature* could have been written. He would not be trying to account to himself for his own moral life, even by reducing it to a natural one; would not be asking what nature is to him, or he to nature, if he were merely the passive receptacle of natural impressions, and not at the same time constructive and free." [1]

However inconsistent, therefore, and unsatisfying Hume's scepticism may be when regarded as a permanent attitude of mind, nevertheless it possesses a deep significance for one who is seeking to understand the progressive movement of philosophical thought in the eighteenth century. By showing conclusively that the Lockian account of the sources of knowledge, and the process of its development, lead by an inevitable logic to a negative position of unqualified scepticism, Hume incites in an inquiring mind the desire to seek a more profound and secure basis for the foundations of knowledge.

This is precisely the effect which the writings of Hume produced in the mind of Thomas Reid (1710–96), the contemporary and fellow-countryman of Hume and the founder of the Scottish School of Philosophy. In his principal work, *Inquiry into the Human Mind on the Principles of Common Sense*, Reid gives an account of the influence which Hume had exerted upon his philosophical

[1] Green's *Philosophical Works*, vol. III, p. 112.

point of view. Originally a follower of Locke and Berkeley, Reid had been led by a study of the *Treatise* to discern the dangerous consequences directly resulting from the fundamental presuppositions of Locke. According to Reid, Hume's analysis is a revelation of the weakness of Locke's position, and consequently calls for a serious re-examination of the ground upon which his philosophy rests. Reid asserts that Locke's explanation of the beginnings of knowledge is not true to experience, and that therefore on purely empirical grounds it will not pass muster. Our knowledge does not start with ideas which are passively received through sensation, but with judgments; and these judgments imply certain first principles, or "natural judgments," which are a common possession of mankind by virtue of the faculty of common sense. Thus Reid introduces the metaphysic of common sense at the very beginnings of knowledge, which imparts to the elements of sensory experience a principle of organisation as well as a principle of reference to a world of reality. Such principles possess naturally a quality of universality and of necessity which sense alone cannot give. Hume stimulated the thought of Reid to the point of a natural reaction from the final position of scepticism in much the same way as he stimulated the philosophical inquiry of Kant. Kant and Reid, in fact, have much in common not only in their general point of view, but in the endeavour of each to supply the essential principles of constructive reason to the scattered elements of the empirical philosophy.[1]

Having traced this movement of thought from its starting-point in the *Essay* of Locke, through the

[1] See Andrew Seth Pringle-Pattison, *On the Scotch Philosophy*, chap. IV, "Reid and Kant."

idealism of Berkeley, to the scepticism of Hume, it will be of interest, both in itself and also by way of contrast, to consider the rise and growth of that materialistic doctrine which is to be referred to the same source in the presuppositions of the Lockian theory of knowledge.[1]

REFERENCES.—R. Adamson: *The Development of Modern Philosophy*, vol. I. Edinburgh, 1903.
J. H. Burton: *Life and Correspondence of David Hume*. Edinburgh, 1846.
T. H. Green: *Introduction to Hume's Treatise of Human Nature. Green's Works*, vol. I. London, 1885.
Green and Grose: Edition of *Hume's Works*. London, 1874.
William Knight: *Hume*. (*Philosophical Classics for English Readers*.) Edinburgh, 1886.
Professor Huxley: *Hume*. (*English Men of Letters Series*.) London, 1902.
James McCosh: *Scottish Philosophy*. London, 1875. New York, 1890.
A. S. Pringle-Pattison: *On the Scottish Philosophy*. Edinburgh, 1885.
E. Pfleiderer: *Empirismus und Skepsis in David Hume's Philosophie*. Berlin, 1874.
M. H. Calkins: *Persistent Problems in Philosophy*. N. Y., 1907.

[1] " In this account of Hume, I have referred throughout to passages from the *Treatise*. I am not unaware that as regards Hume's later work, the *Enquiry Concerning Human Understanding*, which is a reproduction of the *Treatise*, extensively modified and condensed, the author insists that " it alone contains his philosophical sentiments and principles." However, the *Enquiry* does not contain any repudiation of the original principles of the *Treatise*, or its essential doctrines, although there are some significant omissions. The *Treatise*, therefore, as the more systematic and detailed expression of Hume's philosophy, must remain the true source for an intelligent criticism, and according to which his work must stand or fall. See Green's position in this respect in the Preface to his **General Introduction to Hume.**

CHAPTER V

THE MATERIALISTIC MOVEMENT IN ENGLAND AND FRANCE

In the progressive development of thought in the eighteenth century there is a materialistic interpretation of the Lockian idea of substance which exerted a profound influence, not only in England but also in France. It was natural that Locke's fundamental presupposition that the sensations are the primary source of knowledge should become a suggestive formula for materialistic doctrine. Be that as it may, the fact remains that the *Essay* met with such an interpretation; and the development of speculative thought along these lines forms an historical comment upon Locke's philosophical position which is most significant. If one looks solely at the source of knowledge in the sensory framework of man, and is temperamentally averse to all the metaphysical implications which such simple beginnings may contain, and possesses, in addition, a natural tendency toward a materialistic habit of thought, it is quite possible to find in Locke's writings a guide upon a way which the author himself would have been loath to follow. There is a remark which Locke makes in the *Essay* in a somewhat problematical and whimsical manner, as to the possibility that all matter may be endowed with sensibility. He says: "We have the ideas of *matter* and *thinking*, but possibly shall never be able to know whether any material being thinks or no; it being impossible for us, by contemplation of our own ideas, to discover whether Omnipotency has not given to some systems of matter, fitly disposed, a power to perceive and think, or else joined and fixed to matter, so disposed, a thinking immaterial substance; it being, in respect of our notions, not much more remote from our comprehension to conceive that God can, if he pleases, superadd to matter *a faculty of thinking*, than that he should superadd to it *another substance with a faculty of thinking*." [1]

This has been interpreted by many writers in England, France and Germany, not at all in the spirit in which it was originally suggested by Locke, but as though it were the cardinal doctrine of his whole philosophical system. Thus a passing observation of a purely conjectural nature has been magnified out of all proportion, and has been used time and again as valuable ammunition in many a controversy which has waged about the strongholds of materialism. In some of the writers of the eighteenth century who followed this lead there is merely a materialistic drift. With others, and especially as the movement gathers momentum, there is an unreserved avowal of the materialistic creed even in its crudest and most radical form.

One of the earliest and most conspicuous expressions of this materialistic tendency, due, in part at least, to the influence of Locke, is to be found in the writings of David Hartley (1705-57). In his work, entitled *Observations on Man, His Frame, His Duty and His Expectations*, which appeared in 1749, he acknowledges his indebtedness to Locke and New-

[1] Book IV, chap. III, 6.

ton in the opening paragraph of the first chapter: "My chief design in the following chapter is briefly to explain, establish and apply the doctrines of *vibration* and *association*. The first of these doctrines is taken from the hints concerning the performance of sensation and motion which *Sir Isaac Newton* has given at the end of his *Principia*, and in the *questions* annexed to his *Optics;* the last, from what Mr. *Locke* and other ingenious persons since his time have delivered concerning the influence of *association* over our opinions and affections, and its use in explaining those things in an accurate and precise way, which are commonly referred to the power of habit and custom, in a general and indeterminate one. The doctrine of *vibrations* may appear at first sight to have no connection with that of *associations;* however, if these doctrines be found in fact to contain the laws of the bodily and mental powers, they must be related to each other, since the body and mind are. One may expect that *vibrations* should infer *association* as their effect and *association* point to *vibrations* as its cause." [1]

The problem which Hartley took from Locke and developed in his own original way was this: In what way can our complex mental states arise out of the simple elements of sensory experience? Locke's explanation of the unity which characterises the nature of our complex ideas was unsatisfactory, because it presupposed a mental process too external and artificial. He traced the natural history of these complex ideas to combinations of simpler elements. But the resulting mode or composition of these elemental units always appeared to be in itself something more than the mere sum of the component parts. Hartley,

[1] Hartley, *Observations on Man*, etc., vol. I, p. 5.

in his profession (that of a physician), had been, of course, a student of chemistry. By a natural suggestion, therefore, it occurred to him that all complex ideas might be properly conceived after the analogy of a chemical compound rather than that of a mechanical combination. In the chemical compound the elemental parts are no longer discernible, but disappear in the unity of a more complex organisation. Two simple ideas may thus blend together in the course of our experience in such a manner that their original significance is lost as completely as the elemental properties of oxygen and hydrogen when they combine to form water. "It appears also from observation," Hartley asserts in his chapter on "Association," "that many of our intellectual ideas, such as those that belong to the heads of beauty, honour, moral qualities, etc., are, in fact, thus composed of parts, which by degrees coalesce into one complex idea. . . . If the number of simple ideas which compose the complex one be very great, it may happen that the complex idea shall not appear to bear any relation to these its compounding parts, nor to the external senses upon which the original sensations, which gave birth to the compounding idea, were impressed. The reason of this is, that each single idea is overpowered by the sum of all the rest as soon as they are all intimately united together. Thus, in very compound medicines, the several tastes and flavours of the separate ingredients are lost and overpowered by the complex one of the whole mass; so that this has a taste and flavour of its own, which appears to be simple and original, and like that of a natural body. Thus, also, white is vulgarly thought to be the simplest and most uncompounded of all colours, while yet it really arises from a certain pro-

THE MATERIALISTIC MOVEMENT 115

portion of the seven primary colours with their several shades or degrees."[1]

Corresponding to the psychical processes involved in the subtle combinations of ideas through association, there are certain physiological phenomena, according to Hartley, which uniformly accompany them, and which are due to vibrations among the molecules of the medullary substance of the brain. These vibrations differ among themselves in respect to degree, kind, place and line of direction. This furnishes a basis of variety for the qualitative differences which the various combinations tend to produce.[2]

As ideas of a simple nature unite to form a more complex idea, so also certain brain vibrations, after several repetitions together, coalesce into one single vibration. Hartley's endeavour throughout his exposition of the association of our ideas, and its brain basis in medullary vibrations, is to show the possibility at least, if not the detailed *modus operandi*, of the development of our complex ideas from an original source in the simple ideas of sense-perception. I quote his own summary of the explanation of his theory: "The generation of sensible ideas from sensations, and the power of raising them from association, when considered as faculties of the mind, are evident and unquestionable. Since, therefore, sensations are conveyed to the mind by the efficiency of corporeal causes upon the medullary substance, as is acknowledged by all physiologists and physicians, it seems to me that the powers of generating ideas, and raising them by association, must also arise from corporeal causes and consequently admit of an explication from the subtle influences of the small parts

[1] Hartley, *Observations on Man*, etc., vol. I, p. 74 *f*.
[2] *Ib.*, vol. I, p. 30 *f*.

of matter upon each other, as soon as these are sufficiently understood, which is farther evinced from the manifest influences of material causes upon our ideas and associations, taken notice of under the second proposition (that is, whatever changes are made in the brain substance, corresponding changes are made in our ideas).[1] And as a vibratory motion is more suitable to the nature of sensation than any other species of motion, so does it seem also more suitable to the powers of generating ideas and raising them by association." [2]

Hartley's materialism, however, was a qualified one. The implications which the writers who followed him found in his doctrine of vibrations he himself would not allow. His philosophy of "mechanism," as he would call it, is not to be interpreted so as to oppose the immateriality of the soul. That is a question which he insists remains unaffected one way or the other by his point of view.[3]

While it is doubtless true that Hartley may not be justly regarded as a pronounced materialist, nevertheless his writings exerted no inconsiderable influence upon the materialistic drift in the thought of his day.

The one most directly and profoundly affected by his doctrines was Joseph Priestley (1733–1804), who in the year 1775 published certain extracts from Hartley with comments upon them under the title, *Hartley's Theory of the Human Mind on the Principle of the Association of Ideas, with Essays Relating to the Subject of It*. Priestley is, however, more than a mere commentator of Hartley's work. He essays a vigorous defence of materialism in his *Disquisitions Relating to Matter and Spirit* (1777), and

---

[1] Hartley, *Observations on Man*, etc., vol. I, p. 8.
[2] *Ib.*, p. 72.   [3] *Ib.*, p. 510 *f*.

urges that there is no ground whatsoever for assuming two different substances, but, on the contrary, physical and psychical phenomena may be regarded merely as different manifestations of one and the same substance. He insists that solidity and impenetrability are not the essential characteristics of matter, but the properties of attraction and repulsion, which are in no wise incompatible with the various activities of mind such as are exhibited in the processes of sensation, perception and thought. Moreover, the existence of matter in an extended state does not necessarily prove that it is a substance radically different from mind, because the powers of sensation, perception and thought, as belonging to man, have never been found except in connection with a definitely organised system of matter.[1]

Priestley's writings served to popularise the materialistic doctrine and give it a wide circulation not only in England and on the continent, but also in America, where he spent the last years of his life in the enjoyment of a complete freedom from the persecutions which had made his Manchester home no longer tolerable. His materialistic propaganda was announced, however, in the interests of what he believed to be a truer and more profound interpretation of Christianity. He was not slow to attack Holbach's *Système de la nature*, not because of its materialistic point of view, but because of its radical atheism. This, indeed, may be taken as an illustration of the difference in general between the French and English materialists. In England there was a manifest desire among the materialistic writers of the eighteenth century to reconcile their philosophical stand-point with some form of deistical belief. In France, how-

[1] Priestley, *Disquisitions Relating to Matter and Spirit*, vol. I, § 4.

ever, there was a decided tendency toward a philosophy based upon the atheistical implications of the materialistic doctrine. The French attitude of mind, schooled under the influences especially of Montaigne and Pierre Bayle, was decidedly sceptical, and therefore was peculiarly hospitable to the reception of the philosophy of materialism. Locke's fundamental assumption that our sensations form the primary source of knowledge was eagerly hailed by the French writers of the eighteenth century as a new and comfortable gospel. The idea of the sensations as the *primary* source of knowledge readily became transformed into the bolder declaration of the sensations as the *sole* source of knowledge, freed from all implications of metaphysics, and at the same time relieved of the inconvenient intimations of religious or moral obligation.

It would be decidedly over-estimating the influence of Locke, or of Locke as interpreted by Hartley and Priestley, to insist, as some writers have done, that this influence was the beginning and sole cause of the French materialism. The French philosophical thought had its own traditions which were calculated to develop independently the same type of belief, to say nothing of those tendencies which were due to contact with the earlier British philosophy through the writings of the French refugees in England and Holland. It is certainly within the bounds of a conservative judgment, however, in this matter to regard Locke and his followers in England as forces which profoundly influenced and accelerated the general materialistic drift which so conspicuously characterised the French philosophy of this century. As early as 1688, two years prior to the publication of Locke's *Essay*, Le-

THE MATERIALISTIC MOVEMENT 119

Clerc had published extracts from the manuscript of it in his *Bibliothèque universelle*. The *Essay* itself was translated and published by Pierre Coste, one of the French refugees, in the year 1700. Coste, who always expressed an enthusiastic admiration of Locke, was with him in his last illness, and closed the eyes of the great philosopher when death at last claimed him.

Another influence of the most far-reaching consequence in spreading the teachings of "English philosophism" was the publication in 1734 of Voltaire's *Lettres sur les Anglais*. Voltaire, during his visit to England, was deeply impressed by the English thought with which he became familiar, particularly through the works of Newton and Locke. The current of his own thinking was given a new direction and a deeper flow. As Morley has very aptly put it, "Voltaire left France a poet; he returned to it a sage."[1] Through Voltaire's enthusiastic indorsement British philosophy became exceedingly popular in France. In addition to the *Lettres sur les Anglais*, Voltaire published in 1738 an exposition of the Newtonian philosophy under the title, *Elements de la philosophie de Newton;* also later a book in 1764 which contained in popular form much of Locke's general theory of the source and nature of knowledge, entitled *Dictionnaire philosophique portatif*. Voltaire commends Locke most appreciatively in the *Lettres sur les Anglais*. He says of him: "Never perhaps has there ever been a spirit wiser or more scientific, or a logician more exact than Locke. . . . Other philosophers have composed the romance of the soul, but one has now appeared who has endeavoured with modest purpose

[1] *Voltaire*, p. 58.

to write merely its history. Locke has followed the evolution of reason in man, as an expert anatomist explains the springs of the human body." [1]

Among the French writers, the one who perhaps of all others was most directly and most intimately influenced by Locke was Etienne Bonnot de Condillac (1715–80). In his *Traité des sensations* (1754) he elaborates a theory of knowledge which is based exclusively upon the elementary material furnished by the senses, and received in a purely passive manner by the observing mind. In the sensations he finds the ultimate source not only of the varied content of our experience in the field of sense-perception, but also of *all* the more complex activities of our thinking processes. Attention, comparison, discrimination, abstraction, the composition of even the most abstruse of our ideas, are all regarded merely in the light of transformed sensations of a more or less obvious character. His psychology of the sensations became the groundwork for the materialistic writings of the latter half of the century. It was taught in the public schools of France during the Revolution and under the Empire. It exerted a far-reaching influence in preparing the minds of the French people generally for the more radical doctrines of materialism.

Condillac's sensationalism is most graphically depicted by means of his famous figure of a statue growing into consciousness by the gradual awakening of the various senses one after the other. With the birth of the senses there is a corresponding evolution of intelligence which thus arises from the impressions received from without, and not by the development of any native propensity from within.

[1] Voltaire, *Lettres sur les Anglais*, Lettre XIII, "Sur M. Locke."

He insists that "if the first sensation is the scent of a rose, then the soul is the scent of a rose, and naught else." This idea of the transformation of the statue into the living being through a fancied investiture of sense-perception, Lange suggests, may have been taken by Condillac from Lamettrie's *Histoire naturelle de lâme*, and that Lamettrie, in turn, may have borrowed it from a curious conceit of the Church father, Arnobius, in his *Adversus Gentes*. (1) This fiction of the sense-endowed statue of course begs the question as regards the difficulties which attach to a philosophy of sensationalism. These difficulties, however, seem to disappear as the imagination becomes wholly absorbed in following the fortunes of this newly quickened creature which draws its life from the magically acquired sensations. It is a fiction which naturally stimulates the fancy and at the same time silences the critical sense. Through this striking and plausible representation of the origin of the life of consciousness, the philosophy of sensationalism obtained a deep hold upon the French mind. It is always difficult, and often quite futile, to endeavour to dislodge from the mind a metaphor or allegory by means of the straight process of unadorned argument. If one should attempt to show that the statue-man, according solely to the presuppositions of Condillac's own description, would have proved to be an idiot, no doubt such a critic would be regarded as treating the subject flippantly and without a proper and sympathetic appreciation of its significance. And yet the crucial question as to whether mere combinations of passive sensations without a central active organising power could ever come to constitute an intelligent personality, Condillac's

[1] Lange, *History of Materialism*, Eng. trans., vol. II, p. 62.

pleasing fiction completely ignored by tacitly assuming in the finished product that which is nowhere present in the process itself.

Condillac's sensationalism must not be regarded, however, as equivalent to an avowed materialism. While the tendency of his teachings was materialistic, he himself did not appreciate it, nor did he ever profess a materialistic creed.

The ideas of Condillac received further elaboration at the hands of Helvetius (1715–71), who in his famous work, *De l'esprit*, endeavours to show that all of the faculties of the intellect (*l'esprit*) have been developed through experience, and that, too, from the most elemental of sensory beginnings. All moral distinctions are the growth in a like manner from a rudimentary susceptibility to pleasure or pain. The evolution of character and determining forces of conduct depend wholly upon the nature of the education which it is the lot of the individual to receive. Moreover, as education is fostered or hindered by the character of the government, there follows the natural corollary that a government, fast deteriorating, must necessarily prove an undermining influence as regards both public and private morals. Helvetius was exceedingly bitter and at the same time remarkably clever in his arraignment of the governing powers of France in his day. What he most deplored was the evident breaking asunder of the individual and social interests. And this, in his opinion, was largely due to the arbitrary and unjust legislation which had obscured and confused the real interests of life. The health and salvation of society, he declares, rest solely upon the legislator and educator. Although grounding his psychology wholly upon a sensationalistic basis, and evolving a

THE MATERIALISTIC MOVEMENT 123

selfish theory of morals out of pure pleasure and pain elements of feeling, nevertheless Helvetius, with a pleasing inconsistency, maintained a formal belief at least in a religion of deism, and would have repudiated most strictly the materialistic conclusions which his sensationalistic premises seem to imply.

One of the earliest and most pronounced of the French materialists was Julian Offrai de Lamettrie (1709–51). His principal works, *Histoire naturelle de l'âme* (1745), *L'homme machine* (1748), and *L'homme plante* (1748), indicate by their titles his general point of view. He seeks to show by the comparative method that the difference between man and the lower animals, and between the animal and plant life is only one of degree and not of kind; and that the higher forms have been developed from the lower through processes of greater complexity of organisation. He finds the moving force of this development in the desire or wants of the various growing organisms. The mere plant has not as yet attained any kind of psychical life, because it lacks the initial desires necessary for such a mode of existence. Among the sentient organisms, moreover, the greater and more varied the wants, the higher the corresponding development. In man, who possesses the greatest number and variety of wants, and the widest range, we find the most complex and highest form of life. Inasmuch as all states of conscious life in man are accompanied by sensation, Lamettrie infers that sensation is the primary property of all matter, and all our thoughts are merely various modifications of matter. The idea of a spiritual substance he regards as unnecessary and misleading. "The senses!

they are my philosophers." Such is the sentiment with which he most comprehensively expresses his philosophical point of view. He insists that where there are no senses, there are no ideas; and the fewer senses, the fewer ideas. Therefore "the soul depends essentially upon the organs of the body, with which it is formed, grows, decreases."[1]

Concerning the questions as to the being of God and immortality he maintained a wholly agnostic attitude, although he was regarded by many, from a cursory reading of his works, or by common repute, as a professed atheist. His morals, both theoretical and practical, ranged on the low level of a self-indulgence which was free from any of the more rigorous considerations of duty or responsibility. His ideas readily became a recognised charter of unbelief in religion, and of licence in conduct, and were hailed with enthusiastic approval by those who found in it a convenient means of justifying the course of their lives by a show of philosophical acumen. Lamettrie's influence was exceedingly extensive in its scope, and reached not only the various circles of philosophical speculation, but also the popular thought and sentiment of his day.

The leading spirit, however, of the sceptical and reactionary school of philosophical thought in France during the eighteenth century was Denis Diderot (1713–84), a man of most versatile gifts, who, as Rosenkranz, his biographer, characterises him, "combined in his own nature, both consciously and unconsciously, all the modern instincts of French thought."[2]

He had a charm of style which not only adorned

---

[1] Lange, *History of Materialism*, vol. II, p. 57 *f.*
[2] Rosenkranz, *Diderot*, vol. I, p. 5.

his writings, but also made his art of conversation notable among the *salons* of Paris. He was daring in thought and bold in utterance, and that, too, in an age wherein free speech was enjoyed only in defiance of the authorities, and at the risk of public censure or punishment. His nature resented bitterly the lifeless formalism of the church, the tyranny of the priests, their oppression of the masses, their privileges, their casuistry and dogmatism. He welcomed, therefore, a philosophy which should tend to undermine the position and power of an unreasonably favoured class, and reduce mankind to a fair level of opportunity and privilege. To him ecclesiasticism meant dogmatism; and dogmatism meant the traditional metaphysic of sophistry and credulity. The philosophy of sensationalism, therefore, appealed all the more forcibly to a nature which had become embittered by the theological dogmas, urged in support of a decayed ecclesiastical system and inimical to the welfare of the French people.

Early in his career, Diderot came under the literary and philosophical influences of England, "the land," as Diderot himself characterised it, "of philosophers, systematisers and men of inquiring mind." Rosenkranz says of Diderot that "the spirit of English philosophy was embodied in him." [1]

He translated a number of English works into the French, and from the old *Chambers's Dictionary* he received the suggestion and the plan of the great *Encyclopædia*. He was the centre and life of the coterie of authors who wrote for the *Encyclopædia*, that work which not only brought the new knowledge to the masses in France, but also served to quicken in the people a desire to discover for themselves

[1] Rosenkranz, *Diderot*, I, p. 6.

somewhat of the mysteries of nature, and also attain a practical philosophy of life.

Locke exerted no inconsiderable influence upon Diderot's views concerning the primary sources of knowledge. He accepted the Lockian premises, and also his general conclusions. He, however, soon drifted from his original moorings of sensationalism and deism into the darker currents of materialism and atheism. In his article on Locke in the *Encyclopædia* he takes Locke's query as to the possibility of matter being endowed with thought as though it were a positive and established dogma, making the following characteristic comment upon it: "Locke had said in his *Essay Concerning Human Understanding*, that it was not impossible to conceive that matter might have the capacity of thought. Fainthearted men shrank from this statement. But what difference does it make whether matter thinks or not? How can it possibly affect the idea of justice or of injustice, the question of immortality, or any truths of political or religious systems? Supposing sensibility were the primitive germ of thought, and a common property of all matter, scattered through all the products of nature in various proportions, manifesting itself in weaker or stronger degrees according to the varying complexity of different organisms, what evil consequences could any one possibly infer from all this? None. Man would still remain what he is, and would continue to be judged solely by the good or evil uses to which he may devote his activities." [1]

A more detailed account of his philosophical views is given in two of Diderot's essays, the *Entretien entre d'Alembert et Diderot*, and *Le rêve de d'Alembert*,

[1] *Encyclopædia*, article on Locke.

which appeared in the year 1830 under the title, *Mémoires, correspondance et ouvrages inèdits de Diderot*. In these writings he avows a somewhat qualified materialism. Plant and animal, man and beast, the texture of marble and of the living flesh, the forces of nature and the powers of mind, have one and the same source, one and the same explanation. The natural history of his friend d'Alembert is given in the following graphic characterisation: "How has this man accomplished his work? By the simple operation of eating and by other processes as purely mechanical. Here is the general formula in four words: Mangez, digerez, distillez *in vasi licito, et fiat homo secundum artem*. And he who expounded to the Academy the evolution of man and of animals, himself used only material agents of which the successive effects were merely, in the first place, a perfectly inert being, then a sentient being, then a thinking being, a being solving the problem of the precession of the equinoxes, a being sublime, a being marvellous, a being growing old, a being wasting away, then dying, and returning to the dust at last." [1] In another place in this same essay, *Entretien entre d'Alembert et Diderot*, there is a passage in which the materialistic interpretation of human nature is clearly marked. Diderot declares to d'Alembert that "there is but one substance in the universe, in man and in the animal. There is an instrument which a man uses who would teach a canary bird the various notes of its song. The instrument is made of wood; the man is made of flesh. The bird is made of flesh, and the man of flesh, only more diversely organised; but they all have one and the same origin, the same

[1] *Œuvres de Diderot*, Paris, Garnier Frères, 1875, vol. II, p. 109 *f.*

kind of mechanism, the same functions and the same end." [1]

The last word with which Diderot ends this famous conversation is the sombre admonition which he flings at d'Alembert with a curt *Bonsoir, Memento quia pulvis es, et in pulverem reverteris*.[2]

In the *Rêve de d'Alembert*, Mademoiselle de l'Espinasse, who watches by the bedside of d'Alembert during his deep trance, takes down in writing the significant utterances of the philosopher and shows them to his physician, Bordeu, who finds in them not the ravings of delirium, but the sober and serious considerations of one who had profoundly contemplated the mystery of life. The content of the essay is a continuance of the attempt to reduce all psychological phenomena to a physiological basis, and to eliminate all idea of freedom in the thought and affairs of man. In speaking to d'Alembert of his trance-like dream, Bordeu reminds him that throughout the entire period of unconsciousness he had given expression to thoughts which were not only intelligent, but also deeply significant. Moreover, two-thirds of his life had been passed in a similar manner. All the hours of consciousness were nothing but waking dreams. In eating and drinking, sleeping and waking, in meditation and study, in the exactions of work and in the pursuit of pleasure, through the whole round of daily activity, in the purposes of the present and the larger plans for the future, there was a seeming power of initiative, but in reality none at all. Thus man is determined solely by the mechanical processes of mind as well as of body, and the sense of freedom is an illusion

---

[1] *Œuvres de Diderot*, vol. II, p. 117.
[2] *Ib.*, vol. II, p. 121.

which it were well to appreciate and acknowledge once for all.[1]

There is in this essay, however, an indefinite reservation in Diderot's mind concerning the complete vindication of the doctrines of materialism; at least to the extent of expressing through the words of d'Alembert the exceedingly searching and pointed criticism: "Listen, philosopher, I see perfectly an aggregation, a tissue of small beings, each one capable of feeling; but one living being, a whole, a system, a self with the consciousness of its own unity! That I do not see."[2]

Whatever reservations there may have been in Diderot's mind in the earlier expressions of his materialistic doctrine, the critical attitude of inquiry concerning the exclusive claims of materialism wholly disappeared, and in his later years he became sponsor for Holbach's *Système de la nature*, which propounded a materialistic philosophy in its most extreme form. Diderot assisted Holbach in the authorship of this work, and is directly responsible with Holbach for its conclusions. Diderot has been cleverly characterised by Rosenkranz as a realist in his metaphysics, but an idealist in his philosophy of morals.[3]

Diderot would regard man as an automaton, played upon by the forces of nature, to use his own figure, as a musical instrument yields its melody to the touch of a hand which commands it; and yet he would insist upon his responsibility as a moral agent, which has no meaning whatsoever unless based upon some fundamental principle of liberty. There is in Diderot's writings a certain strain of inconsistency

---
[1] *Œuvres de Diderot*, vol. II, p. 175 *f*. [2] *Ib.*, vol. II, p. 124.
[3] Rosenkranz, *Diderot*, vol. II, p. 382.

which is a saving grace rather than an element of weakness. The import of this has been expressed most strikingly in Rosenkranz's admirable estimate of Diderot. He says: "Morality is indeed possible in the creed of an atheist, in so far as he allows the necessity of duty; but the materialist, who, if consistent, must also be an atheist, cannot concede the possibility of any morality so long as he dares to proclaim the mechanical process of material motion as the sole cause of everything. Thinking, willing, self-determination, an independence of motives born of the senses, the direction of one's activities, a feeling of responsibility and the consciousness of obligation, all these are for him impossible. They are mere prejudices. Repentance for any deed of his, as though one at any given moment could act differently from that which he finds himself doing, is for him a complete delusion. There exists for him no *causa finalis*, only a *causa efficiens*. Thus Diderot reasons, as he allows the physician, Bordeu, to speak freely as a consistent materialist. However, How is it with Diderot as a man? How does it happen that he would have been willing gladly to cut off his hand, if only he might have been able to destroy completely his obscene romance of the *Bijoux indiscrets*? In this respect, therefore, he was himself repentant. And Diderot the art critic? How does it happen again that he so vigorously denounced the poverty of artistic ideas and of invention, the perverted tendencies and bad taste of his day? Why was he led to declare that if it were possible to construct a machine which could produce the Madonna of Raphael, we would at once cease to wonder at it? He indeed demanded for art freedom, creative skill and productive intelligence, although he recognised fundamentally only an efficient cause among the atoms. And the dramatist Diderot? Without the freedom of his several characters he could not compose a single scene of one of his dramatic poems; for all action is action only so far as it is the result of free activity. Without action, without responsibility, without retribution, no drama is conceivable. And, finally, Diderot the moralist? How can he define the essence of virtue as sacrifice, how can he demand of human nature the traits of benevolence, pity and heroism, if man is necessitated in all his activities, if the entire language of morality consists merely in self-deception, if our willing and doing are events indeed, but without soul and without freedom? What interest, moreover, has the history of mankind, both in its more terrible aspects, and also in the shallower currents of crime, if it is not the outcome of freedom, and the very antithesis of nature itself? In my opinion it is certainly to the eternal honour of Diderot the man that, despite the inconsistent position in which it put him as a philosopher, nevertheless he clung steadfastly to his belief in the supremacy of the moral life, and rejected the practical conclusions of Lamettrie, whom he despised."[1]

The most pronounced and at the same time the most systematic exposition of materialism among the French writers is to be found in Holbach's *Système de la nature* (1770). This book has been called the Bible of materialism. In its production the author was assisted by Diderot, Lagrange, Naigeon and others of the familiar circle which centred in Holbach's brilliant *salons*. It was too radical for even some of the professed adherents of materialism, for it was not only hostile to the religion of the church

[1] Rosenkranz, *Diderot*, vol. II, p. 385 *f*.

system, but it attacked somewhat bitterly all religions and indeed the very idea of religion itself. Holbach declared the idea of God, indissolubly associated with every spiritualistic hypothesis, to be the source of all tyranny and oppression, and particularly of the evils which were undermining the French nation. In a striking paragraph Holbach declares that "if we go back to the beginning we shall always find that ignorance and fear have created gods; fancy, enthusiasm or deceit has adorned or disfigured them; weakness worships them; credulity preserves them in life; custom regards them and tyranny supports them in order to make the blindness of men serve its own end." [1]

The other materialistic writers before Holbach had held the form at least of a diluted deism or a vague pantheism. Their contention had been with ecclesiasticism rather than with natural religion. Holbach maintained throughout an uncompromising attitude toward every conceivable representation of a supreme being. Even Lamettrie had expressed certain reservations at times which seemed to concede the possibility of a pantheistic interpretation of nature. Holbach, however, consistently held to the atheistic construction of the materialistic position as the foundation of all true thinking in philosophy and all right conduct in morals. He followed the lead of Bayle in his insistence upon the possibility of a high order of morality in connection with the most thorough-going materialism. His ethical doctrines were of course utilitarian; not crudely egoistic, however, but based upon a due regard of the interests and welfare of society as a whole. The ideas of the *Système de la nature* were too advanced for Voltaire and Priestley,

[1] *Système de la nature*, II, p. 200.

both of whom attacked the work vigorously on account of its repudiation of the doctrines of deism in any possible form whatsoever. Politically, Holbach opposed the existing order of things as responsible for the needless suffering and misery of the French people, and insisted that the yoke of bondage could be thrown off, if only the prevalent ignorance and superstition could be dissipated by the light of reason, and mankind be bold to enter upon the full realisation of its natural rights and privileges.

The Abbé Galiani, a Neapolitan, who was the acknowledged wit of the circle of the Encyclopædists, characterises the *Système de la nature* in a most graphic manner as follows: "The author of the *Système de la nature* is the Abbé Terrai of metaphysics: He makes deductions, suspensions of payment, and causes the very bankruptcy of knowledge, of pleasure, and of the human mind. But you will tell me that, after all, there were too many rotten securities; that the account was too heavily overdrawn; that there was too much worthless paper on the market. That is true, too, and that is why the crisis has come."[1]

Goethe also gives a most significant estimate of Holbach. The *Système de la nature* came into his hands while yet a student in Strassburg. He describes the impression of disgust which the gross materialism of Holbach caused in the academic circles there. "But," he adds, "we could not conceive how such a book could be dangerous. It came to us so gray, so Cimmerian, so corpse-like, that we could hardly endure its presence; we shuddered before it as if it had been a spectre. It struck us as the very quintessence of musty age, savourless, repugnant."[2]

---

[1] *Correspondance de Galiani*, I, 142.
[2] *Wahrheit und Dichtung*, Book XI.

Holbach represents the lowest level of materialism, and in its defence his argument is dogmatic and his temper uncompromising. He was not only an author but propagandist as well. Two years after the publication of his *Système* he condensed its chief propositions in a short and popular volume, adapted to a wide circulation, called *Le bon sens, ou idées naturelles opposées aux idées surnaturelles*. This and other pamphlets of his were written to inflame the people against the tyranny of church and state, and exerted a powerful influence in encouraging that desperate frame of mind which made possible the scenes of the French Revolution. Holbach's marked personality and widely extended popularity won for his doctrines at once a large following. Through his generous hospitality he was known as the *maître d'hôtel* of philosophy, and his house was humorously styled the *Café de l'Europe*. Rousseau took him as the prototype for his Wolmar in the Nouvelle Héloïse. All this tended to increase his influence and to give an authoritative tone to his doctrines.

Among the immediate followers of Holbach is the French physician, Pierre Jean George Cabanis (1758–1808), who gave a complete physiological expression to the doctrines of materialism in his *Rapports du physique et du moral de l'homme*. His fundamental thesis is, *Les nerfs—voilà tout l'homme*. His philosophy has no illusions. He crudely and baldly insists, for instance, that the brain secretes thought after the manner that the liver secretes bile. With him philosophy is merely a disguised physiology which would prove more serviceable to mankind if it were frankly stripped of its disguise, and were expressed in unambiguous terms. The materialism of the eighteenth century in France, in its various forms more or less radical, embodied certain tendencies of an unmistakable nature. These tendencies express a movement of thought hostile to any spiritualistic interpretation of nature and to all the established forms of religion; in some cases, as we have seen, even to the very idea of religion itself. The state became an object of attack as well as the church, for it was alleged that the superstitions connected with the creed and rites of the one were used to create a servile fear of the tyrannous authority of the other. The political, religious and social questions of the day were inextricably bound together with the philosophical. To follow these philosophical discussions in that age was not a mere matter of interesting speculation, but of vital concern because they intimately affected not only the individual, but also society, and the very foundations of the state itself. The existing order of things could not assimilate or temper the new philosophy; and, therefore, had to join issue with it to the death. In this respect France differed radically from England. In France the philosophy of materialism was destructive rather than constructive, and, therefore, became a potent factor in an age of revolution.

REFERENCES.—H. Hettner: *Litteraturgeschichte des achtzehnten Jahrhunderts.* Brunswick, 1862.
Lange: *History of Materialism.* London, 1880.
Lévy-Bruhl: *History of Modern Philosophy in France.* Chicago, 1899.
John Morley: *Diderot.* London, 1878.
John Morley: *Voltaire.* London, 1885.
Rosenkranz: *Diderot's Leben und Werke.* Leipzig, 1866.

CHAPTER VI

ROUSSEAU'S PHILOSOPHY OF FEELING

In the midst of the materialistic drift of this period there appeared, within the very circle of the *Encyclopædists* themselves, one who was not content either with the method or with the results of the mere analytical process of dissecting the phenomena of nature and of mind—that process which had succeeded in reducing man to the dust, and the springs of life to their material sources. This protesting spirit was Jean Jacques Rousseau (1712–78). He himself had not been wholly free, however, from certain materialistic tendencies in his thinking, due to the prevailing influences of his day. He had written in the earlier period of his career an essay entitled *La morale sensitive, ou le matérialisme du sage.* Fortunately, or unfortunately as the case may be, the manuscript of this essay was lost. Rousseau accused D'Alembert of having stolen it from his papers in order to make capital of its suspected materialistic teachings in such a manner as seriously to embarrass its author in his exceedingly precarious relations to the church authorities. The general point of view which Rousseau took in planning this particular work he gives in his own words, which are most significant: "It has been remarked that in the course of their lives most men are frequently unlike themselves, and seem to be transformed into beings entirely different. It was not, indeed, to establish so well known a thing that I proposed to write a book; I had a more important and newer purpose. This was to search for the causes of those variations, and by confining my observations to those which are dependent on ourselves, to show in what manner they could be directed by us in order to render us better and thus exert more control over our actions. . . . In examining myself, and in observing others as to the causes of those different dispositions, I found that they depended, in great part, on the preceding impressions of exterior objects, and that, modified constantly by our senses and by our organs, we were feeling, without knowing it, in our ideas, in our sentiments, in our actions even, the effect of these modifications. The striking and numerous observations which I had gathered were beyond discussion, and by their physical principles they seemed to me to provide us with a physical régime which, adapted to circumstances, could place our souls in the conditions most favourable to virtue. . . . Climates, seasons, sounds, colours, darkness, light, the elements, food, noise, silence, motion, rest, everything acts on our machine, and on our souls consequently. . . . I have, however, worked little over that book, the title of which was *La morale sensitive, ou le matérialisme du sage*. Distractions which I shall soon explain prevented me from devoting much time to it, and the reader will be informed later as to what has become of my first draft of this essay." [1]

In this contemplated work, it is possible that Rousseau might have disclosed very positive leanings toward materialism. Be that as it may, the fact remains that Rousseau never published the

[1] *Confessions*, Book IX.

essay, and in the meantime the earlier influences of Condillac's sensationalism upon his point of view began to weaken. At the same time he was also withdrawing from his intimate relations with Diderot and Holbach, and was planning to write a systematic criticism of Helvetius's work, *De l'esprit*, which had been such a potent factor in accelerating the materialistic drift of philosophical thought in France. It is certain that the doctrines of the *Encyclopædists* failed to carry the same weight with Rousseau as they otherwise would have done, had he continued his friendship with them without a break. As it was he not only fell out of their circle, but out of their way of thinking as well.

Rousseau was by nature averse to the cold and unsympathetic attitude of the materialistic writers of the day. The popular philosophy with its implications of atheism as well as of materialism could find no permanent point of affinity in a temperament such as that of Rousseau's, to which life in the wealth and fulness of its content appealed with an overmastering charm. He had no sympathy with those philosophers "who would rather give feeling to stones than grant a soul to man." He had no curiosity concerning the elements which might constitute the basis of life, and out of which life itself might be secretly fashioned. He felt that the human spirit far transcends the bare elements of which it may be composed. The process of reducing all things to their lowest terms which characterised the general habit of the philosophical writers of his day had resulted in destroying the very life which they were interested in examining. While dissection may conserve knowledge of a certain kind, it sacrifices life. The fundamental defect of this group of writers was that they had come to regard the philosophical problem in a wholly abstract way, and they failed to interpret the concrete significance of life as a whole. To them matter was a fetish, and mechanical explanation was considered the only method which could be thought worthy of scientific consideration.

From the time of the renaissance there had been an over-emphasis upon the importance of intellectual culture, and now Rousseau enters a vehement protest —for all of his opinions were vehement in their expression—against the isolated play of the intellect in dealing with the problems of life. He presents a passionate plea for the recognition of something more than naked speculation. He undertakes, as a valiant champion, the emancipation of sentiment. He insists that, deep within the centres of our conscious experience, there is also the play of human feeling, the sense of values, judgments of appreciation and sentiments which sound a lower level than the processes of thought can ever reach. This transition from the cold and impersonal analysis of the intellect to the warmer atmosphere of the feeling is a natural reaction from the age of reason which had followed too exclusively the lead of a mechanical argument, and had remained arrogantly indifferent to the claims of feeling or sentiment. Rousseau had no sympathy with a philosophy of mere negation. "I hate," says he, "this rage to destroy without building up."[1] His peculiar office, therefore, was the attempt to reinstate the factor of feeling in the philosophical thought of his day. He was peculiarly fitted to such a task by native temperament and disposition. Hume writes of him to his friend Burton, "He has only *felt* during the whole course

[1] Mémoire de Mme. d'Epinay, II, 66.

of his life, and in this respect his sensibility rises to a pitch beyond what I have seen any example of." [1]

The French spirit had become extravagantly intellectualised during the eighteenth century, and this was due to a combination of many influences other than the purely philosophical. As early as the middle of the century one of the keenest observers of French affairs and one of the wisest of the French statesmen, d'Argenson, the minister "who had endeavoured to restore a national policy to France," had remarked very pointedly upon this extreme intellectualism of the French life of his day: "The heart," he says, "is a faculty of which we are daily divesting ourselves for want of exercise, while the mind is becoming sharpened and whetted. We are becoming wholly intellectual beings; . . . but I predict that this kingdom will perish through the extinction of the faculties which are derived from the heart. Men no longer have friends; they no longer love their mistresses; how can they love their country? . . . We are daily losing that beautiful part of ourselves styled sensibility. Love and the need of loving are disappearing from the earth. . . . Interested calculations now absorb every moment; everything is devoted to the commerce of intrigue. . . . The internal flame is dying out for want of fuel. Paralysis is gaining the heart. . . . It is by following the gradations from the love of thirty years ago to that of to-day that I prophesy its speedy extinction." [2]

That which d'Argenson detected in the midst of the practical affairs, Rousseau also discovered in the philosophical atmosphere whose pervasive influence had so completely dominated the thought of his con-

---

[1] Quoted by Morley, *Rousseau*, vol. II, p. 299.
[2] *Mémoires de d'Argenson*, p. 417.

temporaries. In the age of the illumination, the light which shines in feeling should not be disregarded. Otherwise the field of vision is limited and the brightness of its light obscured.

In proclaiming the gospel of feeling, Rousseau maintains that by the feelings we are able at times to reach a sphere of truth which a purely intellectual analysis fails to penetrate. The utterances of poet and prophet cannot be expressed in the form of a theorem, nor are they capable of demonstration by any ordinary methods of proof. Rousseau did not urge the obvious commonplace that man feels as well as thinks; his doctrine presents a larger claim, namely, that the feeling is in itself a mode of apprehending the truth. Feeling as an event in our conscious life is as much a psychological fact as the perception of the fall of a stone, or of the existence of a house or tree. It is a fact that likewise must be reckoned with, and its significance must be assessed. There are some situations in life which defy analysis; they are sensed. Their significance is immediately apprehended without an explicit knowledge of the reason which may underlie them. The philosopher, too, may come to see things after the manner of the poet or the prophet, and not be compelled to follow the "dry light of reason" alone. This will be true particularly when the moral or spiritual depths of one's life are sounded, and the resulting experience refuses to be formulated. Such is Rousseau's claim for the element of feeling in a philosophy of life. His point of view and general philosophical method may be gathered from the following passage in his *Profession de foi du vicar Savoyard:* "Moreover I fully understand that, so far from delivering me from my useless doubts, the philosophers only served to multiply the perplexities which troubled me, and could not solve any one of them. I took, therefore, another guide, and said to myself: Let me consult the inner light, it will mislead less than they, or, at least, my mistakes will be my own, and I shall wander less astray in following my own illusions than in committing myself to their lies. . . .

"Possessing, therefore, a love of the truth in my attitude to every philosophy, and having for every method a simple and easy rule which enables me to dispense with the vain subtlety of arguments, I undertake, according to this rule, the examination of all matters of knowledge which interest me, resolved to admit as evident everything to which, in the sincerity of my heart, I am not able to withhold my assent, and to regard as true everything which may seem to me to have a necessary connection with the former; and to leave all else in doubt, without rejecting or admitting their truth, and without disturbing myself to explain that which does not lead to something possessing practical utility." [1]

Here is a direct appeal to the simple deliverances of consciousness, the elemental feelings and instincts of the human heart. Following this method of introspection, and trusting the evidence presented by the simple and unanalysed intimations of his own experience, Rousseau is satisfied that he has discovered abundant evidence of the reality of the inner self, of the compulsion of conscience and of the conscious presence of God. Of his profession of faith, through the words of the Savoyard vicar, Mr. Morley says, "it was not a creed; it was a single doctrine melted in a glow of contemplative transport." [2]

---

[1] *Emile*, nouvelle édition, Garnier Frères, Paris, pp. 298 *f*.
[2] Morley, *Rousseau*, vol. II, p. 265.

There is a touch of mysticism in these inner revelations of Rousseau. "I believe," says he, "that the world is governed by a Will, all-powerful and wise. I perceive this, or rather I feel it, and with me that is equivalent to knowledge. . . . The Being who wills and acts from a power within himself, this Being, in short, whoever he may be, who moves the universe and ordains all things, to him I would give the name of God. To this name I join the ideas of intelligence, power, will, which I have united in one, and that of goodness, which is a necessary consequence flowing from them. But I do not know any the better for this the Being to whom I have given the name; he escapes equally from my senses and my understanding; the more I think of him, the more I confound myself. I have full assurance that he exists, and that he exists by himself. I recognise my own being as subordinate to his, and all the things that are known to me as being absolutely in the same case. I perceive God everywhere in his works; I feel him in myself; I see him in everything about me. But when I fain would seek where he is, what he is, of what substance, he vanishes from me, and my troubled soul discerns nothing.

"In fine, the more earnestly I strive to contemplate his infinite essence, the less do I conceive it. But it is; and that suffices me. The less I conceive it, the more I adore. I bow myself down and say to him, O Being of beings, I am, because Thou art; to meditate ceaselessly on Thee by day and night is to raise myself to the veritable source and fount of my nature. The worthiest use of my reason is to make itself as naught before Thee. It is the ravishment of my soul, it is the solace of my weakness, to feel myself brought low before the awful majesty of Thy greatness."[1]

[1] *Emile*, p. 309.

In such a rhapsody there is a naïve indifference to argument. Rousseau is firmly convinced that there are certain truths beyond the scope of reason, but within the reach and grasp of the instinctive feeling. The belief in God, in self, and in the authority of conscience, may be explained away by the reason, but they persist in the hidden sources of feeling. By a clever reduction of our mental powers to their physiological concomitants, it may be made to appear that man is a mere machine. But Rousseau is thoroughly convinced that such a process of reduction must be regarded as an unwarrantable abstraction, for it considers man apart from those springs of feeling which give him the sense of spontaneity and of freedom, and make him a person rather than an automaton. It is possible to construct a logical machine which will present a fair but crude imitation of certain elementary processes of reason. But who can invent a machine which can express in the faintest degree the simplest and most elemental feeling? I may essay a mechanical explanation of the workings of the intellect, but by what device of gauge or metre can I measure the various degrees of emotional pressure which changing mood or passion may occasion? And by what argument can I demonstrate, and by what formula can I express, the significance of the stirrings within the depths of my nature of impulsive nobility, or the patient broodings of aspiration, or the irrepressible intimations of God and of immortality? The human-machine idea of the materialistic writers of France seemed to Rousseau completely inadequate to illustrate these deeper moods of the heart as well as the finer spirit of reason.

In the application of his doctrine of the feeling element in knowledge to the practical affairs of life,

Rousseau found himself in direct antagonism to the state of society in his day. He skilfully and dramatically prepared a sweeping indictment of the existing institutions of church and of state; this was due to his conviction that government, law, ecclesiastical tradition and social convention all tend to repress the natural and elemental feelings of man, and direct them into artificial channels. He felt that this elemental feeling had in it the touch of reality which the conventionalised customs of society wholly lacked, and that there was a confusion of tongues and a darkening of counsel caused by the very progress of civilisation itself.

His *Discourses, Sur les sciences et les arts* and *Sur l'origine de l'inégalité,* are an appeal from the sophisticated to the natural man. While, from the standpoint of the achievements of civilisation, it may be true that man is gaining the whole world, nevertheless, he is in danger of losing himself. Human progress has not been conducive to the improvement of human nature as regards the things which are inherently excellent. Morality is superficial, and character has lost its true ring. "There is honour," says Rousseau, "without virtue, reason without wisdom and pleasure without happiness." [1]

Civilisation has been a process of corrupting the heart and obscuring the mind; and, subject to its influences, humanity has deteriorated in every respect. Such was the thesis which Rousseau set himself to defend in these discourses. In the preparation of the first discourse his feelings were stirred to the depths, and in such a mood the essay was not an argument of the reason so much as an indictment of the passions. The account of the

[1] *Œuvres*, édition de la Librarie Hachette et Cie, Paris, 1905, I, p. 126.

first suggestions which came to him in reference to this discourse, and of the method of treatment which he determined to adopt, is vigorously described in his own words, and gives an excellent illustration of the manner in which his thought was born of feeling. He tells us that while he was walking along the highway from Paris to Vincennes one hot summer afternoon to inquire for his friend Diderot, who was at that time in prison as punishment for the publication of his *Letter on the Blind*, he chanced to come suddenly across the announcement, in a newspaper which he found by the roadside, of the theme propounded by the Dijon Academy: *Si le rétablissement des sciences et des arts a contribué à epurer les mœurs.* "If ever anything resembled a sudden inspiration," writes Rousseau to M. de Malesherbes, "it was the movement which began in me as I read this. All at once I felt myself dazzled by a thousand sparkling lights; crowds of vivid ideas thronged into my mind with a force and confusion that threw me into unspeakable agitation; I felt my head whirling in a giddiness like that of intoxication. A violent palpitation oppressed me; unable to walk for difficulty of breathing, I sank under one of the trees of the avenue, and passed half an hour there in such a condition of excitement that when I arose I saw that the front of my waistcoat was all wet with my tears, though I was wholly unconscious of shedding them. Ah, if I could ever have written the quarter of what I saw and felt under that tree, with what clearness should I have brought out all the contradictions of our social system; with what simplicity I should have demonstrated that man is good naturally and that by institutions only is he made bad." [1]

[1] Second letter to M. de Malesherbes; also *Confessions*, VIII, 135.

In the white heat of indignation at the social order Rousseau found a light to illumine the course of his thought in the elaboration of his negative answer to the question which the Dijon Academy had propounded. The complexity of the existing social structure had rendered truth unattainable, for the source of truth is to be found in the free and spontaneous feelings of man, and these waters have been polluted or have dried up at their fountain-head. Who, then, can drink of the stream, if there is no flow from the spring? Homely virtue, satisfied desire, a contented spirit, unaffected sympathies, the belief that does not falter for want of knowledge, and the knowledge that does not scorn belief, all belong to a distant age when the world was young. Now the sophisticated and the superficial prevail. This is Rousseau's criticism of the artificial standards and corrupting customs of his day and generation.

The companion *Discourse*, on the *Inequality of Man*, has a similar theme. In its development Rousseau endeavours to prove that the natural differences between man and man have been widened and exaggerated out of all proportion by the artificial social relations which have created class and caste distinctions monstrously degrading and demoralising. "By meditating upon the first and simplest operations of the soul" Rousseau undertook to depict the feelings and ideas of the natural man. His habit of ungrounded speculation concerning the nature of things which lie beyond the scope of observation, and his tendency to fashion facts so as to fit his theory, are conspicuously illustrated in his graphic and detailed description of the ideal state of society when as a child of nature man lived free from the trammels of custom, convention, government and religion. This primitive state of unqualified comfort and content, where desires were few and satisfaction easy of attainment on the part of all, Rousseau describes with the circumstance of an eye-witness. This peculiarly vicious method leads him to strike a balance between the old and the new order of things which is palpably absurd as well as false.

By such a method he necessarily falls into striking inconsistencies and contradictions. His *Contrat Social* is, in fact, a substantial repudiation of the position taken in the *Discours sur l'origine de l'inégalité*, and the *Discours sur les sciences et les arts*. For instance, he says in the *Contrat Social:* "Although man deprives himself in the civil state of many advantages which he holds from nature, yet he acquires, in turn, others so great, his faculties so exercise and develop themselves, his ideas so extend, his sentiments are so ennobled, and his whole soul is raised to such a degree, that if the abuses of this new condition did not so often degrade him below that from which he has emerged, he would be bound to bless without ceasing the happy moment which rescued him from it forever, and out of a stupid and blind animal made an intelligent being and a man." [1]

Rousseau, however, was never disturbed by so small a matter as inconsistency in his oracular deliverances. In this passage there is a spontaneous recognition of the necessity of contributing to the feeling and animal needs of man some saving grace of intelligence. And, although the idea of a social contract is a theory which disregards the past and the historical evolution of society and its institutions, and which bases its central idea upon a set of arti-

[1] *Contrat Social*, I, viii.

ficial conditions conceived in fancy and far removed from fact, nevertheless it is essentially an attempt to rationalise the relations of the individual to his fellows so as to justify a central governing power. It lies outside the scope and purpose of the present study of the movement of philosophical thought in this period of the *Enlightenment* to enter upon a detailed exposition or criticism of the famous doctrine of the Social Contract. Its particular interest for us consists in this, that it furnishes an indication of Rousseau's instinctive and perhaps unconscious appreciation of the natural limitations which the philosophy of feeling is bound to encounter. It is certainly a glaring inconsistency on Rousseau's part to claim everything in a sweeping manner for the spontaneous play of the feelings, all insight, all knowledge, all direction of conduct and final decisions in the perplexities of thought and action, and yet at the same time to attempt a rational justification of the foundations of that civilisation which, according to his fundamental point of view, tends to check the free development of these same feelings, and to neutralise their native power. Rousseau's attitude in this respect is something more than an instance of inconsistency. It possesses a deeper philosophical significance. It represents a natural return of the feeling element in experience upon itself, and the finding of itself in the larger sphere of its intellectual relations and implications. For feeling, after all, is a function of the intelligence, that is, as the contributions which it receives from the intellect are found to vary, so also will the corresponding feeling vary in intensity and in significance. Rousseau did not succeed in his attempt to abstract the feeling elements from the concrete whole of life any more than the

Encyclopædists were able to abstract the intellectual elements in disregard of the claims of feeling.

The tendency to allow some place in his philosophy of feeling for the balancing function of the reason is noticeable in a number of places throughout the *Confession of Faith of the Savoyard Vicar*. In referring to the sensations, Rousseau qualifies their exclusive claims in the following statement: "I am, however, not merely a sensitive and passive being, but a being likewise active and intelligent; and whatever philosophy may say to the contrary, I shall at least dare to lay claim to the honour of thought." [1]

He places man above all other animals because he alone is able to contemplate them all. "It is therefore true that man is lord of the earth which he inhabits. For not only does he dominate all creatures and dispose all of the elements by his industry, but he alone knows how to conduct himself in the world; and, moreover, he can appropriate through contemplation the very stars themselves, although he is not able to approach them. Who can show me another animal upon the face of the earth who understands the use of fire and who can gaze in admiration upon the sun? What! I am able to observe and understand all creatures and their relations one to another. I am able to recognise order, beauty and virtue. I am able to contemplate the universe and raise my thoughts to the hand which governs it, and I am able to appreciate the good and pursue it. And yet shall I stoop to compare myself to the beasts?" [2]

Moreover, he clearly recognises a moral order in the world, and the necessity for the individual to regulate his own life according to its laws. He says:

[1] *Emile*, p. 302.   [2] *Ib.*, p. 310.

"There must be definite moral order wherever there is sentiment and intelligence. The difference between the good and evil man is that the good man orders his life in accordance with the whole, and the evil man would order the whole in accordance with the interests of his own individual life. The latter makes himself the centre of all things; the former takes the measure of the radius and holds himself at its circumference. Therefore he finds his proper place at once in regard to the common centre, which is God, and in respect to all the concentric circles which represent his fellow creatures." [1]

As a corrective of the dictates of pure subjective feeling, Rousseau would place above the particular experience of the individual and the sentiments which would naturally control his will a *raison commune*, of which there are abundant intimations in the conscience of every human being, and which should exercise a superior authority. This appeal from the particular to the universal reason may be clearly recognised in the following passage from a letter to one of his correspondents: "You bid me distrust this internal assent, but I find in it a natural safeguard against the sophisms of my understanding. And I fear that on this occasion you are confusing the secret inclinations of our heart which lead us astray with that more secret, more inward voice which reclaims and murmurs against these interested decisions, and brings us back, in spite of ourselves, to the way of truth." [2]

In a similar manner in the *Contrat Social*, Rousseau states that the individual will must always recognise

---

[1] *Emile*, p. 328.
[2] See Caird's Essay on "Rousseau," in his *Essays on Literature and Philosophy*, vol. I, p. 133.

and acquiesce in the *volonté générale*, to which it is related as ~~the particular~~ to an all-comprehending and ~~univer~~sal. However, while recognising ~~the char~~acter of the intellectual factors ~~combine~~d with the forces of feeling in our ~~life, n~~evertheless, does not give this idea ~~any~~ very certain place in his thought. ~~T~~his is not far to seek. The tide ~~run~~s too strong in his nature for ~~him to resi~~st the pressure of particular feel-~~ing with~~ deeper universal significance. While insisting that Emile, in the course of his ideal education, must at all times respect reason and preserve an open mind, nevertheless in his own thinking he yields invariably to the overmastering power of a sentiment which is impatient of any rival. On this account he fails to give a satisfactory account of the relations of man to his fellow man in society. He never wholly frees himself from an innate tendency to magnify the feeling element in the determination of the life of the individual. Consequently he regards the individual, thus controlled in a large measure by the feelings peculiar to his own nature, as separate and isolated both as regards the essential characteristics of his personality and also the conduct of his life. He is, therefore, capable of entering into political relations only in an artificial manner. Rousseau regards man neither as a political nor as a social animal; for the feelings always exercise a tendency toward undue particularisation. Therefore one who emphasises the feeling element in experience, always tends to an extreme individualism. And the units of society, thus differentiated, do not draw together. The individual, according to Rousseau, who lives according to nature, is one guided by inclination and even at times by caprice, and who has not learned the secret of a life which is ordered by reason and the sense of obligation.

To form an adequate philosophy of life there must be some attempt at rationalising its phenomena, that is, of discovering the universal significance and organic relations of its scattered and separate experiences. But while the universal may be expressed in terms of thought, the feeling element cannot so readily be exhibited in its wider bearings, and it resists all attempt at generalisation. My feeling is mine and may not be yours; its significance, therefore, remains for me alone. Rousseau himself is aware of this, as may be seen from his confession that "a proof of sentiment for me cannot become a demonstration for others, and it is not reasonable to say to any one, 'You ought to believe this, because I believe it.'"[1] The particular feeling so holds Rousseau's exclusive attention that he always fails to appreciate its larger significance and bearing which thoughtful reflection alone can disengage. His *Confessions* bear witness to his abnormal interest in the play of his own feelings, and also to his evident conviction that it is a matter of supreme importance to acquire the habit of making an exact assessment of every passing sentiment and changing mood. The *Confessions* represent the abstract consideration of the anatomy of the feelings in its most extreme and exaggerated form. In this record of his own life there is a veritable idolatry of sentiment. The exposition of the play of passion and appetite with such prodigality of detail, the analysis of emotions ignoble as well as noble, and the self-regarding attitude which the author consistently maintains throughout his nar-

[1] Caird, *Ibid.*, p. 134.

rative are an offence not only to the reason but to the imagination as well. Extreme individualism is the dominant note in all of Rousseau's writings; it is the natural product and expression of the exaggerated egoistic sentimentalism which is emitted from every page of the *Confessions* like the heavy palling odour of over-luxuriant and rank vegetation.

This tendency on the part of Rousseau to regard the feeling element of experience in a wholly abstract manner, despite his concessions at times to the corrective and steadying power of the reason, may be seen also in the practical separation of feeling from action which is one of the most conspicuous features of his character and which gives to his life its fundamental defect of inconsistency.

Rousseau is capable of noble feeling, and quite as capable also of ignoble action. He perfectly illustrates in his own nature the characteristic remark of Hume, that "reason is and ought to be only the slave of the passions." For him feeling never became a law to the will; but there was always a weak compliance with the desire of the moment. Sentiments which imposed obligation of any kind were exceedingly distasteful to him. "In everything," he confesses, "*gêne* and subjection are insupportable to me, they would make me hate pleasure itself." [1]

Again, he states that "in order to do good with pleasure, it is necessary for me to act freely, without restraint; and to take away all the sweetness of a good work from me it is only necessary that it should become my duty. Be it man or duty or even necessity that lays a command upon me, when my heart is silent, my will remains deaf, and I cannot obey; I see an evil threatening me, but I let it come rather

[1] *Confessions*, I, 5.

than agitate myself to prevent it. In every imaginable thing, what I cannot do with pleasure it is impossible for me to do at all." [1]

With Rousseau virtue is something to be admired, but not practised. He who wrote so convincingly of the supreme duty of the maternal care of children that the mothers of all France turned instinctively to the neglected responsibilities and privileges which an awakened conscience no longer dared to deputise, was himself so indifferent to the natural claims of his own children that he was willing to place them in a foundling hospital, and to dispose of them in such a manner as to destroy any possible clue of the recognition of them in after years, thus severing all paternal ties whatsoever completely and irrevocably. He who graphically pictured the ideal home of domestic simplicity and happiness never made a home for his own. He who could be easily reduced to tears at the very thought of virtue and of honour, felt at the time no compunctions of conscience in unjustly accusing a young serving-maid of stealing in order to shield himself; and again, in basely deserting his friend and teacher who had been overcome suddenly by an apoplectic seizure in a crowded market-place, he followed the impulse of convenience rather than the dictates of decency, to say nothing of the demands of friendship.

Loyalty to friends was a theme which stirred his eloquence to extravagant expression, and yet in all of his friendships he was never able to pass beyond the shadow of himself. With a profound sympathy for the unfortunate and oppressed, and valiantly championing the rights of the people, nevertheless the actual presence of the individual person, the con-

[1] *Reveries*, VI.

crete representative of humanity in general, was irritating and intolerable to him. He indulged himself in the reverie of feeling as a form of intoxication. In fancy Rousseau was able to regard life from the stand-point of a disinterested spectator, and in his speculative moods things assumed normal proportions; the noble and the ideal were then seen in their true light, and were regarded with an enthusiastic appreciation which provoked in him a spirit of exaltation. But immersed in actual experiences of life, Rousseau became acutely sensitive to the sordid, the distorted, the mean and base side of human nature. His own bodily comfort appealed to him so strongly that he was disinclined to take any part in those affairs which might offend his taste or depress his spirit. There was no co-ordination of the ideal and the real in his philosophy of life. His general point of view in this regard is described in a somewhat paradoxical manner, and yet most significantly withal, in *La nouvelle Héloïse*. Through the words of Julie he gives expression to his creed concerning happiness: "People are only happy before they are happy. Man, so eager and so feeble, made to desire all and obtain little, has received from heaven a consoling force which brings all that he desires close to him, which subjects it to his imagination, which makes it sensible and present before him, which delivers it over to him. The land of chimera is the only one in this world that is worth dwelling in, and such is the nothingness of the human lot that, except the being who exists in and by himself, there is nothing beautiful except that which does not exist." [1]

The feelings which find play solely in the sphere of the imagination, and are completely divorced from

---

[1] *La nouvelle Héloïse*, VI, viii, 298; *Confessions*, XI, 106.

that action which is their natural mode of expression, and at the same time are uninfluenced by those intellectual associations which are wont to give them depth and direction, may well be regarded as an exceedingly uncertain light in guiding us to the sources of truth. The discrepancy between the ideal and the actual in Rousseau's case is the more marked because of the insistence throughout his various works upon the pragmatic test of truth.[1] He freely indulged in such assertions as these: that "he will not burden his mind with any difficult problems which do not lead to practical results," and that "goodness should spring from the heart as well as show itself in one's conduct," and again, that "the true reward of justice is the consciousness that one has practised it";[2] nevertheless he never was able or never cared to order his own life so as to illustrate the noble sentiments which his thought devised with such facile skill.

In the endeavour to form a just estimate of Rousseau's contribution to the philosophical thought of his day, it must be borne in mind that he did not succeed in establishing a philosophy of feeling. In that he failed. However, he did succeed in his efforts to draw attention to the necessity of including the feeling element in an adequate philosophy of man. If it should be objected that this is not a new or original idea, it will be at least allowed that Rousseau brought the play of his genius to bear upon this neglected factor in the speculations of his philosophical colleagues, and by the charm and vogue of his writings kept it well in the foreground of contempo-

---

[1] See a recent article by Prof. Albert Schinz on *Jean Jacques Rousseau, A Forerunner of Pragmatism*.

[2] *Emile*, pp. 299, 322.

rary thought. In the age of reason he entered a plea for the claims of feeling. It is true that these claims were exaggerated, and the urgency of his contention overwrought, and yet it may have been necessary to over-emphasise the importance of the feeling factor in order that his cause might gain even a hearing. Mr. Morley has given an estimate of Rousseau which, both as an appreciation and as a criticism, is most expressive and adequate: "Rousseau awoke emotion to self-consciousness, gave it a dialect, communicated an impulse in favour of social order, and then very calamitously, at the same time, divorced it from the fundamental conditions of progress, by divorcing it from disciplined intelligence and scientific reason." [1]

It is true, as we have seen, that Rousseau was not wholly indifferent to the high offices of reason, and yet in protesting against the extreme position wherein reason had grown mechanical, and contemptuous of the actual experiences of life, he naturally fell into the counter error of substituting one extreme position for another. But sentiment is not a substitute for wisdom, nor emotion for law. Rousseau's word, therefore, cannot be considered as final. While drawing attention to a neglected factor, he commits the fatal blunder of regarding that factor as though it were the whole, and of placing an exclusive emphasis upon it. In the rôle of the champion of feeling he challenged reason as a foe, whom however he should have endeavoured to win as an ally and friend.

Rousseau's direct influence upon the subsequent philosophical thought is illustrated most conspicuously in the effect which his individualism and his protest against the exaggerated valuation of the intellect produced in the mind of Kant. In a notable

[1] Morley, *Rousseau*, vol. II, p. 49.

passage in the *Fragmente*, Kant expresses his appreciation of Rousseau and his personal indebtedness for a timely suggestion which radically affected his general disposition and attitude of thought. He says: "I myself am by inclination an inquirer. I feel an absolute thirst for knowledge and a longing unrest to advance ever further and to enjoy the delights of new discovery. There was a time when I thought that this was what conferred real dignity upon human life, and I despised the rabble who knew nothing. Rousseau has shown me my error. This dazzling advantage vanishes, and I have come to honour man, and should regard myself as of much less use than the common labourer if I did not believe that this speculative philosophy will restore to all men the common rights of humanity." [1]

It is no inconsiderable debt that Kant owed to Rousseau. His respect for the individual and his appreciation of man's worth as an end in himself; his democratic feeling for the rights and the needs of the people; his belief in the intimations of the practical as well as of the pure reason; and his conviction that happiness is not a matter of culture alone, but depends quite as much upon the sound heart and the simple nature of the more lowly conditioned in the march of humanity,—this, in part at least, Kant gained from the inspiration of Rousseau.

Wherein Rousseau failed, namely, in his inability to recognise the constructive power of reason, in this very respect the critical genius of Kant restored the true balance of thought by producing a synthesis of intellect and feeling which merits the distinction of a philosophy of human nature in its fully rounded capacity.

[1] Hartenstein's second edition of Kant's Works, vol. VIII, p. 642.

THE ENLIGHTENMENT

REFERENCES.—Edward Caird: *Essay on Literature and Philosophy*, vol. I. Glasgow, 1892.

Thomas Davidson: *Rousseau and Education according to Nature*. New York, 1902.

T. H. Green. *Philosophical Works*, vol. II, pp. 386–396. London, 1885.

H. Höffding: *Rousseau und Seine Philosophie*. Stuttgart, 1897.

L. Lévy-Bruhl: *History of Modern Philosophy in France*. Chicago, 1899.

J. R. Lowell: *The Sentimentalism of Rousseau: Among My Books, Series* I. Boston, 1876.

Frederika Macdonald: *Jean Jacques Rousseau, A New Criticism*. London, 1906.

Frederika Macdonald: *Studies in the France of Voltaire and Rousseau*. London, 1895.

John Morley: *Rousseau*. London, 1873.

Saint Marc Girardin: *Rousseau, sa vie et ses œuvres*. Paris, 1874.

Sainte Beuve: *Confessions de J. J. Rousseau. Causeries du lundi*, III. Paris, 1874.

M. G. Streckeisen-Moultou: *J. J. Rousseau, ses amis et ses enemis*. Paris, 1861.

Joseph Texte: *Jean Jacques Rousseau and the Cosmopolitan Spirit in Literature*. London and New York, 1899.

George Saintsbury: *Rousseau* in *Encyclopædia Britannica*.

CHAPTER VII

THE PHILOSOPHY OF LEIBNIZ

There is a type of mind radically different from that of Rousseau, quite different also from that of Locke or of his school, which is illustrated in the writings of Gottfried Wilhelm Leibniz (1646–1716). In his philosophy, the empirical point of view gives place to the rationalistic—a method of inquiry which, in spite of its seeming opposition, is really the natural complement of empiricism. The rationalistic method of constructing a systematic body of knowledge profoundly affected the movement of the philosophical thought in the eighteenth century; and no one contributed more brilliantly or more significantly than Leibniz to the stream of its influence. The rationalistic attitude of mind regards the reason as a source of knowledge, as well as the senses; but more than that, it holds that even the material furnished by the senses would prove wholly unintelligible, were it not for the interpreting capacity of certain fundamental ideas and principles which are born of the reason alone. Leibniz, therefore, supplies an element which is wanting in the presuppositions of Locke and in the development of the Lockian principles at the hands of his followers, and he appears as the natural critic of Locke from the stand-point of rationalism. His *Nouveaux Essais* present a detailed criticism of Locke's *Essay Concerning Human Understanding*.

In the *Nouveaux Essais* two friends, Philalethes and Theophilus, converse together; the first states the views of Locke, the second replies from the stand-point of Leibniz. Locke, it will be remembered, had insisted that *nihil est in intellectu, sed non fuerit in sensu;* and Leibniz, in commenting upon this declaration of Locke's, had added, *nisi intellectus ipse*. This supplementary clause expresses in a phrase the fundamental point of view of Leibniz's philosophy. In his Preface to the *Nouveaux Essais* Leibniz comments thus significantly upon the differences between his point of view and that of Locke: "Our differences are upon subjects of some importance. The question is to know whether the soul in itself is entirely empty, as tablets upon which as yet nothing has been written (*tabula rasa*) according to Aristotle and the author of the *Essay*, and whether all that is traced thereon comes solely from the senses and from experience; or whether the soul contains originally the principles of many ideas and doctrines which external objects merely call up on occasion, as I believe with Plato, and even with the Schoolmen, and with all those who interpret in this way the passage of St. Paul (Rom. ii. 15), where he states that the law of God is written in the heart. The Stoics call these principles *prolepses*, *i. e.*, fundamental assumptions, or what is taken for granted in advance. The Mathematicians call them *general notions*, κοιναὶ ἔννοιαι. Modern philosophers give them other beautiful names, and Julius Scaliger in particular named them *semina æternitatis*, also *zopyra, i. e.*, living fires, luminous flashes, concealed within us, but which the encounter of the senses makes appear like the sparks which the blow makes spring from the steel. And the belief is not without reason, that these inner illuminations indicate something divine and eternal which appears especially in the necessary truths. Whence another question arises, whether all truths depend upon experience, *i. e.*, upon induction and examples, or whether there are some which have still another foundation. For if some events can be foreseen prior to any proof which may have been made of them, it is manifest that we ourselves contribute something thereto. The senses, although necessary for all our actual knowledge, are not sufficient to give it all to us, since the senses never give us anything but examples, *i. e.*, particular or individual truths." [1]

This represents the line of departure from Locke, which Leibniz follows throughout the whole course of his criticism. The intellect furnishes certain basal ideas, as being, unity, substance, identity, cause, perception, reason and the like, and these ideas, moreover, are constitutive in the process of interpreting the crude material supplied by the senses.[2]

The knowledge which is given by the senses is obscure and confused until it is illumined by the light of reason, where alone the truth shines clear and in its own light. Leibniz, moreover, holds that "the intellectual ideas which are the source of necessary truths do not come from the senses. . . . The ideas which come from the senses are confused, and the truths which depend upon them are likewise confused, at least in part; whereas the intellectual ideas and the truths which depend upon them are distinct, and neither the one nor the other have their origin in the senses, though it is true we should never think of them without the senses." [3]

[1] *The New Essays*, translated by Alfred Gideon Langley, p. 42 *f*.
[2] *Ib.*, p. 45.   [3] *The New Essays*, p. 82.

It appears also that these simple ideas, clear and distinct, because born of the reason, contain potentially many necessary truths according to which the very universe itself is fundamentally determined. If one only possesses the proper insight, it is possible for him to deduce from the self-illuminating activities and dispositions of the reason itself, the fundamental nature of the essential principles which underlie both the appearance and the reality of the world. Far from believing that knowledge has its origin from without through the inlet of the senses, Leibniz, on the contrary, traces its beginnings to the sources which are hidden in the depths of the mind. Truth is there held fast in a potential state, as yet undeveloped and undiscovered. It is not a possession, but a possibility. It can be elicited, however, by the penetrating and informing power of thought.

Truth, therefore, is to be deduced through a strictly logical process which starts with certain indefinables, that is, those primary ideas which cannot be proved, and, indeed, have no need of proof.[1] Thence, through various combinations and manipulations of these self-evident axioms and principles, Leibniz believed that new truths could be indefinitely evolved, somewhat after the manner of a geometrical method. The ideas which thus hang together admit of an indefinite elaboration.

This finds a conspicuous illustration in his *Characteristica Universalis*, which is a method of symbolical representation and of logical calculation by means of certain character symbols. Thus Leibniz endeavours to reduce the processes of reasoning to forms and operations similar to those which are employed in the familiar algebraical methods, and

---

[1] *The Monadology*, § 35.

with the expectation of correspondingly fruitful results. When only twenty years of age he published an outline of this method in his *Dissertatio de Arte Combinatoria*. Such was his belief in the utility of a symbolical device in reasoning that he declares: "If controversies were to arise, there would be no more need of disputation between two philosophers than between two accountants. For it would surfice for them to take their pencils in their hands, to sit down to their slates, and to say to each other (with a friend as witness, if they liked), 'Let us calculate.'"[1]

This conception of Leibniz opened the way for the modern Symbolic Logic, and yet it never developed the fruitful results which its author had expected. He was, throughout his life, however, deeply interested in its possibilities, and was always confident that a completely satisfactory method of such a kind would be some day devised.[2] His belief in the possibility of a procedure of thought from primary truths of an axiomatic character through symbolic terms and operations to an indefinite elaboration of a consistent body of knowledge, serves to illustrate in a pre-eminent degree his peculiar type of mind. Its rationalistic character is thus sharply defined. Unless one can appreciate, in some measure at least, this habit of mind which is "able to reason in metaphysics and morals in much the same way as in geometry and analysis," it will be quite impossible to understand the significance of Leibniz's rationalistic point of view and method in

---

[1] *Die philosophischen Schriften von G. W. Leibniz*, herausgeben von C. J. Gerhardt, Berlin, 1875–90, vol. VII, p. 200. (Subsequent references to Leibniz's works will be to this edition.)

[2] See Couturat, *La logique de Leibniz*, chaps. II, III and IV.

contrast with the principles and procedure of an empirical philosophy.

We may study Leibniz merely as a critic of Locke, and gain much by such an exercise. And yet we, on the other hand, should lose much if we failed to regard him also in reference to the distinctly constructive vein of thought which characterises his philosophical writings. It is necessary to take this into consideration if we are correctly and adequately to estimate the worth of his peculiar contribution to the philosophy of the eighteenth century.

That contribution, to put it briefly, is the idea that in some way the processes of thought represent the real relations and connections of things, and that an understanding of the one furnishes a suggestive key to the nature of the other. Proceeding, therefore, to a more minute examination of his philosophy, it appears that its central doctrine is his conception of the fundamental nature of substance. We have already observed how important a rôle the idea of substance plays in the philosophy of Locke, and that of Berkeley and of Hume. Leibniz's theory as to the characteristic features of substance was provoked originally by the complete dissatisfaction which he felt with Descartes's account of the nature of substance, wherein it is maintained that the essence of external things is extension. Leibniz, on the contrary, was convinced that a substance is never an aggregate of parts such as the very idea of extension, that is, the idea of spread-outedness, would seem to necessitate. If it is to have anything more than a verbal significance, substance must possess some essential unity in itself. The idea of the extension of matter is one which is given by the senses, and, indeed, by the very grossness of the senses, and is never the conception which is the product of our thinking faculty; thought indeed gives a more profound insight. On this point Leibniz says: "It can be inferred that corporeal substance does not consist of extension or divisibility; for it will be admitted that two bodies remote from one another ... are really not one substance. ... Now, every extended mass can be considered as composed of two or a thousand others; we have merely extension by contact. From this point of view we shall never find a body of which we can say that it is truly one substance. It will be always an aggregate of many. ... Extension is an attribute which cannot constitute a complete being; no action or change can be derived from it, it expresses merely the present state, but not at all the future or the past, as the notion of a substance should." [1]

If the characteristic feature of matter is not extension, what other property can be suggested? Leibniz insists that the idea most intimately associated in our minds with the essential nature of matter is that of force. Out of mere extension it is impossible to derive the idea of motion, and motion is the most conspicuous and constant property of that kind of matter of which our type of minds at least can be cognisant. The observation of the sensible properties of matter, however, will not discover to us the essential nature of the substance which underlies all perceived properties. It is not patent to empirical observation or experiment. Locke himself concedes the impossibility of attaining any true knowledge of the nature of substance through sense perception.

How, then, does Leibniz reach this conception of substance as a centre of force? By a method which

[1] *Die phil. Schriften*, II, 71.

is peculiarly characteristic of his general point of view and habit of mind. It is not by outer observation but by the inner analysis of the nature of his thought processes that the secret is revealed to him. His inquiry is exceedingly subtle. It is an indirect way of disclosing the mystery of nature, as it is revealed in the operations of the mind, for he is convinced that the mind forms "a living mirror of the universe," and that the necessities of thought reflect as well as determine the nature of things. In the analysis of our logical processes it will be found that the natural form through which our thought manifests itself is the judgment, namely, the form in which a predicate is asserted of a subject. It happens that in the varied phases through which thought in its rapid shifting continually passes, that which may be a subject in one context becomes a predicate in another. However, there is an unique kind of subject, of which many predicates may be asserted, but it can never be considered itself as a predicate of any other subject. A subject, thus peculiarly constituted, is the true type of substance. Substance, therefore, may be precisely and adequately defined, according to Leibniz, as that which is the subject of all its various predicates, but is itself the predicate of no subject.[1]

Now the question naturally suggests itself, What is the most perfect illustration of this description of substance? Is it not the idea of the self which underlies all my mental states? These states are various; but they have one constant object to which they may be severally referred. I am a subject always, and can never be properly regarded as the mere predicate of any other subject. Moreover, I

[1] Leibniz, *Schriften*, IV, 432.

have an intimate and immediate knowledge of my own nature, which I cannot gain through external observation in reference to any other object whatsoever. Therefore the idea of substance in general will be formed after the analogy of the soul, or self substance. As this substance, moreover, is subjected to a deeper analysis, it reveals its innermost nature as essentially a force centre. It is continuously active, and the energy which it draws from its inner springs needs no re-enforcement from without. The essential feature of substance, as represented by the Ego, is its self-originating and self-determining nature. This dynamical quality of substance Leibniz indicates by characterising it as an *entelechy*, because in every substance there is "a sufficiency ($αὐτάρκεια$) which makes it the source of its internal activities."[1]

Every substance, as an *entelechy*, therefore, contains the potential power of its own development. And this characteristic feature of substance not only is revealed by the direct intuition of the dynamics of one's own spirit, but can be discovered also through a strictly logical mode of procedure. It is possible to deduce the idea of the self-sufficient nature of every true substance by a consideration again of the essential function of the subject-predicate relation in every judgment. For every complete subject comprises within itself all of its predicates. A true predicate is never external to the subject, but is implied in the nature of the subject itself, and falls wholly within the circle of its essential significance. Any predicate which may be regarded as added to a subject is

---

[1] *The Monadology*, § 18.
As to the relation of Leibniz *entelechy* to the ἐντελέχια of Aristotle, see Robert Latta, *Leibniz, The Monadology and Other Philosophical Writings*, p. 229, footnote.

artificially related to such a subject, and is so far forth unreal. If our knowledge of any subject were complete, then an analysis of its concept in all of its properties and implications would reveal all of its predicates. Therefore, as Leibniz declares, inasmuch as every true predication has some foundation in the nature of things, every substance will be found to partake of this characteristic feature of a subject after the manner of the logical necessities of thought. Consequently, every substance is self-contained. It has within it the potential of whatever actual manifestation it may ever exhibit. Every substance, therefore, has its own individuality completely marked, and sharply differentiated. In their ultimate elements things are as individual as persons. And these elements of the world, self-sufficient and self-determined in their power of initiative and capacity of resourceful originality, Leibniz designates by the name of *Monads*.[1]

Leibniz's *Monadology* contains a complete description of the nature of the monads. In this account the monad is represented as the unit of substance, but with an intensive rather than an extensive nature. No two monads are alike, and every one, true to its individual character, is a little world within itself. It preserves its own unity in the midst of the never-ceasing flux in which the various phases of its activity are constantly occurring. According to the fundamental principle of Leibniz's philosophical method, that the nature of the logical processes is a key to the nature of reality, the monad in respect to its unity finds

[1] The term monad Leibniz did not borrow from Giordano Bruno, as is commonly supposed, but from one of Leibniz's own contemporaries, François Mercure van Helmont (1816-99). For a detailed treatment of the whole subject, see L. Stern, *Leibniz und Spinoza*, chap. VI. pp. 111-219, also the *New Essays*, p. 101, footnote.

a corresponding prototype in the essential features of the logical concept, which always expresses a unity in the midst of variety, or an identity in difference.

Leibniz graphically expresses the self-sufficiency of the monad in declaring that "it has no windows." [1] The meaning of this is, that nothing contributes to the nature of the monad from without; on the contrary, the monad contains in its own being the promise and potency of its complete development. It not only contains within itself power for all its activity, but the forecast of its history as well. The differences, moreover, which exist among the various monads are intrinsic; they are not like the atoms, which are supposed, after the manner of the ancient philosophy, to vary according to differences of position in time and space, and also according to the nature of the combinations into which it is possible for them to enter.[2]

The theory that the individuality of the monad is determined by an "internal principle of distinction" and not by external circumstance, Leibniz defends by his closely related theory of the *identity of indiscernibles*, namely, that "things qualitatively undistinguishable are absolutely identical, and therefore would not count as different things, but really one and the same thing." This principle of Leibniz is a corollary of the principle of sufficient reason. As he himself says of it: "I infer from that principle [that of sufficient reason], among other consequences, that there are not in nature two real, absolute beings, indiscernible from each other; because if there were, God and nature would act without reason in ordering the one otherwise than the other." [3]

[1] *Monadology* § 7.   [2] *The New Essays*, p. 238 *f*.
[3] *Schriften*, VII, 393

Thus Leibniz proves that every monad must possess an individuality due to an inherent principle of inner distinction. Moreover, as the monad experiences change, and passes from one state to another, this is due to its constitutional *appetition*, as Leibniz calls it—that is, an inner tendency to realise the full measure of its possibilities; consequently the monad proceeds from change to change in a course of progressive development. When such a tendency appears in a monad attended with consciousness, it is then akin to desire.[1]

In the process of development, moreover, every present state of a simple substance is a natural consequence of its preceding states, so that "every present is big with its future." Consequently every monad is determined solely by what it is and never by what may happen to it. Its progress is necessary and not contingent, because its store of energy, its impulse and directive force, are all from within.

The question at this point may be very properly asked: If every monad is driven by an inner power, and unaffected by the forces which may play upon it from without, how, then, is it possible to explain the evident interconnection and interaction between the various phenomena of nature? To this, Leibniz would reply: "In the case of simple substances, the influence which one monad has upon another is only ideal. It can have its effect only through the mediation of God, in so far as, in the ideas of God, each monad can rightly claim that God, in regulating others from the beginning of things, should have regarded it also. For, since one created monad cannot have a physical influence upon the inner being of another, it is only through this primal

[1] *Monadology*, § 15.

THE PHILOSOPHY OF LEIBNIZ

regulation that one can be dependent upon the other." [1]

While Leibniz holds that the monads have no windows, this statement cannot be interpreted in a literal manner; for each monad after all has a single window opening to the light above; and each monad is dependent upon this light as a principle of life which streams into its being from the supreme Monad, God. While independent of all others, the monad nevertheless has its origin and support in the divine Monad.

The independence, however, of one monad as regards another does not signify in the least that the several monads are out of all relation one to another. On the contrary, they are most intimately connected in the following manner: Each monad in itself is a "perpetual living mirror of the universe," [2] as Leibniz puts it.

Each monad, in its way, expresses a certain phase of the universe. That phase may be very insignificant, and yet it is so much a part of the "scheme of things entire" that if perfectly known it would inevitably lead the thought by necessary implication to the part most intimately connected with it, and that in turn to another and another without limit, until the widening circles of knowledge would comprehend the universe. Each monad is in this sense a microcosm, so that whatever is particular in any one substance is at the same time common to all. This function which every simple substance exercises, of expressing in its own nature some phase of the great world without, Leibniz calls the faculty of perception. This term is used in a most comprehensive sense, including not only the processes of

[1] *Monadology* § 51.   [2] *Ib.*, § 56.

consciousness through which we are aware of the world about us and ourselves as well, but also the various modes in which also mere unconscious things may reflect in their own natures the larger world of which they are through this very capacity an integral part. In reference to this function of "expression" or "perception," Leibniz declares that "God at first so created the soul, or any other real unity, that everything must arise in it from its own inner nature, with a perfect spontaneity as regards itself, and yet with a perfect conformity to things outside of it. . . . And accordingly, since each of these substances accurately represents the whole universe in its own way and from a certain point of view, and the perceptions or expressions of external things come into the soul at their appropriate time, in virtue of its own laws, as in a world by itself, and as if there existed nothing but God and the soul, . . . there will be a perfect agreement between all these substances, which will have the same result as if they had a communication with one another by a transmission of species or qualities, such as the mass of ordinary philosophers suppose." [1]

Not only are there these expressive "perceptions" throughout the universe of things; but also among persons as well there are determining forces in consciousness, though we ourselves may be unconscious of them, which partake of the nature of actual "perceptions" themselves. Of these Leibniz speaks as follows: "There are a thousand indications which make us think that there are, at every moment, an infinite number of *perceptions* in us, but without apperception and reflection, *i. e.*, changes in the soul itself of which we are not conscious, because the im-

[1] *Schriften*, IV, 484.

pressions are either too slight and too great in number, or too even, so that they have nothing sufficiently marked to distinguish them from each other; but joined to others, they do not fail to produce their effect and to make themselves felt at least confusedly in the mass. . . . These minute perceptions are, then, of greater efficacy in their results than one supposes. They form I know not what—these tastes, these images of the sense qualities, clear in the mass but confused in the parts, these impressions which surrounding bodies make upon us, which involve the infinite, this connection which each being has with all the rest of the universe. We may even say that in consequence of these minute perceptions, the present is big with the future and laden with the past, that all things conspire together (σύμπνοια πάντα as Hippocrates said), and that in the least of substances eyes as penetrating as those of God could read the whole course of the universe.

"Quæ sint, quæ fuerint, quæ mox futura trahantur." [1]

This doctrine of representation, according to which one monad may express the nature of another, and indeed of all others, was naturally suggested to Leibniz by his mathematical studies and habit of mind. He relates the monads one to another after the analogy of the various properties of geometrical figures such as the circle or ellipse. Every property of a circle, for instance, so adequately expresses the nature of the circle as a whole, that if any one property should be given, all the others could be deduced from it. In this sense every property reflects in itself all the others. Any one can be taken as a correct definition of the circle itself. In a similar manner precisely, the various

[1] *New Essays*, p. 47 *f*.

parts of the universe so hang together that any one is a representation in a certain sense of all the others. The implication is not always obvious, nor do we ever comprehend its full significance. A monad reflects or expresses only that part of the whole of things which lies nearest to it, and is by nature most intimately associated with it. All beyond is confused and obscure, and yet connected by necessary relations. To the mind of God alone, the *Monas monadum*, does every other monad reveal its secret, and the secret of each one is, in its own peculiar way, the secret of the universe.

The particular relation which seems to connect things together by some external bond, namely, that of cause and effect, Leibniz explains merely as a particular instance of his general theory of representative function. Both cause and effect being the result of an inner activity in each case, the one cannot be regarded as acting upon the other. The relation which they sustain to one another, as we observe them, is the noticeable difference in capacity between the two, of expressing the nature of the universe of which they are parts. The substance whose inner change brings about the more complete representation of the universe is to be regarded as active, *i. e.*, the cause; the other, whose inner change brings about a less complete expression, is to be regarded as passive or being acted upon, *i. e.*, the effect.[1]

Causation, therefore, in this view of it, is a process of striking the balance between two substances as regards their relative capacity to manifest through the channels of their own nature the world of which they are both essential parts.

[1] *Discourse on Metaphysics*, §15.

While every monad is instinct with the life of God, whether consciously or unconsciously, as the case may be, still the conscious manifestation is of a superior order to that which occurs in the various forms of the inanimate nature, and through the entire range of the lower phases of animal life. There is, therefore, a certain hierarchy of substances, inasmuch as "the virtue of a particular substance is to express well the glory of God, and the better it expresses it, the less is it limited." [1]

Leibniz elaborates this idea more in detail in the following notable passage: "For assuredly spirits are the most perfect of substances, and best express the divinity. Since all the nature, purpose, virtue and function of substances is, as has been sufficiently explained, to express God and the universe, there is no room for doubting that those substances which give the expression, and are at the same time conscious of it and consequently are able to understand the great truths about God and the universe, do express God and the universe incomparably better than do those natures which are either brutish and incapable of recognising truths, or are wholly destitute of sensation and knowledge. The difference between intelligent substances and those which are not intelligent is quite as great as between a mirror and one who sees." [2]

In this account which Leibniz gives of the nature of the monad it is exceedingly difficult to comprehend how each single monad can exercise a complete independence in all of its varied activities, and yet at the same time be capable of reflecting in itself all the changes which occur in the monads directly associated with it, and, indeed, in all other monads also,

[1] *Discourse on Metaphysics*, § 15.   [2] *Ib.*, § 35.

though in an indirect manner and, it may be, in an inappreciable degree. In other words, how is it possible to reconcile inner spontaneity with co-ordinate activity? To such a problem Leibniz finds the appropriate solution in his doctrine of *pre-established harmony*. This doctrine also has its origin in certain fundamental principles of mathematics. In his mathematical studies Leibniz had become familiar with the device of regarding two wholly independent systems of relations from a common point of view, in such a manner that every relation of one system is capable of suggesting and expressing a corresponding relation in the other. The two systems, therefore, can be regarded throughout as functionally co-ordinated. The conspicuous illustration of functional co-ordination in mathematics is the method of the Cartesian geometry, by means of which all geometrical relations find their appropriate expression in the algebraical. In the theory of the co-ordinate geometry, the various figures and their properties may be represented by algebraical equations, which correspond to them not only in a general way but also in all minuteness of detail. Such an equation as $x^2 + y^2 = 36$ represents a circle, in the sense that every property of this equation is an exact representation of a corresponding property of a circle, so that we can study the nature of a circle indirectly by investigating the characteristic features of its equation and interpreting them in terms of their geometrical concomitants. Moreover, if in the given equation of the circle, we imagine certain changes to occur, so that it appears now as $4x^2 + 9y^2 = 36$, instead of simply $x^2 + y^2 = 36$ as before, then the transformed equation no longer represents a circle, but an ellipse. Conceive this new equation to undergo an additional change, this time simply a change of sign from plus to minus, then the equation thus modified, $4x^2 - 9y^2 = 36$, now represents an hyperbola.

Thus every change, however slight, in the one system represents a corresponding change in the other, which is precisely co-ordinated with it. Obviously the two systems are independent, and yet completely interrelated. No one would think of saying that a change in one system *causes* a change in the other. The notion of a functional relation such as this is merely that of suggestive representation. It would be absurd to conceive of any cause and effect relation which could possibly obtain between an algebraical modification of an equation and a corresponding spatial change in the nature of a circle or an ellipse, in the sense that the one becomes, in some mysterious manner, transformed into the other. While there is no underlying causal connection between the two systems of relations, there is, however, an exceedingly nice adjustment. This adjustment has been called a functional co-ordination. This is merely the mathematical phrase for the concept of pre-established harmony. The harmony between the algebraical and geometrical systems of relations is not artificial or arbitrary. It is one which grows out of the fundamental nature of the two sets of relations themselves. By their very nature they admit of an exact co-ordination. And it is in this sense that Leibniz uses the term pre-established; all concomitance of relations may be traced back to an inherent common basis in the heart of things which show the possibilities of co-ordinate development.

The doctrine of pre-established harmony, therefore, is to be regarded in the first instance as Leibniz's explanation of the relations which the monads in general sustain one to another. The activity of every monad is thus functionally co-ordinated with every other. A change in one expresses a change in the others after the same manner that a modification of an algebraical equation by changing a plus to a minus sign expresses the series of characteristic differences between the fundamental nature of an ellipse and that of an hyperbola. It is in this sense that every monad is "a mirror of the universe." Its own inner changes are functionally co-ordinated with other corresponding possible changes throughout the whole range of created substances. Thus Leibniz would explain the striking paradox of his philosophy—the attempt to show how universal order can be conserved by the most extreme form of individualism.

In the telegraphic apparatus for the transmission of wireless messages, the discharging instrument must be "toned" to an exact correspondence with the receiving instrument. The two must be accurately "syntonised," or no message can be transmitted. This is only a sort of pre-established harmony. One instrument *expresses* the symbolical message which is sent forth from the other because there is the possibility of intelligible co-ordination based upon the common "tone." So also in every system of symbols which serve to express certain ideas corresponding to them there is an illustration again of the relation of pre-established harmony, the most perfect example of this being the comprehensively co-ordinated system of relations between thought and language. Every change in words, and in the indefinite variety of combinations which they may form, expresses varying shades of meaning in the corresponding thought. The idea of a pre-established harmony, therefore, among the monads signifies a co-ordination of a similar kind, so that any change of relation experienced by any one can be regarded as representing possible changes in some or all of the others, provided only that the key of interpretation be known. In an unknown language, whose sounds convey to our ears no intelligible message, there is nevertheless a pre-established harmony of sound and thought in every uttered syllable. We who are ignorant of the language fail to comprehend its meaning. So, also, if we only could understand the language, we might be able also to understand, through the significant symbolism of nature, the mystery of God, of the world and of man.

Not only does Leibniz attempt to explain the general nature of the monads in their relation one to another, by his doctrine of pre-established harmony, but he also applies it to certain special relations as well, in which his theory seems to be conspicuously illustrated.

The first of these is the relation of mind to body. Of these two intimately associated parts of our being, each is a closed system. Changes in bodily states are caused solely by preceding bodily states; likewise changes in mind by preceding mental states. Each is, after its own manner, sufficient unto itself, and the one does not in any sense act upon the other; mind cannot produce physical effects, and the body cannot of itself produce mental effects. Each, however, in the development of its own distinct activities, expresses, in every possible change which is due to its own inherent nature, a corresponding change in the other. The two are functionally co-ordinated. Every relation which exists in the one series has a definite significance when interpreted in terms of the other. Of this co-ordination of mind and body,

Leibniz says: "We can also see the explanation of that great mystery 'the union of the soul and the body,' that is to say, how it comes about that the passions and actions of the one are accompanied by the actions and passions or else the appropriate phenomena of the other. For it is not possible to conceive how one can have an influence upon the other, and it is unreasonable to have recourse at once to the extraordinary intervention of the universal cause in an ordinary and particular case. The following, however, is the true explanation: We have said that everything which happens to a soul or to any substance is a consequence of its concept; hence the idea itself or the essence of the soul brings it about that all of its appearances or perceptions should be produced out of its own nature, and precisely in such a way that they correspond of themselves to that which happens in the universe at large, but more particularly and more perfectly to that which happens in the body associated with it, because it is in a particular way and only for a certain time according to the relation of other bodies to its own body, that the soul expresses the state of the universe. This last fact enables us to see how our body belongs to us, without, however, being attached to our essence. I believe that those who are careful thinkers will decide favourably for our principles because of this single reason, viz.: that they are able to see in that which constitutes the relation between the soul and the body, a parallelism which appears inexplicable in any other way." [1]

In this significant passage the relation between soul and body is stated as a special and peculiar case of the soul's relation to the universe at large, and may

[1] *Discourse on Metaphysics*, § 33.

be regarded, therefore, as a kind of corollary to the main doctrine of pre-established harmony. It is also of interest to note that Leibniz regards the co-ordinate relations of body and of soul as constituting a kind of "parallelism." This is a foreshadowing, not only in name but in significance as well, of that psycho-physical parallelism which was first suggested by Spinoza, and which has been so fruitfully developed in modern times.

The seeming reaction between mind and body is explained by Leibniz along the lines of his general theory concerning the nature of causation. When a change in one monad is capable of explaining a change in another, the first is said to be active, the second passive, activity and passivity being wholly relative characterisations. Moreover, as monads differ in clearness of perception, and those which have the clearer perceptions are the more active, therefore the soul having clear perceptions is more active than the body in this sense, and therefore can be said to act upon the body and dominate it. Moreover, so far as the soul is perfect and has clear perceptions the body is subject to it, but in so far as it is imperfect it is subject to the body.[1] This is in accordance with the general principle of Leibniz that the "domination and subordination of monads, considered in the monads themselves, consists only in the degrees of their perfections."[2]

There is, moreover, a second special case which illustrates the doctrine of pre-established harmony, namely, the co-ordinate relations which exist between the two spheres of efficient and final causes. As a result of the pre-established harmony between soul and body, Leibniz finds a resulting harmony between

[1] *Schriften*, VI, 138.   [2] *Ib.*, II, 451.

these two kinds of causation, inasmuch as efficient causes have to do with the activities of the body, and final causes, on the other hand, represent the purposes of the mind. "Souls," says Leibniz, "act in accordance with the laws of final causes through their appetitions, ends and means. Bodies act in accordance with the laws of efficient causes or motions. The two realms, that of efficient causes and that of final causes, are in harmony with one another." [1]

There is still another case of pre-established harmony, that which obtains between the world of nature and the world of the divine purposes. It is, indeed, merely an illustration in its most comprehensive form of the general relation of efficient to final causes. There is a world of a moral and spiritual order which has its being within the world of nature. This inner world of moral order and purpose Leibniz very significantly calls the "city of God." "As we established above," says he, "that there is a perfect harmony between the two natural realms of efficient and final causes, it will be in place here to point out another harmony which appears between the physical realm of nature and the moral realm of grace, that is to say, between God, considered as the architect of the mechanism of the universe, and God considered as the Monarch of the divine city of spirits." [2]

In this attempt to reconcile the spheres of efficient and final causes, Leibniz gives the promise at least of effecting a synthesis between the empirical and rationalistic points of view. He emphasises the point that the one cannot be considered solely to the exclusion of the other. In a letter to M. Remond

[1] *Monadology*, § 79. [2] *Ib.*, § 87.

(1714) he states most clearly the complementary relations of these two methods of thought: "I have found that most of the philosophical sects are right in a good part of what they maintain, but not to the same extent in what they deny. The Formalists, such as the Platonists and the Aristotelians, are right in seeking the source of things in final and formal causes. But they err in neglecting efficient and material causes and in inferring (as did Mr. Henry More in England, and some other Platonists) that there are phenomena which cannot be explained on mechanical principles. But, on the other hand, the Materialists, or those who hold exclusively to the mechanical philosophy, err in setting aside metaphysical considerations and in trying to explain everything by that which is dependent on the imagination. I flatter myself that I have discovered the harmony of the different systems, and have seen that both sides are right, provided they do not clash with one another; that in the phenomena of nature everything happens mechanically and at the same time metaphysically, but that the source of the mechanical is in the metaphysical." [1]

While all credit must be given to Leibniz for his discerning insight in insisting that these two methods of interpreting the phenomena of nature must be regarded as mutually complementary, nevertheless, the harmony which he declared assuredly characterises the different systems, he himself never adequately established or satisfactorily revealed. For, after all, any real reconciliation after the manner of a direct synthesis of these two spheres of being was altogether impossible according to the central doctrine of Leibniz's philosophy. For in general he does not

[1] *Schriften*, III, 607.

allow the possibility of any substance acting upon any other whatsoever, and, particularly, nothing really affects the substance we call mind from without.

Moreover, Leibniz is very careful to define with a nicety of precision the particular sense in which it can be correctly said that our knowledge is received by us from external sources. It is in the sense merely, he distinctly states, that "certain exterior things contain, or express more particularly, the causes which determine us to certain thoughts."[1]

The empirical elements in knowledge, the material of fact which is given in sense perception, Leibniz regards merely as thought in a confused and obscure form, the adumbration of a truth which comes to an adequate revelation only in the clear light of reason. That which seems to be presented to us from without must not be regarded as so much crude material upon which the reason works, and out of which it constructs ideas as the finished product. On the contrary, Leibniz very emphatically maintained that there are in the intellect itself such traces of the world without, of its laws and its organisation, the lines of its progress, and the measure of its possibilities, that, whatever the material may be which is presented to it through the senses, it is already anticipated, in its inner significance at least, by certain elements, native to the nature of thought itself, which lie concealed in a potential state within the deeper recesses of the mind. This idea Leibniz explicitly develops in the following paragraph: "Nothing can be taught us of which we have not already in our minds the idea. This idea is as it were the material out of which the thought will form itself. This is what Plato has excellently brought out in his doctrine of reminis-

[1] *Discourse on Metaphysics*, § 27.

cence, a doctrine which contains a great deal of truth, provided that it is properly understood and purged of the error of pre-existence, and provided that one does not conceive of the soul as having already known and thought at some other time what it learns and thinks now." [1]

In every perception, therefore, according to Leibniz, there is a supra-sensible element which constitutes its reality. Every observation of sensible fact must be interpreted, consequently, in terms of the idea which it awakens. Leibniz thus places the weight of his emphasis upon a rationalistic view of things. Facts are the symbolical expressions of ideas, in some such a fashion as the mere physical lines and set of a face express a man's character.

Moreover, Leibniz regards the object of knowledge as never immediately known, or connected with the observing mind by any direct process whatsoever. Between what is given in perception and what is perceived, therefore, there is no possibility of a genuine synthesis. The two terms are harmonised only in an indirect manner, so far forth as each is functionally co-ordinated with the other according to the fundamental principle of things in the universe at large. There is a relation, therefore, between the external world and the observing thought only as each has the capacity to "express" the nature of God and the universe, and thus each indirectly to express the nature of the other. Indeed, Leibniz reminds us of Berkeley, and actually speaks his language in the doctrine of divine concurrence within the process of sense perception itself. "We may say, therefore, that God is for us the only immediate external object and that we see things through him.

[1] *Discourse on Metaphysics*, § 26.

For example, when we see the sun or the stars, it is God who gives to us and preserves in us the ideas, and whenever our senses are affected according to his own laws in a certain manner it is he who, by his continual concurrence, determines our thinking." [1]

It is, after all, no direct and real synthesis of subject and object—to come to a knowledge of nature through the intervention of God. Leibniz in reality holds nature and the observing mind quite apart, and a divine mediation alone serves to bring them into relation.

While the actual synthesis of the empirical and rational elements was attempted by Kant in a more direct manner, and with more satisfactory results than Leibniz had attained, yet the work of Leibniz is not to be regarded merely as furnishing certain convenient elements for the great constructive work of his illustrious successor. He did that, but more. He also established certain fundamental truths which have affected profoundly the current of philosophical thought, not only throughout the eighteenth century, but even to the present day. His doctrine of substance as a centre of energy agrees in an almost prophetic manner with the modern theory of the ultimate energy unit, which is supposed to be the basis of all material phenomena; and also with the corresponding point of view which sees within the seemingly passive objects of our observation a ceaseless activity, and within the sphere of the inconceivably minute particles of matter a world of moving elements. The one point of difference, however, is that the monad of Leibniz, as a unit of energy, is intensively individual, and all qualitative differences are due to the original and inherent

[1] *Metaphysics*, § 28.

differences of the various elementary substances themselves—no two in the whole universe being alike. According to the modern theory, on the contrary, it is supposed that there is a certain uniformity of the ultimate energy characteristics, and differences are accounted for by the various combinations which the original units may chance to form. Leibniz's units, however, are never qualitatively indifferent. Whatever their development, and into whatever combinations they may enter, there is throughout a complete conservation of individuality as well as of energy.

It is, indeed, a most singular inconsistency on Leibniz's part that he failed to derive variety of substance by a method of arranging like elements in different combinations, inasmuch as, by his *Ars Combinatoria*, he regards it as quite possible to reach an indefinite variety of true judgments through various combinations of symbolic characters representing simple and fundamental concepts of thought. Now, Leibniz held as a central principle of his philosophical system that the processes of thought indicate the essential nature and the real connections of things, therefore, inasmuch as the development of thought in his symbolic system proceeds according to a method of devising various significant combinations, what would have been more natural than for Leibniz to fall in with the obvious suggestion that in all probability variety of substance throughout the universe may be also due to a certain variety of combinations which the simple elements are capable of undergoing among themselves?

Leibniz, however, held most tenaciously to his conviction that each monad is a simple substance, and in no wise composite; therefore the possibility of qualitative differences among simple substances being accounted for by the differences due to various forms of combination, was necessarily excluded from his thought.

There is still another conception of Leibniz which was a prophecy of results of a most comprehensive character, which were to be reached at a later day and in other fields of thought. This is his idea of a natural evolution of the essential characteristics of every substance according to the law of their inner nature. Leibniz believed in a fundamental principle of continuity operative throughout the universe in such a manner that there cannot possibly be any leap in nature. This continuity, he held, is unbroken throughout every phase of activity, whether mechanical or mental. Moreover, the evolution which Leibniz had in view was not merely that of the single substance, but of all substances co-ordinately related in one and the same system—the realisation of a great cosmic program. In this world system he emphasises the unity of nature, whose various parts are interconnected each to each, and each to the whole. While every substance is individual, no substance is isolated; and all conspire together to serve a common end. The following passage of Leibniz, if its theological interpretation and also certain crudities of biological expression were to be eliminated, might well appear in some modern essay on the theory of evolution:

"Commencing from ourselves and proceeding even to the lowest things, a descent is made by *very small degrees*, and by a continued series of things, which in each remove differ very little one from the other. There are fishes that have wings, and to whom the air is not strange, and there are birds inhabiting the water whose blood is cold like that of the fishes, and whose flesh so strongly resembles theirs in taste that the scrupulous are allowed to eat them on fish days. There are animals so closely approaching the species of birds and of beasts that they hold the middle ground between them. The amphibia contain both terrestrial and aquatic animals. Seals live upon the land and in the sea; and porpoises (whose name signifies sea-hog) have the warm blood and the entrails of a hog. Not to speak of that which is reported of sea-men, there are *some animals* who seem to have as much knowledge and reason as some that are called men; and there is so close a relation between animals and vegetables, that if you take the most imperfect of one, and the most perfect of the other, you will scarcely perceive any considerable difference between them. Thus, until we reach *the lowest and least organised parts of matter*, we shall find everywhere species bound together and differing by degrees almost imperceptible. And when we consider the wisdom and infinite power of the Author of all things, we have reason to think that it is conformed to the magnificent *harmony of the universe* and to the great design as well as to the infinite goodness of this sovereign Architect, that the different species of creatures ascend, also, little by little from us toward his infinite perfection." [1]

In commenting upon Leibniz and the other pioneers of the philosophical interpretation of nature in the seventeenth and eighteenth centuries, Professor Osborn remarks: "It is a very striking fact that the basis of our modern methods of studying the Evolution problem was established not by the early naturalists, nor by the speculative writers,

[1] *The New Essays*, p. 332 *f*.

but by the philosophers. They alone were upon the main track of modern thought."[1]

True to his fundamental principles of interpretation, Leibniz's thought is concerned with the final as well as the material and efficient cause of evolution. His rationalistic point of view leads him to regard the end toward which the whole creation moves as the essentially determining factor in its beginnings and throughout the whole course of its development, so that what may prove to be last in execution must have been first in conception. All things work together on this hypothesis to conserve the *harmony of the universe*. It is natural that if Leibniz held any theory of evolution, he should tinge it with a philosophical colouring. This may seem to the strictly scientific evolutionist of to-day wholly gratuitous. But it is an interest which Leibniz, by his mental temperament, could not possibly conceal. Whatever may be the comment upon its philosophical and theological ground, Leibniz's theory of evolution, as a sketch roughly outlined, and in parts vaguely suggested, must be regarded as an idea which anticipated an age whose spirit the great philosopher of that remote generation felt, and in a measure expressed.

While Leibniz supplies, as we have seen, the rationalistic *motif* which was necessary to correct the unbalanced character of Locke's too exclusive empiricism, he is also strongly of the opinion that a synthesis of the rationalistic and empirical elements in knowledge should be effected. Though his attempt in this regard is not wholly satisfactory, it serves a purpose in the progressive movement of thought by contributing significant material and suggestion to the master mind of Kant. In a more

[1] H. F. Osborn, *From the Greeks to Darwin*, p. 87.

direct manner also Leibniz has furnished the philosophical world at large with a wealth of ideas which have proved eminently suggestive and of incalculable value. The conception of a unity in the midst of difference, of a harmony underlying seemingly opposed phenomena, of profound relations which exist among elements superficially separate and distinct, of an unbroken continuity in the process of unfolding the treasures of nature and of mind, the conviction, moreover, that there is a reason and meaning in everything, the idea also of a world of order and of purpose whose significance is revealed alone in God, and the consequent creed of optimism, and its cardinal doctrine of the best possible world—this is, in part at least, the heritage which comes to us through the works of Leibniz, and which has generously enriched the permanent possessions of philosophical thought.

REFERENCES.—R. Adamson: *The Development of Modern Philosophy.* Vol. I. Edinburgh, 1903.
Ernst Cassirer: *Leibniz's System.* Marburg, 1902.
Louis Couturat: *La logique de Leibniz.* Paris, 1901.
John Dewey: *New Essays Concerning Human Understanding. A Critical Exposition.* Chicago, 1888.
E. Dillmann: *Eine neue Darstellung der Leibnizschen Monadenlehre.* Leipzig, 1891.
C. T. Gerhardt: *Die Philosophischen Schriften von G. W. Leibniz.* Berlin, 1875-90.
George M. Duncan: *The Philosophical Works of Leibniz.* New Haven, 1890.
A. G. Langley: *New Essays.* London and New York, 1893.
Robert Latta: *Leibniz. The Monadology,* etc. Clarendon Press, 1898.
J. T. Merz: *Leibniz. (Philosophical Classics for English Readers.)* Edinburgh, 1884.
Bertrand Russell: *The Philosophy of Leibniz.* Cambridge Press, 1900.
W. R. Sorley: *Leibniz* in *Encyclopædia Britannica.*
Frank Thilly: *Leibnizens Streit gegen Locke.* Heidelberg, 1896.
Kuno Fischer: *Leibniz's Leben, Werke und Lehre.* Heidelberg, 1902.
M. H. Calkins: *Persistent Problems in Philosophy.* N. Y., 1907.

CHAPTER VIII

THE CONFLICT OF TYPICAL PHILOSOPHICAL TENDENCIES IN GERMANY

Germany was the common ground where the various philosophical forces of the eighteenth century met. Here they appeared, now in conflict, and again in attempt at reconciliation. It was a period of confusion and uncertainty, of controversy in some quarters, and of an artificial eclecticism in others, but withal a period of preparation for the necessary work of reconstruction which was later to be accomplished by the profound insight of Kant. For this task the great philosopher also was preparing, through an intimate contact with the various philosophical influences of his day, and through a growing appreciation, on his part, of their several glimpses of truth as well as their corresponding limitations. Kant's critical estimate of this period is significantly revealed in his pointed characterisation of it: "*Wenn denn nun gefragt wird: leben wir jetzt in einem aufgeklärten Zeitalter? So ist die Antwort: Nein; wohl aber in einem Zeitalter der Aufklärung.*"

The influence which most conspicuously dominated the German thought of this century was that of Leibniz as systematised and formulated in the writings of his follower, Christian Wolff. It was primarily, as we have seen, an intellectualistic point of view, emphasising the supreme significance and value of the unmistakably clear ideas of the reason as the ultimate source of knowledge. At the same time, the empirical view of Locke appealed more strongly to a large circle of the younger philosophers, who had been introduced to this way of thinking directly through the German translations of Locke's *Essay*, and indirectly through the Lockian doctrines which had come into Germany through the widely growing influence of the French writers.

Not only was there the old controversy as to whether truth is to be sought by the analysis of the clear ideas of the reason, or through research in the psychological origins of our more complex mental states; but also there was in certain quarters an emphatic protest against the search for truth at all in the sphere of the intellect, and an earnest plea for the deeper insight, as it was believed, which the feelings alone are capable of giving. This influence was intensified in part by the writings of Rousseau, and in part also by the wave of pietism which swept over Germany. This religious movement had its beginning with the teachings of Spener (1635–1705), and was developed and furthered by the more systematic efforts of Francke (1663–1727). In the midst of the various philosophical stirrings of thought, this Teutonic Quakerism exerted a profound influence both upon the philosophical thought and the religious conviction of Germany throughout this period of unrest and controversy. It had at least two essential characteristics in common with the doctrines of the Wolffian philosophy, namely, a disregard of creeds, and the insistence upon the supreme worth of a moral life as the essence of religion. The philosophy of the *Aufklärung* tended to substitute morality for religion; and where this tendency was not completely realised, at least the moral aspects of religion were placed conspicuously in the foreground. Pietism, as a rule of life showing its fruits in a personal morality, sympathetically expresses, and that too with all the earnestness and fervour of an established sect, this characteristic tendency of the *Aufklärung*. Moreover, pietism insists upon religion as the immediate personal concern of the individual, and in this respect emphasises another essential and conspicuous factor in the general philosophical movement of thought of that day,—a trait also of the German spirit which had manifested itself so persistently in the marked individualism of Luther and the age of the Reformation. The university of Halle, founded in 1694, was the home and centre of this pietistic movement in Germany.

Martin Knutzen (1713–51), who was the teacher of Kant in the University of Königsberg, had a strain of pietism in his exposition of the Wolffian philosophy, and the common ground between these widely different points of view was emphasised by the prominence which he gave in his teaching to the ideas of individualism and subjectivity. There was still another type of mind which appeared in this period, and which, like the pietistic temperament, found in the feelings the source of inspiration and consequently of knowledge. I refer to the rising school of German poets who believed that certain ideas are grasped intuitively, and that such ideas resist all attempts to analyse them into simpler elements or to trace their origin to earlier forms. They were of the opinion that such truths can neither be explained nor yet explained away. They come through flashes of visions, through mystic insight and sympathetic appreciation. From this point of view it is urged that the poet is to be regarded as the true philosopher.

After this brief survey of the various intellectual forces which meet in Germany during this century, we now proceed to a more particular examination of them severally. The philosophy of Leibniz was the most significant and wide-reaching influence of this period. Unfortunately it became known to the German people through the interpretation of his writings which finds expression in the works of Christian Wolff (1679–1754). I say unfortunately, because the so-called Leibniz-Wolffian philosophy presents the letter of Leibniz's thought without its spirit. In order to render the doctrines of Leibniz adaptable to the needs of instruction in the schools and universities Wolff reduces them to very distinct definitions and convenient formulas, and consequently he wholly depotentiates their original vitality and significance. Wolff was by nature a systematiser. He knew how to arrange the dead bones of philosophy in their proper order and to give them their precise articulation. But he failed to quicken them with the breath of life. The remarks which Herder makes concerning the Wolffian adaptation of the Leibnizian philosophy are most striking and apposite. He writes in 1776 in the *German Mercury*: "Leibniz loved to make comparisons, to make novel use of other men's ideas, and frequently to couple the most contradictory opinions; thus he revealed his whole system not otherwise than as it presented itself to him, as it lived in his soul, in glimpses of wit and imagination, in short essays and in ever familiarising us with other men's ideas. It had to be felt in the warmth of this origin and of this connection, otherwise Leibniz's spirit was gone, and with it all the original and primitive truth of the impression. Wolff, who was incapable of feeling this, or who, as follower and commentator, had no time for feeling, made theorems out of these prospects and glimpses of wit. They were so much easier to demonstrate, as they had lost their spontaneousness and had become trivial and might mean everything or nothing. The followers of this school-dissector dissected further: the Germanised Latin language of philosophy stood there as a tree on which caterpillars and beetles had left on each leaf a metaphysic of dry threads, so that the dryad wept for mercy—Leibniz, Leibniz! where was thy spirit?" [1]

It is always the case that the simplified ideas of a great teacher fail to represent him adequately. Leibniz's rationalism was tempered and balanced, not, it is true, in any systematic manner, for Leibniz never reduced his philosophy to a formal system; nevertheless, he was keenly sensible of the wealth of significance hidden in the concrete and particular experiences of life, which the cut and dried formulas of a scholastic mind are powerless to express. Wolff demonstrates the inadequacy of a purely logico-metaphysical inquiry which loses itself in the empty phrases of a barren rationalism. His *Vernünftige Gedanken* concerning logic, metaphysics, ethics, psychology, physiology and politics cover the entire field of philosophy and cognate sciences and form a complete "philosophical encyclopædia." While their influence was extensive, forming the basis of instruction throughout all the higher schools of Germany, nevertheless, because they were superficial and scholastic, that influence was never deep or permanent.

Leibniz did not reduce his philosophy to a system, because it was too deeply penetrating, too subtle, too vaguely suggested at times, too delicately shaded in

[1] Merz, *Leibniz*, pp. 198 *f.*

its discriminations, too elusive in the thoughts which were profoundly felt, yet impossible adequately to express. It was, in short, too instinct with life to admit of the laying bare of its bone and tissue by the scalpel of a scholastic logic. Leibniz's intellectualism was balanced and modified, if not by actually expressed reservations and limitations, at least by the unexpressed implications of his point of view and general attitude of mind. Wolff, however, despite his obvious limitations as an expounder of the doctrines of Leibniz, rendered an incalculable service to the philosophical thought of Germany. He wrote in the German language; his style was clear; his treatment of the extensive range of philosophical topics was comprehensive. Consequently a mass of philosophical doctrine became available to a large popular following whose interest in the deeper problems of thought and of life it was the means not merely of stimulating, but also of creating. Through Wolff, therefore, the German people were made familiar with a philosophical vocabulary and received an orientation in the typical philosophical disciplines. Germany's secure grounding in philosophical doctrines was due in no slight measure to the contribution which the works of Wolff made to the national education of his day.

In looking for the true follower of Leibniz we would naturally seek one who was able to appreciate the deep undercurrents of his philosophy, and to give his thought an adequate expression in a form which possesses more life and significance. Such a follower we do not find in Wolff or in any member of his school, but in one who combined in a remarkably versatile nature the gifts of a poet, philosopher, dramatist, critic, historian and theologian, namely, Gotthold Ephraim Lessing (1729–81). With Lessing in the line of philosophical descent from Leibniz may be placed that other philosopher poet, Johann Gottfried Herder (1744–1803). The delicate *nuances* of Leibniz's thought which Wolff failed wholly to appreciate were revealed to the artistic insight both of Lessing and of Herder. What the bare logical faculty misses altogether, the sympathetic instinct is able to apprehend. This in itself is an indication that clear thought capable of expression in convenient formula is not the sole source of knowledge. The light of reason, which the philosophers of the *Aukflärung* in Germany regarded as the one and only guiding star, might shine on the high places of thought, but it failed at times to penetrate the more obscure regions of the lower valleys. Lessing was one who found in Leibniz valuable suggestions as to the illumination of those stretches of thought whose darkness the conventional formulas of the Wolffian system were wholly incapable of dispelling. Of the difficulty in expressing the thought of Leibniz in the exact formulas of the school Lessing says, in a conversation with Jacobi: "Leibniz's ideas of truth were so formed that he could not bear to see too narrow limits set to it. From this mode of thought many of his statements have flowed, and it is often hard for the most acute student to discover his real opinion. For that very reason I think so highly of him; I mean, on account of this great manner of thinking, not on account of this or that opinion which he appeared to hold, or even actually held." [1]

According to Leibniz's doctrines of continuity and of progressive development, the objects of thought

---

[1] Jacobi, *Werke*, Part IV, § 1.

which are not capable of shining in their own light may, nevertheless, possess a deep significance when regarded in the light of an unfolding process of which they themselves are essential stages. The age of reason in Germany, as in France, despised the past achievements of thought and of deeds, because they had failed to measure up to the advanced standards of the *Aufklärung* ideals. In Germany the break with the past was not actually brought about by a decided rupture with church and state, as it was in France during the period of the Revolution. Protestantism in Germany was more elastic and adaptable. The church was able to accommodate itself to the new phases of thought, namely the Wolffian philosophy and pietism. In the generation following Wolff's activity as author and teacher most of the professors of theology in the various German universities were adherents of the Wolffian system. The sympathies of the state were with the new philosophy; for was not the great Frederick himself a philosopher of the *Aufklärung* and the first patron in his time of philosophy, the arts and letters? Nevertheless, the sense of historical continuity and the appreciation of its debt to the past were wholly foreign to the thought of that age. While there was no revolution in Germany, the ties with the past were but lightly regarded, and there was a general declaration of independence in reference to all the historic phases of thought, as well as to all the thinkers who were not of the living present. Lessing's contribution to the age in which he lived was the insistence upon the unbroken continuity of the historical development of the world, both of the world of thought and the world of action. Lessing approached the philosophy of Leibniz not from its speculative but from its practical side. He was not primarily interested in the metaphysical significance of the doctrine of the monad or its epistemological applications. But he was interested most enthusiastically in the idea of evolution, which was the essential characteristic of the life of the monad. He appreciated with a keen insight the value of the doctrine of evolution as a method of historical criticism. While the age of the *Aufklärung* could lightly dismiss all past achievement as insignificant because inferior to the standards of the present, Lessing insisted that its value must be assessed according to its part and place in the development as a whole. What is not according to formula and rule may still possess a value and interest when regarded in its own setting, and as a phase, even though a passing phase, of an onward movement toward a more and more complete expression of truth.

Lessing was convinced that light may be found to illuminate present problems, not merely in the inner reason, but also in the external records of history. This idea is developed at length in his *Erziehung des Menschengeschlechts*. For Lessing regards history as a continuous revelation of God, and he was of the opinion that the education of the race is a divine leading, a pillar of cloud by day and a pillar of fire by night. Lessing in the search after truth in religion demands a return to the sources in a study of the religion of Christ as the proper corrective of the misconceptions and abuses of the Christian religion. Moreover, he regards as particularly valuable the investigation of the evolution of the religious idea among savage tribes and heathen peoples and the great religions of the East. As each monad, in Leibniz's theory, is considered as representing, in some slight degree at least, certain phases of the great whole,

—the universe itself; so also, according to Lessing, every form of religious belief, every symbol of rubric and ritual, even every clouded superstition may be regarded as a more or less complete expression of religious truth. No positive religion has an exclusive claim to absolute truth, but each has a relative value. As the famous fable of the three rings in *Nathan der Weise* portrays, truth appears in many forms, none of which admits of perfect defence and complete adherence in the scorn and defiance of the others. In 1815 Goethe wrote of Lessing and his *Nathan der Weise:* "May the well-known tale, happily represented, forever remind the German public that it is called not only to see, but to hear and to understand. At the same time may the divine feeling of tolerance and forbearance therein expressed remain sacred and precious to the nation." [1]

By his cosmopolitan attitude to the religions of the world Lessing naturally drew upon himself the sharp fire of opposition and abuse from the camp of the dogmatic orthodoxy of his day. His publication of the *Wolfenbüttler Fragmente* precipitated a bitter controversy between himself and the theologians. This work, purporting to be a manuscript found by chance in the library at Wolfenbüttel, was really written by Reimarus, a reputed orthodox teacher and writer, and a recognised champion of natural religion and of the prevalent deism of that age. The manuscript was given to Lessing by the daughter of its author after his death. This work marked the beginnings of the higher criticism in biblical literature. It gave to Lessing himself an impetus in the historical study of the sources of the Christian religion. The idea of a gradual unfolding of the religious concept in a

[1] Sime, *Lessing*, vol. II, p. 260.

progressive order of development became the basis of all of his critical studies. He saw the same principle also working in the evolution of the truths of philosophy, of art and of all knowledge.

There was in Lessing, moreover, an unusual combination of the critical and poetical temperaments. To his judicial mind and the ability to express his thought in a clear and lucid style there was joined a rare capacity of sympathetic insight and appreciation. He supplied in his own person, and as a conspicuous object lesson, that combination of the elements of mind and heart which the cold, rigorous logic of the *Aufklärung* wholly lacked. And it was by no means at the expense of the strict demands of logical canon and precept that he succeeded in supplying this warmer tone of poetical insight and enthusiastic appreciation. The tendency in the manner of thinking during this period was to dismiss as worthy of no consideration whatsoever the particular instance which was not obviously intelligible through a ready reference to some general principle or standard; or at least to grasp only so much of an object's significance which might be thus easily and formally interpreted, and to discount altogether its finer shades of meaning and import. Thinking always becomes mechanical when the particular instance is seen only in the light of doctrine or theory. An age such as that of the *Aufklärung* failed to appreciate the poverty of the formula and of the general principle in dealing with actual concrete experiences rich in content and warm with life. Leibniz's theory that each monad has its own peculiar individual nature and is incapable of complete subsumption under a general group or class, is an idea which appealed most strongly to the keen sensibilities of Lessing. Although Lessing's mind was exact, it was not mechanical. Not only as a critic did he regard the particular experience as worthy of a special consideration for its own sake, but also as an artist he felt that the recognition and appreciation of æsthetic values come not by rule and formula, but by the indefinable and inexpressible impressions which arise from the deep places of one's being in the presence of the beautiful, whether in nature or in art.

An entire region of thought as well as of feeling was thus opened to the eyes of the *Aufklärung* philosophers, somewhat bewildered and dazed by the bright light of rationalism. Lessing found in the æsthetic appreciations something which was at least extra-rational. His masterly exposition and defence of this essential phase of human nature served to counterbalance the excessive and exclusive claims which were so stoutly urged by the adherents to a purely intellectual philosophy of the spirit of man. Lessing declares that man cannot live by thought alone, and that by swinging clear of the ties with the past, the age of the *Aufklärung* had shut out a whole world of accumulated experience which had been funded in the classical models of antiquity. He was convinced that one needs the inspiration of the ideals which men of other ages, striving after the truth, have sought to realise in permanent forms of beauty and of power. To live for a season in the atmosphere of noble attainment, and to catch, in a slight measure at least, the spirit of those men who have seen visions and dreamed dreams, and have wrought their ideals into symbols of truth and of beauty, is an experience which in itself serves to deepen the thought, and to free it from the deadening effects of empty phrase and barren formula.

Lessing endeavoured to show that there is a vast region of truth which cannot be intellectualised. He thus indicated the inadequacy of an exclusively rationalistic method in the search for truth, and in this most practical manner, by an appeal to a wide range of experience which can never be comprehended under the forms of definition and dialectic. Such a region may be ignored, it is true, but it is always at the expense of true vision and of a deep knowledge of the significance of life.

Lessing, moreover, discriminated between the essentials of religion and its accidents. He refused to follow any convenient error; he believed that no labour of inquiry was too arduous or too exacting. He was uncompromisingly the foe of superficial thinking, and of dumb acquiescence in the authority of custom and tradition. His was a militant spirit in the affairs of the mind. His enemies were ideas —ideas whenever they showed the flaws of inconsistency or the taint of insincerity. Of his prowess as a dialectic swordsman Heine speaks with a grim humour: "No head was safe from him. Many a skull he struck off from pure wantonness, and then was mischievous enough to hold it up to the public to show that it was empty." [1]

The spirit of Leibniz's philosophy was revealed not only to Lessing but also to Herder. Herder's type of mind was, however, affected by it in a somewhat different manner. While he also was profoundly impressed with Leibniz's doctrine of development, he was more interested in the search for the beginnings of that development than in the study of its more perfect models. His peculiar interest was in the study of origins, in the *petits perceptions* of human

[1] Weber, *Deutschland*, Part I, p. 168 (Volksausgabe).

thought. He held that what men feel instinctively is of more importance than what they can attain by deliberate effort or through the accumulated experience of the race. The latter is oftentimes conventional, strained and hampering. The free spirit of man is thus weighted with the burdens of custom and of authority. This of course is essentially Rousseau's point of view. Herder found in the early folklore and songs of primitive peoples material for his inquiry. The primitive religions also offered him the means of studying the religious idea in its forms of instinctive expression. What a man feels, what he gains through a native poetical insight, or what overpowers his soul through an instinctive faith, here, according to Herder, are the sources of truth. They may be deeply hidden in the past, but from their springs flow the clear and healing waters of true wisdom.

Moreover, Herder interpreted the significance of Leibniz's monads as indicating the interconnection of all things in the universe, both in the course of history and in the phenomena of nature. This dependence of individual upon individual, of generation upon generation, constitutes the fundamental principle of a true philosophy of history. This is the ground motive of his *Ideen zur Philosophie der Geschichte der Menschheit*. His biographer Haym characterises this work of Herder's as follows: "The changing play of vital forces, striving ever toward a higher and more complete manifestation, and thereby conserving the harmony of the great All, this is the theme of the Leibnizian *Monadenpoem;* likewise the upward movement of all the organic forces of nature to their ultimate realisation in humanity, and the progressive development of humanity itself toward ever higher and more complex forms, is the theme of Herder's history of philosophy, concealed at times though it may be by fugitive thoughts which flit athwart the path of his main purpose. In a word, the *Ideen* form a bolder development of the ideas contained in the work entitled *Vom Erkennen und Empfinden*. As the latter is the natural history of the soul according to the doctrines of Leibniz, from the phenomena of sensation to the higher functions of intelligence and of freedom, so also the former seeks to comprehend within the scope of a similar historical evolution the natural and moral world in general, the earth and its creatures from the lowest to the highest, the vocation of man both in this world and in the next, also finally the past, the present and the future of his earthly career." [1]

The idea of the harmony of the world appealed strongly to Herder's poetical temperament as well as to his religious feeling. The concept of evolution which has, for the most part, a strictly scientific connotation in the thought of our modern world, is for Herder a theme of inspiration. In it he hears the music of the spheres and reads the law of life, the decrees of God and the destiny of man.

Both Herder and Lessing came under the influence of Spinoza as well as that of Leibniz. They believed in an inner and immanent relation between God and the world, which was an idea quite foreign to the deistical doctrines of their day; but, on the other hand, expresses completely the point of view of Spinoza.

Lessing and Herder were not alone in their more sympathetic interpretation of the phenomena of experience. The feeling element in knowledge was

[1] Haym, *Herder*, vol. II, p. 267.

PHILOSOPHICAL TENDENCIES 209

illustrated further in the works of Hamaan, Lavater and Jacobi. The latter particularly emphasised the element of faith in religion which transcends the sphere of knowledge and appropriates stores of truth wholly inaccessible to the reason alone.

This movement of thought with its various phases, artistic, poetic and religious, brought to the fore the claims of naïve feeling in opposition to the rival and exclusive claims of the pure intellect. It appealed strongly to the German mind and left an indelible impression upon the German thought. It served to temper the spirit of a too formal and barren rationalism. It drew attention to living, struggling humanity, with its pleasures and pains, its perplexities and cares, its purposes, aspirations and hopes, as well as to the general laws which are supposed to govern the world and regulate the thought and life of man. It was the appeal to actual fact from the inadequacies of conventional principles. It was the particular case in protest against the attempt to force it to fit some ready-made universal. Leibniz had taught that the individual may be regarded as belonging to a class or group, but not wholly or essentially. He is, after all, an unclassified unit. He is within his own nature unique. He may be associated with the general, but he belongs to himself. The law, the principle or formula may describe him, but cannot comprehend him. It is this doctrine which the combined extra-rational tendencies of the poet philosophers, Lessing and Herder, especially emphasised. They, in a peculiar manner, freed the teaching of Leibniz from the stereotyped setting which it had found in the scholastic system of Wolff, and gave a warmer and richer tone to the thought of their day. In this sense they are the true successors of Leibniz, and form the natural line of connection between the great teacher and the subsequent development of philosophical thought in Germany.

Moreover, this movement of thought, which demanded a place for the feeling element in the account of the phenomena and principles of human nature, was strongly reinforced by the widely reaching influences of pietism; for in pietism, too, there was a natural protest of the starved spirit of man against the lifeless formalism of church dogma and the tyranny of ecclesiastical authority. It served also to emphasise the need of some deeper knowledge of the inner light of human nature.

The philosophy of the *Aufklärung* in Germany is further illustrated by a movement of eclecticism in philosophical thought, exceedingly popular and widespread in its influences. Its leading spirit at the beginning of the century was Christian Thomasius (1655-1728), professor of law at the University of Halle from its foundation in 1694. He emphasised a common-sense appeal in philosophical questions, a spirit of tolerance for the truth which may be concealed in seemingly opposed systems of thought, and the supreme importance of a practical philosophy of life.

Thomasius was a pioneer in this field of popular philosophy; he was followed by a group of clever and graceful writers, as Mendelssohn, Nicolai and others, who sought to give to their thought an attractive and interesting form, whatever might be the inconsequence of its content. Their writings became the *Philosophy for the World*, a name given by Engel, one of the foremost advocates of the doctrines of this school. Concerning this phrase, Engel himself says: "These words mean by a *philosopher* a man who brings forward any truth that belongs to philosophy or that is considered philosophically, it matters not what it may be or in what form; and they mean by the *world* the whole mixed public, where one man favours one set of objects, another another, where one man has a liking for one particular tone, another for another." [1]

The idea which is suggested in this explanation is characteristic of this school of *Popular Philosophers*, namely, that life and its problems must be judged from many sides, and that there must be an open-mindedness in the approach to all philosophical questions. This eclectic and popular tendency is conspicuously illustrated in the works of Moses Mendelssohn (1729-86), a man of the people, self-taught and self-disciplined. He was an intimate friend of Lessing, and joint author with him of the essay submitted in competition for the prize offered by the Berlin Academy of Sciences, entitled *Pope, ein Metaphysiker*. The Academy had proposed as subject for this prize essay the philosophical system of Pope. Lessing and Mendelssohn took the position that Pope's *Essay on Man* did not contain a *system* of philosophy at all; moreover, that truth cannot be found in any one system whatsoever, and that poetry can never be the vehicle for systematic expression of any kind. By its very nature, poetry transcends the limitations of proposition and formula, and by intimation and suggestion enables us "to feel what it can ne'er express yet cannot all conceal."

This interpretation of the poet's function in philosophy characterises the essential features of Mendelssohn's efforts to present a popular philosophy to the thoughtful minds of his day. The rationalistic and empirical tendencies which appear throughout his

[1] Erdmann, *History of Philosophy*, Modern, p. 311.

philosophical discussions are variously mingled, but are never treated in a manner which shows an attempt at synthetic construction or the appreciation even of the possibility of it. Associated with Mendelssohn, and also an intimate friend of Lessing, is the great editor, Friedrich Nicolai (1733–1811). For over twenty-one years he was the sole editor of the *Allgemeine Deutsche Bibliothek*, a series of volumes, essentially critical, which became the organ of the "enlightened philosophers," for the expression of a common-sense view of things in the field of religion, philosophy, art and literature. Nicolai always maintained that, as a man of business and of affairs, he was able to form a more critical and practical estimate of philosophical values, because he was free from all academic tradition and prejudice. His worth in the history of thought is to be assessed more by what he inspired in others than by what he succeeded in accomplishing himself.

There was in Germany during this period still another distinct current of thought which found expression among a group of young teachers and authors who approached the subject of philosophy in a more systematic manner. They were convinced of the inadequacy of a pure intellectualism, and based their protest, not upon religious or practical grounds, but upon a conscious philosophical need of a more serious study of empirical psychology. Wolff had emphasised unduly the significance of the rational psychology; and a decided reaction from this exclusive point of view naturally occurred. Prominent in this circle of inquirers who were not satisfied with the hard and fast lines of the Wolffian system, was Johann Nicolas Tetens. In his preface to his *Philosophische Versuchen über die menschliche Natur und ihre Entwickelung* he expresses very forcibly the limitations of the purely metaphysical method: "Metaphysical analysis must conclude, not begin, our inquiry as to the nature of the soul. It must be preceded by psychological analysis. Once this has been accomplished, metaphysical analysis is reduced to that of a few fundamental faculties and modes of operation, and is then, in this abridged form, to be carried as far as may be. Where this empirical knowledge of the fundamental faculties is still lacking, however, it is useless to attempt to explain them by means of so obscure an organisation as the soul. Moreover, however far we proceed in metaphysical psychology, the authenticity of its propositions must always be tested by empirical knowledge." [1]

Thus various influences combined to indicate the inadequacy of a too exclusive intellectualism. While empiricism was exhibiting its natural limitations through the development of the materialistic philosophy in France, intellectualism, on the other hand, was passing through a similar trying-out process in Germany. In view of all these various tendencies of thought, each with its obvious limitations as an adequate philosophy of life and of knowledge, the question naturally suggests itself whether out of these diverse and often contradictory fragments it may not be possible to reconstruct a philosophy which will bring together the seemingly incongruous parts and order them in a harmonious whole. The attempt to answer this question brings us to the critical method and philosophy of Kant, in which the light of the *Aufklärung* is by no means extinguished, but the rather is absorbed within a brighter centre of illumination.

[1] *Philosophische Versuchen*, I, p. xiii.

REFERENCES.—G. G. Gervinus: *Geschichte der deutschen Dichtung*, vol. IV. Leipzig, 1853.

H. Hettner: *Litteraturgeschichte des achtzehnten Jahrhunderts.* Brunswick, 1862–70.

J. Sime: *Lessing: His Life and Writings.* London, 1873.

R. Haym: *Herder nach seinem Leben und nach seinen Werken.* Berlin, 1877.

J. T. Merz: *Leibniz.* Part II, chap. IV, *The Fate of Leibniz's Philosophy.* Edinburgh, 1884.

Kuno Fischer: *Leibniz's Leben, Werke und Lehre Drittes Buch, von Leibniz zu Kant.* Heidelberg, 1902.

CHAPTER IX

THE CRITICAL PHILOSOPHY OF KANT

The philosophical movement of the eighteenth century, as we have seen, discloses two underlying currents, the one of empiricism and the other of rationalism. These philosophical points of view represent two distinct types of mind which are radically different, and which would seem, on the surface at least, in irreconcilable opposition. From the standpoint of either one, a fire of criticism may be trained upon the other with most telling effect. And yet, notwithstanding this, each in turn reveals its own inherent inadequacy as a method of constructing a complete body of knowledge; and the historical development of the philosophical thought during this period clearly proves it. The many attempts, however, to solve the problem of knowledge, and the interminable controversies which they engendered, were not altogether futile and unsatisfactory. They helped at least to eliminate certain errors, and to establish here and there preliminary and partial statements of truth, whose complementary elements were to be disclosed later. They formed necessary stages in the development of a more complete and adequate solution of the philosophical problem, and they served also to prepare the way for a more profound insight by which the elements of opposition in clashing systems might be harmonised so as to reveal underlying relations of a truly reciprocal nature. The important office of reconciliation and reconstruction fell to the lot of Immanuel Kant (1724–1804).

He was eminently equal to the task, for his was essentially a synoptical mind, that is, a mind which naturally tends to see things together, rather than apart; to see things as related which a merely surface observation would regard as wholly unrelated and disconnected.

In his first published work in 1746, *Gedanken von der wahren Schätzung der lebendigen Kräfte*, Kant gives expression to a conviction which is particularly characteristic of his general point of view concerning opposed schools of thought: "We are in a way defending the honour of human reason when we reconcile it with itself in the persons of different writers of high intelligence, and discover the truth, which by such men is never entirely missed, even in their contradictory utterances." This remark referred originally to Kant's attempts to reconcile the different views of Descartes and Leibniz concerning the nature of *vis viva*, and yet it may be fairly regarded as typical of the attitude of thought which he maintained throughout the whole course of his philosophical studies. This mediating tendency in his thinking may be observed in a conspicuous manner in his efforts to harmonise the empirical and rationalistic methods in the pursuit of truth. And for our discussion this particular phase of his general point of view is most pertinent and significant. He recognised the natural limits which were inherently connected with either method, and yet at the same time he fully appreciated that the relations which they sustained one to the other might be regarded as complementary, each supplying that which had proved wanting in the other. Such a reconciliation, however, could be brought about only on a higher level of thought. It is a level difficult to attain, and yet eminently worth attaining. It is not gained however by unreflective minds. It is only the arduous labour of thought which achieves such an end as its reward. The different systems which the philosophy of the *Aufklärung* had produced all tended, in various ways, to separate the knowing mind from its object of knowledge, and to insinuate a wedge of cleavage between thought and reality. The many controversies had been like so many blows to drive the wedge deeper home. It was Kant's function to bring together the separated elements and to restore them to their proper settings as parts of a unified whole.

Kant was peculiarly fitted for this work of reconstruction, not merely on account of his natural habit of mind, that of seeing the congruence of the seemingly disparate elements of knowledge, but more particularly because in his own thinking he had passed through the various phases of thought which on a larger scale had characterised the philosophical movement of the eighteenth century. This would seem to illustrate, in the field of philosophy at least, the famous theory of recapitulation which Lessing insisted upon, that the path by which the race reaches its perfection every individual man must sooner or later traverse. The high vantage ground from which opposed philosophers could be discerned as friends rather than foes was not reached by Kant at a single bound. His thought passed through a natural process of evolution in which it is possible to note three distinct stages:

1. A period of rationalism.
2. A period of empiricism.

3. A period in which Kant endeavoured to effect a synthesis of these two opposed systems, which resulted in the so-called critical philosophy.

In the first period Kant was a follower of the prevalent Wolffian philosophy of his day. Even in this early period there were intimations of a spirit of protest on Kant's part concerning the inadequate features of dogmatism. The chief work expressing the rationalistic attitude of his thought is that with which in 1755 he "habilitated" as privat-docent in the University of Königsberg, entitled *Principiorum primorum cognitionis metaphysicæ nova dilucidatio.*

In the second period he reacted substantially from the Leibniz-Wolffian influences, as may be seen in the essays which he published in 1762-63, *Die falsche Spitzfindigkeit der vier syllogistischen Figuren erwiesen; Der einzig mögliche Bweisgrund zu einer Demonstration vom Dasein Gottes; Untersuchung über die Deutlichkeit der Grundsätze der naturlichen Theologie und Moral; Versuch den Begriff der negativen Grössen in die Weltweisheit einzuführen.*

In this period Kant questions the traditional demonstrations of metaphysics concerning the being of God; and takes the significant position that it is absolutely necessary that one should convince himself of the existence of God, but not so essential that one should demonstrate it. He draws the distinction, moreover, between the contradiction of concepts and the opposition of facts; and insists that, while two contradictory ideas cannot exist together in thought, it is quite possible that a negative force may neutralise a positive one, or modify it, in the world of actual facts. He appreciates also the difficulties in the traditional account of the nature of causation as contained in the Wolffian philosophy of the day, and in all of these essays there is a growing sceptical attitude toward all speculations which are not grounded in experience.

The break with Leibniz and a leaning toward the empiricism of Locke is even more strongly marked in Kant's *Träume eines Geistersehers erläutert durch Träume der Metaphysik*, which he published in 1766. This is a still more decided protest against all theories in philosophy which transcend experience.

The third period begins in 1770 with the publication of Kant's Inaugural Dissertation, *Disputatio de mundi sensibilis atque intelligibilis forma et principiis;* and it extends to the year 1781, which marks the appearance of the great *Kritik der reinen Vernunft*. In this period we find a gradual development of his critical method. The point of view finally reached in the *Kritik* was the result of a slow process of the most earnest labour of thought extending over some eleven years, from 1770 to 1781. In the *Dissertation* there is an obvious tendency to regard the sensible and the intelligible worlds as wholly distinct. Leibniz had regarded the difference between the two worlds as consisting in the relative clearness of the knowledge which is given by them. According to Leibniz, sensation is only a confused form of thought. Kant, however, does not regard the difference as one of degree but of kind, and insists that the two spheres are distinct and separate. Kant at this period in the development of his philosophical system regards the intelligible world as constituting the world of reality, somewhat after the manner of Plato, and through its ideas he is convinced that one might determine, on the grounds of pure reason alone, the general nature and characteristic features of experience; that is, this point of view represented a strictly rationalistic interpretation of the world of knowledge. This position, however, brought to Kant certain misgivings which he could not satisfactorily explain. These are expressed in his famous letter to his friend Marcus Herz, of the 21st of February, 1772. He says in part: "I noted that something essential was wanting, something which I myself, in my long metaphysical researches, and all others, had left out of account, and which in fact gives the key to all the mysteries of metaphysics; for I asked myself on what rests the reference to the object of that which we call ideas in us? . . . Our understanding does not produce the object which it apprehends, nor is the object the cause of its ideas (*in sensu reali*).

"Thus the pure concepts of the understanding cannot be abstracted from the feelings of sense, nor are they simply the expression of the character of our passive receptivity.

"They have their sources, indeed, in the nature of the soul, but they are neither the result of the action of the object upon it nor do they produce the object. In my *Dissertation* I was content to explain their nature in a negative way, and to say only that they are not modifications of the soul produced by the object. But now I must ask in what other way an idea is possible, which refers to an object, without being the effect of an impression from that object. I had asserted in the *Dissertation* that ideas of sense represent things as they appear, and ideas of the understanding represent things as they are. But how can these things be made known to us if not by the manner in which they affect us? And if the ideas of the understanding arise from the inner activity of thought, whence comes the agreement which such ideas must have with those objects which, however, they do not produce? And how can the axiomatic truths of the pure reason conform to these objects without this agreement being in any way dependent upon experience? In mathematics this is possible, for the objects with which it deals are quantities and can be so represented, simply because we are able to form ideas of them by taking a unit several times over. The mind actively constructs its ideas of quantity, and therefore we can understand how the fundamental principles underlying the concept of quantity can be developed in a purely *a priori* manner. But as regards the concept of quality, how is it possible for my understanding to form an idea of the nature of things with which idea the things themselves must of necessity agree; how shall it lay down real principles as to their possibility to which experience must exactly conform, and which nevertheless are independent of experience? Such a question always leaves the problem in obscurity as to how the possibility of conforming to the nature of things themselves can belong to the faculty of the understanding." [1]

This is the dilemma of the transition period of Kant's thought, How can an idea in the mind refer to an external object? No satisfactory answer to this question was possible so long as the position of the *Dissertation* was maintained which separated the world of sense from the world of intellect. The new position of the *Critique*, however, no longer allows that these two spheres are separate and distinct, but regards them from the point of view of their reciprocal functions. Thus in the process of sense perception there must be the co-operative activity of the

[1] Kant's *Werke*, Hartenstein, VIII, 689 *f.*

intellect; but, on the other hand, the activity of the intellect has play only within the sphere of experience, and is wholly unable to go beyond or back of that experience as it is disclosed in the ordinary phenomena which constitute the warp and woof of our lives. This position marks the new point of view established by the *Critique*, and represents the result of the evolution of Kant's thought in this decade between the *Dissertation* and the publication of his great work in 1781.

The characterisation of Kant's philosophy as "critical," and his method as the "critical" method, admits of a various interpretation. And yet, amidst all the different shades of meaning of which the term is capable in the Kantian usage, there is, however, a fundamental meaning which is consistently maintained, whatever may be the more subtle *nuances* associated with it. The critical method is an examination of the knowing processes of the mind for the purpose of discovering some satisfactory basis of discrimination between the *a priori* and the *a posteriori* sources of knowledge; that is, between the material which the mind discovers to be necessary and universal, and the material which is given through particular experiences, and whose nature no activity of the mind could possibly forecast. The critical method seeks, therefore, to establish the exact scope and function of each of these two sources of knowledge.

In this sense the *Critique of Pure Reason* may be regarded as a logic of limits. It is essentially the function of our critical faculty to set defining boundaries and draw precise lines of discrimination, for it is only through a fine sense of discrimination that the true relations which underlie the surface appearance of things can be discovered. Moreover, discrimination does not necessarily set the objects of its inquiry in opposition the one to the other; it quite as often results in effecting their union as their separation. And in the case of the critical reflections of Kant the results are constructive rather than destructive. His argument was no polemic either against rationalism or empiricism. He held no brief for the exclusive interests of either one in the field of knowledge. Kant's effort to determine the definite limits of these sources of knowledge was for the very purpose of establishing more clearly and precisely their co-ordinate functions and powers. The critical philosophy has an essentially irenic character; it seeks to harmonise rather than antagonise; to bring together rather than to hold apart; and to show that surface contradiction may merely conceal a more fundamental relation of complementary and reciprocal functions. However, this peculiar insight which is able to bring about a reconciliation of opposites is not possible on the lower levels of reflection. It is not something which is obvious, and even when finally apprehended, it is not easy to express or explain. Kant himself did not apprehend it at a glance, but only by a slow and patient evolution of thought.

There is another characterisation of the method of Kant's philosophical inquiry, which, when understood, throws further light upon the task of interpreting the *Critique;* it is the designation of the Kantian method as the "transcendental" method, and the logic which supports it as the "transcendental" logic. The transcendental logic takes the point of view that there are certain universal and necessary elements in all knowledge, whose origin is to be found in the nature of our thought and not in the objects of experience themselves. The word transcendental does not imply that knowledge of this kind *transcends* experience; it refers rather to that unique kind of knowledge which is common to all experience, and without which experience would be impossible. Moreover, no single experience, nor any mass of experience, either individual or racial, is capable of revealing such knowledge, or of furnishing a sufficient ground for it. Because it determines experience, it cannot be the result of experience. We must the rather seek its source and warrant in the nature of those necessary and universal forms of thought which condition the very possibility of experience itself, as well as constitute its essential character and scope. Given the type of mind such as that which we possess, its nature determines the peculiar kind of experience of which we are capable. The characteristic features of the mind which determine the nature of experience in this respect are revealed to us in an *a priori* manner. The priority, however, according to Kant, is logical and not chronological. We do not first become aware of these principles of thought, and then observe them as they may be illustrated afterward in experience. But inasmuch as they appear constantly in every actual experience, and as it is impossible to eliminate them from any conceivable experience whatsoever, we therefore come to regard them as possessing a necessary and universal character which renders them a determining factor in all experience, and constitutes in this respect their essential priority.

Moreover, this *a priori* element in knowledge is not derived, on our part, by the analysis of some concept which we discover in the field of knowledge. It is not a rediscovery in our ideas of something previously obtained by experience. Experience, of course, records itself in ideas, and these ideas, in turn, when closely scrutinised, reveal truths whose particular origin in experience we may fail wholly to remember. The *a priori* element in knowledge has a clearer title, however, than this. There is a radical difference which Kant expresses by referring the *a priori* element to a *synthetic* rather than an *analytic* process of thought. The distinction between analytical and synthetical judgments is one which lies at the very centre of the entire argument of the *Critique*. In the analytical judgment the predicate is merely explicative, that is, it exhibits some obvious and essential characteristic of the subject; in the synthetical judgment, on the other hand, the predicate is ampliative, that is, it adds some characteristic attribute to the nature of the subject which no process of analysing the idea of the subject as known to us could ever possibly suggest. The synthetical judgment possesses the peculiar function of extending the content of our ideas, and thus increasing our store of knowledge. The fact that water under normal circumstances will boil at 212° F. is a synthetical judgment. It gives us exact information of which the bare concept of water by itself could never possibly disclose through any process of mental analysis, however subtle and acute it might be. And the same is true of all those judgments of experience by which our ideas are enlarged and the range of knowledge extended. The synthetic judgments of this type, therefore, all have an *a posteriori* origin. The information which they impart is given to us by the things which we actually see or hear or taste or touch.

But the point which Kant suggests is the possibility of our forming any synthetic judgments which have a purely *a priori* origin, that is, judgments which thought itself discovers to be the necessary and indispensable conditions of the very possibility of any sense experience whatsoever. This is the central and most fundamental problem of the *Critique*. Upon it the entire discussion hinges. It is the attempt to furnish an answer to this question in all of its bearings that virtually constitutes the subject-matter of the critical philosophy. To understand the argument of the *Critique* it is necessary to appreciate fully the significance of this problem. And the significance of this problem will be the better appreciated if we consider it in the light of Hume's insuperable difficulty concerning the nature of causation. Kant himself made Hume's argument the point of departure for his discussion, both in the manner of stating the question concerning the possibility of synthetical judgments *a priori*, and also in his efforts to think out a satisfactory solution of the problem. In speaking of Hume in this connection Kant says: "How is it possible, says that acute man, that when a concept is given me, I can go beyond it and connect with it another which is not contained in it, and in such a manner as if the latter *necessarily* belonged to the former? Nothing but experience can furnish us with connections of that sort (this was his inference from that difficulty, which he held an impossibility), and all that supposed necessity, or, what is the same thing, all cognition *a priori* (held to be such) is nothing but a long habit of finding something true, and hence of holding subjective necessity to be objective."[1]

[1] Kant, *Prolegomena to Any Future Metaphysic*, Mahaffy's translation, p. 28.

Hume contends that all the phenomena of experience are separate existences, and that separate existences, for the very reason that they are separate, cannot in themselves give any evidence of a necessary connection between them, and that the idea of necessary connection so indissolubly associated with the events of our experience is one which our minds, long immersed in custom, have projected upon experience without any objective warrant. Consequently, that which we thus read into the phenomena of life must be regarded as wholly illusory. It is precisely at this point that Kant joins issue with Hume, and insists that there are certain judgments which the very nature of thought itself constrains us to form, and which force upon us the idea of a necessary connection among the various events of our experience, whatever these events in particular may be. Such judgments, therefore, have a purely *a priori* origin. The idea of necessary connection does not rest upon the scope of our experience, however exhaustive and painstaking an induction we may pursue; for experience always falls short of the universal, and if the universal validity of an idea cannot be maintained, its necessity is also invalidated. Not only is the idea of necessity not the result of experience, but the very possibility of any experience at all is inconceivable, unless we presuppose that it will occur in connection with other experiences before and after, which are bound together with it by those necessary ties of sequence and coexistence which the mind by its very nature expects, and whose existence it imperiously demands.

From this point of view Kant's *Critique* may be regarded as a metaphysic of induction. By this I refer to the obvious limitation of all inductive procedure, wherein we have given at most a multiplicity of special cases, with the theoretical possibility, at least, that exceptions beyond the range of our observation may exist; nevertheless, our generalisations, based solely upon the array of special cases before us, do actually carry with them the conviction of necessity and universality. No mass of particular instances, however imposing, can of itself constitute a universal. No process of adding special case to special case can of itself evolve the idea of necessity. The truth is, Kant maintains, if the single instance did not give a clear intimation of a necessary origin and a universal validity as a part of an ordered and systematic whole, then no multiplying of such instances could possibly give a sufficient warrant for formulating a universal law as necessitated by them. Inasmuch as it is evident, on the one hand, that the mere repetition of experiences is incapable by itself of creating the idea of necessity, and, on the other hand, that no single experience, however simple, can be satisfactorily interpreted by us without supposing that it must have occurred through some law of necessity, we cannot escape the obvious conclusion that the idea of the necessary connection of the events of life is the condition of experience and not the result of it. A world of detached and unrelated events is not the kind of a world which we are capable of experiencing, or which our minds are capable of conceiving. We do not think in such a world, we do not plan for it nor do we act in it. Constituted as we are, we can apprehend things only as necessarily connected, and as sustaining certain relations which must prove universally valid.

Even where the necessity is veiled and the supposed universality is confronted with outstanding exceptions, nevertheless, it is the fundamental belief in some underlying necessity and universal significance which spurs our endeavour to persevering research, and renders the mind impatient of inexact methods and inadequate results. The spirit of all scientific inquiry bears witness to this. There is a natural urgency of the mind which demands order, system, consistency and the sufficient reason in investigating the phenomena of nature and the events of life.

This idea, therefore, of the necessary connection of things is one which can never arise as the result of experience merely, but is itself the presupposition and condition of the very possibility of any experience whatsoever and which has its origin in the fundamental nature of the knowing processes of the mind. Consequently such an idea must be regarded as possessing an essentially *a priori* character. It has also a strongly marked *synthetical* property, not merely because there is added a new idea to the manifold of the phenomena of consciousness, but because the new idea which is added is one of unique instrumental value in fashioning the otherwise unrelated parts of knowledge into a systematic whole. As such, it represents essentially an organising function of thought.

Kant, however, in dealing with the problem of the possibility of synthetic judgments *a priori*, is not satisfied with considering it merely in the light of Hume's sceptical attitude in respect to the doctrine of causation. This is merely a point of departure from which the way is opened to a more thorough and comprehensive treatment of the synthetical functions of the mind in general. Kant conceives the fundamental nature of thought in all of its phases as synthetical, that is, as possessing a capacity to build together the elementary fragments of knowledge which are given in experience so that they form a systematic and ordered whole and thereby become intelligible. This integrating power of thought, however, is not confined to the familiar processes of reason wherein ideas already completely formed and definitely determined are massed in the most effective manner for the purposes of argument, or it may be wrought into plans for enterprises of large scope and significance, or are so combined as to suggest policies which possibly may concern the life of a nation or the welfare of a people. This conception of the mind's activity Locke developed at length in the *Essay*. Kant's idea of the constructive power of the understanding is far more fundamental than this. Not merely are the fully formed products of thought skilfully ordered by the mind, but at the very threshold of knowledge itself, where the crude elemental material is furnished through the senses, the mind is already *actively* engaged in fashioning and informing the given material according to its own native powers. The simplest perceptions in the field of consciousness are not received passively by the mind, but are produced by the active working of thought upon the sensory material. In the process of the simplest perception, though it be only a momentary sweep of vision or the mere glance of the eye, the many crude and separate elements of sensation are transmuted into the ordered parts of a single, complete and unified object of thought. It is essentially a process of *transmutation*, and not of mere *passive reception* and *transmission*. Kant has no sympathy with what I would characterise as the photographic theory of sense perception, namely, that the mind receives through the mechanism of our sense organs an impression of external objects in somewhat the same manner that a photographic plate receives upon its sensitive surface the picture of the object to which the camera may be directed. Without the constructive function of thought to organise the chaotic mass of sensory elements, our perceptions could never be other than a confused blur of a hopelessly clouded vision. In a very significant and true sense, therefore, seeing is thinking.

This synthetic function of thought Kant treats at length, and endeavours to determine its characteristic features in three distinct spheres: (1) In the processes of sense perception; (2) in the processes of relating our various perceptions one to another, in such a way as to develop a systematic body of judgments, and (3) in the more complex processes of inference. According to a natural division of our mental powers, these three phases of our thought activity find their proper scope in the three faculties, respectively, (1) of the sensibility; (2) of the understanding, and (3) of the reason. And Kant treats the various problems which arise in these several spheres in the three main divisions of the *Critique:*

1. The Transcendental Æsthetic.
2. The Transcendental Analytic.
3. The Transcendental Dialectic.

These three spheres of thought cannot be kept rigorously and consistently separated, and Kant himself does not succeed in doing it, for their essentially co-operative functions do not admit of it. For the purpose of Kant's discussion, however, and as outlining in a broad, general way the characteristic features of the play of thought in these several spheres, it is a satisfactory and adequate division of his subject. These three spheres of thought present different philosophical problems, each after its own nature; but in all there is a common point of view, namely, that of the *transcendental* way of viewing things. The *transcendental* method, however variously it may be applied, always sets itself the one task of determining those necessary and universal elements in our thinking which possess synthetic significance and can be traced to an *a priori* origin. As these transcendental elements discover themselves in the sphere of the sensibility, of the understanding, and of the reason, they form the basis for those detailed systems of knowledge which we have come to recognise under the familiar names of:

1. Pure Mathematics.
2. Pure Natural Science.
3. Metaphysics.

By *pure* in this connection, as well as in the title of his work, the *Critique of Pure Reason*, Kant refers to that peculiar kind of knowledge which is given by the immediate processes of thought in a wholly *a priori* manner, that is, whatever is discovered to be universal and necessary. Kant therefore puts to himself the following question: In the sphere of sense perception, what elements are in all the sensory processes and yet are not qualities of any particular objects of perception themselves, but are recognised directly as indispensable and necessary in the perception of all objects whatsoever, and consequently possess an *a priori* and not an empirical origin? Kant's answer to this question is that there are two such elements, namely, space and time.

In all knowledge which comes to us through the senses there are two distinct kinds of elements, a variable and a constant. The variable elements are the different qualities of the particular objects which appear in the field of sense perception. Every object has its own peculiar qualities which determine it, and differentiate it from all others. But all objects, however they may differ among themselves, present certain constant elements. They all appear in space, and their appearance is connected with some point or period of time. These two elements of space and of time, the one observed by the outer sense and the other by the inner sense, Kant calls the common forms in which all objects of sense perception show themselves in experience. Now the very fact that they are constant forms, invariable and indispensable in all experience, is an indication to Kant that they have their origin in the very nature of thought itself, and are therefore strictly *a priori* forms of the mind, according to which the mind arranges and orders the crude materials mediated by the senses.

If the ideas of space and time had been derived from the nature of the objects perceived and not from the nature of the perceiving mind, then the characteristic features of space and time would appear to be indefinitely variable and consequently uncertain; but they are, on the contrary, constant and certain. Any object of knowledge we can think away from any given time or space, but time and space themselves resist the utmost efforts of fancy to efface them from any possible sense experience which we are able to conceive. All experience is conditioned by them, but no experience can alter their fundamental characteristics in the least particular.

Moreover, there is but one space and one time. There is no such thing as an individual space which differs from another individual space, of which the idea of space in general is the universal concept. The understanding does not derive the concept of space as it does its other concepts which are born of experience, and which are therefore merely the generalisation of a number of particular instances. Space may be divided into a number of parts, but not into a group of particulars. The various parts of space show no qualitative differences. Space is perfectly homogeneous throughout and is without limit in extent. The same is true of time. These ideas are unique. They are unlike all other ideas which result from the inductive generalisations of experience. And, therefore, we must trace them to some other source, which Kant declares must be in the very nature of thought itself.

To picture objects of sense in a world free from all space and time limitations, or in a world with essentially different space and time conditions, is a task which even the wildest flight of the imagination would essay in vain. It is impossible for us to conceive of the world, as we know it, under the conditions of four dimensions, or of history as subject to a reversible time process. Our sensible experiences must assume the forms of space and time as they inevitably force themselves upon our thought.

In pure geometry, therefore, there is not merely a formal process of unfolding the truth implied in a body of analytical judgments, that is, where the predicate is obviously suggested by the nature of the subject. The truths of geometry rest upon a number of synthetical judgments which are given by the direct intuition of the nature of space. Space being what it is, the tridimensional geometry results. The necessary connections and relations which it presents are not subject to the variations of experience for the very reason that they are not the result of experience, but do themselves condition experience. No experience can possibly occur which will swing clear of their limiting conditions. Given the kind of space relations which our minds of necessity impose upon all of our experiences uniformly, it must follow that the straight line is the shortest distance between two points, and that the sum of the angles of a plane triangle will always equal two right angles. If we were compelled to construct our experiences under other space conditions, as, for instance, upon spherical surfaces, or within a world of four dimensions, these propositions would not then be valid. Every object, therefore, in the world of sense must correspond strictly with the theorems of geometry, because they depend upon necessary and universal space conditions, and these space conditions in turn rest ultimately upon the nature of the mind which conceives them.

Upon this theory of Kant's the ideality of space and time is a necessary implication. These forms, to which all experience must inexorably conform, have then a reality essentially subjective. All objects which move into our ken, the mind invests with the characteristic features of space and time. If any objects should show themselves under any other possible conditions, they could find no place in consciousness. While space and time are subjective conditions imposed upon experience, they are, nevertheless, real; as real as the objects themselves which appear in consciousness. What may be behind the series of appearances which constitute experience and what may be the real nature of things in themselves is another question. This, at least, can be said, that whatever reality the appearances of objects in consciousness may possess, the same reality attaches to the ideas of space and time, which are the necessary presuppositions of the possibility of such appearances.

Kant next proceeds from the world of sensibility and its space and time construction to the world as interpreted by our body of systematic judgments, the world which our understanding builds up out of the materials given in sense-perception. This world of the phenomena of nature as the mind comes to know it is a world whose various parts appear as necessarily connected in an orderly and coherent manner. The idea of causation, as we have seen, is the central idea according to which the various phenomena of our experience become arranged in a system of logical sequence and coexistence.

There are, moreover, other *a priori* ideas which are intimately associated with the idea of causation, and which subserve a similar function, that of organising our knowledge along certain fixed and determinate lines. These *a priori* concepts which show this essentially *synthetic* or constructive function, are the Kantian *categories of the understanding*. The table of categories is formed by Kant according to the general nature of the various types of judgment, on the ground that every distinct variety of judgment form represents a distinct function of the understanding. The table thus constructed is as follows (the corresponding judgment types being placed in parentheses throughout):

TABLE OF THE CATEGORIES

I. Quantity—
    (1) Unity (Universal)
    (2) Plurality (Particular)
    (3) Totality (Singular)

II. Quality—
    (1) Reality (Affirmative)
    (2) Negation (Negative)
    (3) Limitation (Infinite)

III. Relation—
    (1) Substance and Accident (Categorical)
    (2) Cause and Effect (Hypothetical)
    (3) The Reciprocity of Action and Reaction (Disjunctive)

IV. Modality—
    (1) Possibility—Impossibility (Problematical)
    (2) Existence—Non-Existence (Assertory)
    (3) Necessity—Contingency (Apodictic)

The co-ordination of the categories with the various forms of judgment is somewhat of a *tour de force* on Kant's part, and yet we must not fall into the error of overlooking the significance of the table of categories as a whole on account of the obviously artificial and strained character of certain parts. The categories of substance and of causation bear the main weight of his argument. Together with the forms of space and time, they determine, in broad lines at least, the kind of experience which our minds are capable of apprehending. To the rationalist Kant would say, You cannot build up a world of ideas which is independent of experience. And at the same time he would turn to the empiricist and would say quite as emphatically, But your experience cannot become an object of knowledge to the mind at all unless it fulfils the requirements of space, time and causation, which are the conditions imposed by the inherent nature of thought itself. It is this thought which is expressed in Kant's notable dictum;

"*Gedanken ohne Inhalt sind leer, Anschauungen ohne Begriffe sind blind.*" [1]

Kant in this same context insists that the understanding lacks wholly the function of perception; while, on the other hand, it is quite as true that the senses are wholly incapable of the constructive function of thinking. The two processes, therefore, must be regarded as complementary. One supplies the material and the other the form of our thought. However, the material furnished by the senses to the understanding is not unformed material; for already in this preliminary process the informing activity of thought has subjected the mass of sensory elements to the conditions of space and time. Even in the simplest perception itself the categories of the understanding begin to function at least in an incipient manner.

The world, therefore, as it appears to us, that is, to thinking beings, must be made up of objects which appear in space and in time, and which sustain orderly and coherent relations one to another. But is the world as it appears, the world as it really is? This question, Kant maintains, the mind on account of its essential nature can never answer. Our thoughts can only become cognisant of the world which experience presents in our consciousness, and experience can only discover to us things as they appear to be, that is, mere *phenomena*. What they may be really in themselves, the *noumena*, our thought is not capable of apprehending.

The phenomena of experience are all mind conditioned. And it is in this sense that a pure science of nature is possible. Whatever the particular phenomena of nature may be they must all conform to certain universal laws of cause and effect, substance

---

[1] K. d. r. V. Adickes, p. 100.

and attribute, and other *categorical* conditions, which the character of the mind itself imposes. What may be behind nature as its ultimate ground, thought can never explore. The thing as it really is, in contrast to the form which it must necessarily assume in order that it may appear in consciousness at all, the *Ding-an-sich* of the Kantian terminology,—that can never become a proper object of our investigation; because, to become an object of knowledge, it must comply with the time, space and causal necessities which are the inevitable conditions of any possible experience whatsoever.

There is, indeed, as Kant himself claimed, something completely revolutionary in an idea so bold and original as this. There is a Copernican audacity about this adventurous thinker who would place mind in the centre of the world of experience, and would thus determine nature by mind rather than mind by nature. Nature can reveal herself to mind only upon the conditions and after the manner prescribed by the mind itself. Every object of knowledge is naturally viewed according to the mind's interpretation of it; and the mind's interpretation of it must always be in accordance with the fundamental and unvarying principles which have their source in the activities of the understanding as an organ of knowledge. Kant's whole argument turns upon his conception of the nature of mind, which may be briefly summarised in a sentence: the sensory material is not *transmitted* to the mind, but passes through a process of *transmutation* due to the activity of thought; also the mind never pictures its objects of knowledge, but interprets them according to the suggestions of its own nature and the determination of its own laws.

If, therefore, we allow that all experience is limited to things as they must appear in order that thought can apprehend them, there is still a further question which insistently presses upon us. Is it not possible that our thought in some preternatural manner can transcend the ordinary modes of experience so as to attain a knowledge of the nature of things as they are in themselves? This is the problem of the possibility of a metaphysic. Kant maintains that the traditional speculations of metaphysics have all been based upon mere conjecture as to the probability of the truth of certain ideas, and are therefore wholly unsatisfactory; or else they have appealed to common sense, which is absurd, because this appeal to common sense is essentially a demand for the presentation of some concrete example in experience, and this procedure upon the face of it can throw no light upon the possibility of acquiring knowledge of something which, by its very nature, transcends all experience.

Kant, therefore, seeks to examine the higher processes of the reason in order to determine whether it may not be possible to discover some intimation, at least, concerning the ultimate nature of things in themselves. This is the problem of the *Dialectic of Pure Reason*. The *reason* (*die Vernunft*), according to Kant, is a higher function of the mind than the *understanding* (*der Verstand*). The *understanding* is always occupied with objects of knowledge which are given in experience, relating them, connecting them, discriminating between them, referring particulars to their appropriate universals and forming universals out of a mass of particulars. *Reason*, on the other hand, is that phase of the mind's activity which is concerned solely with the inquiry as to its own nature. Kant defines metaphysics as "the occupation of reason with itself." [1]

The reason does not exercise its activity by means of the categories, as is the case of the understanding; it contains within itself the source of certain *Ideas*, which are inherent in the nature of reason, and which cannot be given through the ordinary channels of experience. They do not come by observation but by contemplation.

Kant regards the processes of reason as essentially syllogistic, and therefore he finds in the three typical forms of syllogistic procedure, the categorical, the hypothetical and the disjunctive, the three corresponding *Ideas* of the pure reason:

1. The Psychological Idea—that of the Self.
2. The Cosmological Idea—that of the World.
3. The Theological Idea—that of God.

Here again, as in the case of the categories and the typical forms of judgment, the correspondence of the Ideas of the pure reason to the three logical processes of the syllogism is artificial and strained. However, allowing for this in our minds, it is possible to see that the very nature of the syllogistic procedure itself might naturally suggest these metaphysical Ideas, of God, of self and the world. For it is of the essence of the syllogistic process to refer particular cases to the universal which comprehends and accounts for them, or to refer a more specific concept to a more generic one as its proper explanation and warrant in a coherent system of knowledge. This is an indication of a natural compulsion of the mind to require for its own satisfaction that its knowledge should be capable of unification and systemisation. Thought is always impatient of any process of reasoning which

[1] *Prolegomena*, p. 90.

stops short of some complete, central and all-comprehensive idea. We are not content to refer one state of consciousness to another as its proximate explanation, and so ground one experience in another. The mind constrains us to seek a common ground for all phenomena whatsoever which may occur in consciousness, and this common ground is found in the central self, which may be regarded as the absolute subject of all of our various experiences. This idea of self seems, moreover, to satisfy the supreme test of an absolute substance, namely, as that which is to be regarded always as a subject, and never as a predicate of some other subject. This, it will be remembered, is Leibniz's definition of a true substance, and Kant avails himself of it in this phase of his general discussion.

As all states of consciousness seem to find a complete unification in the central self, so also all the various objects of knowledge seem to require a like grounding in some underlying system of order and of law to which they may all be referred. This idea of a comprehensive world system is a conception which is so much more profound and ultimate than any group of actual experiences could ever adequately illustrate that it merits the designation which Kant gives to it of a transcendental Idea of the reason.

Profound and comprehensive as the idea of a perfect world system may be, it is not adequate, however, as a final idea in which the thought can rest satisfied. The same urgency of the mind toward some higher centre of unification constrains the thought to refer both the self and the world to some all-comprehensive idea which is the adequate ground of them both, and this Kant finds in the transcendental Idea of God.

These *Ideas of the pure reason*, however, do not possess that ultimate character which seems at first to belong to them by virtue of the native necessities of thought. While these Ideas seem to penetrate to a lower depth than any mass of cumulative experience, however extensive, is able to disclose, nevertheless, upon a more critical analysis, it is seen that there is involved in them all a fundamental illusion, and that this is due to the very nature of the reasoning process itself. There is a tendency in the very momentum which thought in its activity acquires, of carrying the reason beyond its own boundaries. This is the tendency particularly of assuming that what proves itself to be valid of phenomena must also be true concerning things in themselves. What is gained through the offices of experience is not necessarily applicable in a region which experience cannot penetrate. Thus reason gives us the Idea of the central self, but it is, after all, merely the self as circumstanced and conditioned by the experiences in which it finds its sole sphere of manifestation. So far as the self is an object of consciousness it is empirically related and connected, and so far as it is not empirically related and connected it ceases to be a proper object of knowledge. We can never get the self out of its setting, which was Hume's contention. We have come to know self in its setting, and to abstract it from the states of consciousness with which it is essentially bound up is to do violence to the integrity of thought. Reason may discover intimations of the permanent character of the inner self, of a continuous personal identity, and yet this permanence is assured only within the bounds of experience. The self has a history which indicates an individual personality amidst the shifting scenes of life and the successive states of consciousness, but only within that stretch of experience which lies within the confines of birth and of death. Kant draws attention to the fact that the complex and varying experiences of life are the condition of our unitary self-consciousness, and that therefore we have no warrant for the inference that the self will survive the cessation of our sense experience. Any metaphysical speculation, consequently, concerning the immortality of the soul is altogether illusory.

The *cosmological Idea*, moreover, involves a like contradiction and confusion of thought. Speculation concerning the nature of the world tends to land itself in certain inevitable *Antinomies;* the thesis and antithesis of the *Antinomies* are each seemingly capable of conclusive proof, and yet the one contradicts the other. The Kantian *Antinomies* are as follows:

I. Thesis: The World has, as to Time and Space, a Beginning (Bounds).
Antithesis: The World is, as to Time and Space, infinite.
II. Thesis: Everything in the World consists of simple part.
Antithesis: There is nothing simple, but everything is composite.
III. Thesis: There are in the World causes acting through Freedom.
Antithesis: There is no liberty, but all is Nature.
IV. Thesis: In the series of World Causes there is some necessary Being.
Antithesis: There is nothing necessary in the World, but in this series all is contingent.

The first and second antinomies, which Kant calls the mathematical antinomies, are regarded by him as based upon an original concept which is self-contradictory. Consequently the two opposed statements which reason may derive from such a concept must both be false. In the first *Antinomy* the self-contradictory concept which thus seems to give rise to the two contradictory theses, each equally defensible, is the following: Objects appearing in space and time, after the manner which our mind is constrained to think them, have also a self-subsisting existence beyond and apart from the thought which expresses them. This is an unwarrantable inference, for things in themselves may be wholly independent of time and space conditions. In the second *Antinomy* there is a like confusion of the world of experience, and the world which is conceived as lying beyond experience. The division of phenomena into parts is a process which falls wholly within experience, and the possibility of a similar process beyond experience or prior to experience is wholly gratuitous. The first and second antinomies therefore must be regarded as presenting contradictory statements, both of which, however, are false. In the third and fourth antinomies, which Kant calls dynamical, the two seemingly opposed conclusions must both be regarded as true. There may be a complete determinism as regards things as they appear in nature, but at the same time a complete liberty as regards things in themselves. So also within the natural series everything is contingent, but there is still a possibility of a necessary Being behind and underlying the entire series itself. Therefore freedom and natural law are not necessarily incompatible. Each has its own sphere, and each must be regarded from its own distinctive point of view. A resolution of their surface contradiction is thus possible. The theological Idea does not receive its warrant as the other ideas we have just considered by merely enlarging the bounds of experience, but rather by swinging clear of experience altogether; the reason, in order that it may comprehend more adequately the connection, unity and order of experience, feels compelled to form the idea of a most perfect primal Being as the ground of all other beings and as the warrant of all knowledge. The fundamental fallacy here, as Kant shows, is the gratuitous assumption that we can make the subjective conditions of our thinking the objective conditions of things as they are in themselves. God in the mind is not necessarily God in the world. It is in this connection that the impossibility of a pure metaphysic is most conclusively shown.

Is there then no function which these Ideas of reason may perform? In answering this question Kant draws the distinction between the constitutive and the regulative use of Ideas, such as these, in building up our world of knowledge. He maintains that although these Ideas do not enable us to constitute a new world which transcends the actual world of experience, and thus forms the ultimate ground and explanation of the phenomena of life; nevertheless they do possess a certain regulative function, in that they furnish a norm or standard to which the organising processes of the understanding are compelled to conform. They place a compulsion upon thought to view its experiences not as scattered fragments of fleeting impressions, but as constituting a world of knowledge which shall be a world of unity, order and system, even though it be only a world of mere appearance. Moreover, these Ideas of reason stand as a perpetual protest against certain philosophical attitudes which arise from a superficial and unreflecting observation of the experiences of life. The Idea of a central self within the stream of consciousness, wholly irrespective of its possible destiny beyond, cannot be accounted for adequately by the doctrines of materialism which would eliminate the soul from this world as well as from the world to come.

The cosmological Idea of a world system of order, coherence and unity indicates at least the unsatisfactory character of all the argument of naturalism which assert that nature is sufficient for itself. Moreover, all natural necessity in the sensible world refers one phenomenon to another, and so on indefinitely, and in this circle of explanation it is impossible to satisfy the higher demands of reason, which insist that unconditional necessity must be sought for in the unity of some kind of a cause essentially distinguishable from the chain of sensible phenomena. Consequently the theological Idea serves to free the reason from any form of fatalism. "Thus the transcendental Ideas," Kant declares, "serve, if not to instruct us positively, at least to destroy the rash assertions of *Materialism*, of *Naturalism*, and of *Fatalism*, and thus to afford scope for the moral Ideas beyond the field of speculation." [1]

Through these negative offices of reason the way is cleared, therefore, for the consideration of those moral ideas which operate in a sphere wholly free from the limitations imposed upon the purely knowing processes of the mind. This account of the wider scope of our moral ideas contained in the *Kritik der practischen Vernunft* must not be regarded as an after-thought, on Kant's part, by which

[1] *Prolegomena*, p. 133.

he seeks to regain through the compulsion of the moral sense all that had been destroyed through his criticism of the pure reason. It must be remembered that the task of the *Kritik der reinen Vernunft* is to establish the well-defined limits of our experience of the world of nature, and by so doing to demonstrate that there are certain ideas which can never be expressed in terms of natural phenomena or explained by the nature of such phenomena, but which have a significance transcending the conditions and circumstances of the time and space series of natural events. Kant regards the *Critique of Practical Reason* as establishing these ideas of the moral sense upon a higher plane; and its offices begin at the point where those of the pure reason end. The nature of the will in the conduct of life reveals a depth of reality which the mind in its purely intellectual functions is incapable of sounding. While all objects of sense experience are conditioned by the limitations of the phenomenal world, the acting subject, in its self-determining and self-directing powers within a world of moral law and responsibility, rises above the conditions and limitations of the world of nature. Man is something more than a thing among things which are inevitably determined by the play of the cosmic forces.

Man is more than a mere phenomenon; as a moral agent acting in the midst of his various states of consciousness, he manifests a certain *noumenal* aspect. I find myself under constraint to act as though I were free and possessed a power of initiative. In this consciousness my whole being resents any attempt to reduce my self-asserting personality to the level of the forces of nature which it consciously directs and commands. It belongs to a higher order and fulfils a higher purpose. Man's moral and religious consciousness can never be explained by science, for it belongs to a sphere which lies beyond the province of natural science, and which the principles and methods of natural science can never penetrate. The ideas of God, freedom and immortality which Kant maintains are the inevitable postulates of moral responsibility and endeavour, are inviolable, therefore, as regards any possible attempt to explain them away by reducing them to a purely naturalistic basis. While science cannot justify the ideas of our religious and moral consciousness; no more can science disprove them. Their higher warrant, therefore, is secure, because it is forever freed from any criticism which a sceptical empiricism may chance to offer.

We are conscious, however, of a certain dualism of the theoretical and the practical reason in Kant's treatment. The two spheres, which seem at times to be wholly separate and distinct, Kant endeavours to unite through the mediating offices of the æsthetic judgment. In his *Kritik der Urtheilskraft* he completes his systematic discussion by an analysis of the essential nature and functions of the judgments which deal with our sense of evaluation and appreciation. In the æsthetic judgment there is an unique combination of the subjective and objective elements of consciousness. When we assert that any object in nature or of art is beautiful, the idea of beauty is in no sense conditioned by objective necessities, for it is essentially a subjective feeling. However, it is a subjective feeling which is peculiar in this respect, that it is free from the particular colouring of the personal nature and character of the individual who may entertain the notion of the beautiful. True beauty has an impersonal and universal strain which it compels us to acknowledge. In an object of beauty, therefore, there is a concrete embodiment of the universal. The universal, as it were, shines through this phenomenal representation, and thus gives us an intimation of the nature of things as they are. In other words, the essence of beauty is not in the phenomenal appearance merely, but lies at the heart of the object as the secret of its reality.

The æsthetic judgment, moreover, expresses purpose as well as beauty. In the various organisms of nature Kant is impressed with the marvellous adaptations which subserve their appropriate ends—an internal teleology. And this suggests to him the following antinomy: Experience knows only mechanical causes; but organisms of plant and animal life exhibit a mode of interconnection of parts and adaptation to the ends of the whole which cannot be satisfactorily explained by mechanical causes. Kant's solution of this difficulty is that the teleological interpretation of nature gives us an intimation of a power working through phenomena to produce definite ends, which may be regarded possibly as one phase, at least, of the activity of the true *noumenal* reality, and therefore fairly representing a fundamental characteristic of the nature of things as they are in themselves. Such a teleological principle as this in nature is capable of harmonising the mechanical causes which are required by the categories of the understanding on the one hand, and on the other, those processes which realise certain definite ends, and which in their operation significantly resemble the various activities springing from the free purposes of the practical reason. Thus Kant endeavours to effect a synthesis of the theoretical and practical reason through an analysis of our æsthetic and teleological judgments, and thereby bring into harmony seemingly opposed and discordant elements.

Whether Kant wholly succeeded in his ambitious effort to construct a self-consistent system out of the seemingly disparate elements of knowledge is a question which has been, and always will be, variously answered. Whatever may be the final estimate, however, every student of the Kantian philosophy must concede that the line of his endeavour indicates a direction of thought, and a method of critical analysis, which the philosophy of the *Aufklärung* had failed to discover. That movement of thought culminates in him, for he conserves in his philosophy the elements of truth which it had evolved, and at the same time he overcomes its obvious defects and limitations. To mark the scope and function of experience, to establish its complete dependence upon the interpreting, informing and ordering mind, to discover a world of moral law and life, wherein the free spirit of man moves toward his determined ends, modifying the mechanical conditions of the causal series of events so as to compel them to obey his will; to find, moreover, in such a world the presence of a divine compulsion, and to discern within the beauty and purpose of nature the presence of a kindred spirit—such has been, in part at least, the high office which Kant has performed in presenting to the philosophical thought of his age, and, indeed, of all ages the truth as he saw it.

REFERENCES.—R. Adamson: *The Development of Modern Philosophy*, vol. I. Edinburgh, 1903.
R. Adamson: *The Philosophy of Kant*. Edinburgh, 1879.
Edward Caird: *The Critical Philosophy of Kant*. London and New York, 1889.

T. H. Green: *Lectures on the Philosophy of Kant. Philosophical Works,* vol. II. London, 1885.
Kuno Fischer: *Criticism of Kant.* Eng. trans. by Hough. London, 1888.
George S. Morris: *Kant's Critique of Pure Reason.* (*Grigg's Philosophical Classics.*) Chicago, 1882.
Friedrich Paulsen: *Immanuel Kant.* Stuttgart, 1898; translation, New York, 1902.
J. Royce: *The Spirit of Modern Philosophy.* Part I, chap. IV. Boston and New York, 1892.
J. H. Stirling: *Text Book to Kant.* Edinburgh and London, 1881.
W. Wallace. *Kant.* (*Philosophical Classics for English Readers.*) London, 1882.
J. Watson: *Kant and His English Critics.* London, 1881.
J. Watson: *Selections from Kant.* New York, 1888.
J. Watson: *The Philosophy of Kant Explained.* Glasgow, 1908.
M. H. Calkins: *Persistent Problems in Philosophy.* N. Y., 1907.

CHAPTER X

THE PRACTICAL INFLUENCES OF THE ENLIGHTENMENT

We have been pursuing in the foregoing chapters an historical study of the theory of knowledge. In the theoretical discussions of the eighteenth century, however, there necessarily emerged certain problems which have an exceedingly practical interest, and which exerted an influence of wide extent upon the character and life, not only of the educated classes, but also of the masses. While the practical tendencies of all speculative thought inevitably appear in the opinions and customs of a general public far removed from their sources, it is particularly true of the philosophy of the *Enlightenment*, that its influences had no small part in shaping the popular point of view concerning the moral, religious and political convictions of that age. And the reason of this lies in the fact that this philosophical movement, especially in France and Germany where it culminated, assumed a form which made it intelligible to the general reading public. Indeed, it was the express purpose of many of the writers of this period, as we have already seen, to present their speculative inquiries in such a manner as to merit the characterisation of a "philosophy for the masses."

As regards these three practical influences of the *Enlightenment*, the moral, the religious and political, the main tendency of each may be comprehensively described as that of *utilitarianism*, of *deism* and of *individualism* respectively. The beginnings of these practical influences as well as of the theoretical speculations are to be found in the philosophy of Locke. The *Essay* is to be regarded as the "Philosopher's Bible," as Green styled it, not only as a rule of faith for the writers of this century, but as a rule of practice as well.

Locke's theory of morals is the logical outcome of his psychology of the senses. If all of the complex ideas of our knowledge are traceable at the last analysis to primary sensations, then the pleasure or pain tone of these sensations will eventually colour and determine the nature of those particular complex ideas which we call moral. The distinction between good and evil from this point of view is one which is based upon the more primitive distinction between pleasure and pain. Locke very clearly defines his position in this particular. He says: "Things then are good or evil, only in reference to pleasure or pain. That we call *good*, which is apt to cause or increase pleasure or diminish pain in us; or else to procure or preserve us the possession of any other good or absence of any evil. And, on the contrary, we name that *evil* which is apt to produce or increase any pain, or diminish any pleasure in us, or else procure us any evil, or deprive us of any good. By pleasure and pain I must be understood to mean of body or mind, as they are commonly distinguished; though in truth they be only different constitutions of the *mind*, sometimes occasioned by disorder in the body, sometimes by thoughts of the mind.

"Pleasure and pain and that which causes them, good and evil, are the hinges on which our passions turn. And if we reflect on ourselves, and observe how these, under various considerations, operate in us; what modifications or tempers of mind, what internal sensations (if I may so call them) they produce in us, we may thence form to ourselves the ideas of our passions." [1]

Further, Locke recognises as the ideal of good the quantity rather than the quality of our pleasures. He says: "*Happiness*, then, in its full extent, is the utmost pleasure we are capable of, and *misery* the utmost pain; and the lowest degree of what can be called happiness is so much ease from all pain, and so much present pleasure as without which any one cannot be content. . . . Further, though what is apt to produce any degree of pleasure be in itself good, and what is apt to produce any degree of pain be evil; yet it often happens that we do not call it so when it comes in competition with a greater of its sort; because, when they come in competition, the degrees also of pleasure and pain have justly a preference. So that if we will rightly estimate what we call good and evil, we shall find it lies much in comparison; for the cause of every less degree of pain, as well as every greater degree of pleasure, has the nature of good, and *vice versa*." [2]

Moreover, in Locke's account of the will as the source of the moral as well as of all other activity, he substantially eliminates those higher considerations, as we are wont to designate them, from the forces which are capable of exerting any influence upon us in the face of moral issues. In this respect Locke states his position very clearly: "To return then to the inquiry, What is it which determines the will in regard to our actions? And that, upon second

---

[1] *Essay*, Book II, chap. XX, § 2, 3.
[2] *Essay*, Book II, chap. XXI, § 43.

thoughts, I am apt to imagine is not, as is generally supposed, the greater good in view; but some (and for the most part most pressing) *uneasiness* a man is at present under. This is that which successively determines the will, and sets us upon those actions we perform. This uneasiness we may call, as it is, *desire;* which is an uneasiness of the mind for want of some absent good. All pain of the body, of what sort soever, and disquiet of mind is uneasiness; and with this is always joined desire, equal to the pain or uneasiness felt; and is scarce distinguishable from it." [1]

Now, inasmuch as the pleasures of the mind, or its uneasiness and disquietude, must be, according to Locke's fundamental principles of interpreting the complex ideas of thought, merely modes of the primary sensations whence they originally arise, this pleasure-pain basis of Locke's ethical theory is of such a comprehensive nature as to explain fully, from his point of view, the complete range of our moral principles and sentiment.

However, this position is not maintained consistently by Locke. He endeavours to connect it, quite impossibly, with the idea of a body of ethical principles which are demonstrable according to the method of mathematics. Locke always insisted this could be done, but never succeeded in doing it. His friend Molyneux, in one of his letters, urges him to apply himself to this undertaking: "One thing I must needs insist on to you, which is that you would think of obliging the world with a Treatise on Morals, drawn up according to the hints you frequently give in your *Essay* of their being demonstrable according to mathematical method. This is most certainly

[1] *Essay*, Book II, chap. XXI, § 31.

INFLUENCES OF ENLIGHTENMENT

true; but then the task must be undertaken only by so clear and distinct a thinker as you are, and there is nothing I should more ardently wish for than to see it."[1]

Locke, however, never acceded to the desire of his friend, but contented himself with the various hints which the *Essay* contains. It is perhaps well that Locke did not adventure upon this difficult undertaking, peculiarly difficult for him, because of the presuppositions of his theory of knowledge. There is an inevitable dilemma which would have confronted him upon the very threshold of his task:—If there is an essential and unalterable distinction between right and wrong, so that from certain fundamental concepts it is possible to deduce rigorously a self-consistent system of inviolable moral principles, then the sensational basis of Locke's theory of knowledge is wholly inadequate to account for it; but if, on the other hand, it is possible to reduce all of our complex ideas, including the moral, to the elementary experiences of a sensory nature, then the effort to discover mathematically demonstrable principles of morality would be wholly futile.

In relation to his idea of the possibility of a morality capable of demonstration, Locke is obviously inconsistent, although it is an inconsistency which his unconscious appreciation of the constructive powers of the mind compels him to embody in his discussion, despite the demands of a rigorous logic. This is seen in the following passage: "The idea of a Supreme Being, infinite in power, goodness and wisdom, whose workmanship we are, and on whom we depend; and the idea of ourselves, as understanding, rational creatures, being such as are clear in us, would, I suppose,

[1] *Molyneux to Locke*, August, 1692.

if duly considered and pursued, afford such foundations of our duty and rules of action as might place *morality* amongst the *sciences capable of demonstration:* wherein I doubt not from self-evident propositions, by necessary consequences, as incontestable as those in mathematics, the measures of right and wrong might be made out, to any one that will apply himself with the same indifferency and attention to the one as he does to the other of these sciences." [1] The ideas of God and of self, as thus conceived, cannot be consistently allowed as the foundation of demonstrable morality, if the original presuppositions of Locke are to be maintained seriously.[2]

Locke, moreover, regards our moral life as controlled by the commands of a law which is imposed upon us by a law-giver. That law is threefold: the *divine* law, the *civil* law and the law of *opinion* or *reputation.* Our ideas of personal pleasure and pain must therefore give place to the higher dictates of law, the divine law being "the true touchstone of moral rectitude," as Locke characterises it.[3]

To this divine law is added the sanction of divine rewards and punishments as an incentive to action. There is here a kind of theological utilitarianism, similar to that of Paley, though not so shamelessly pronounced.

The mingled elements of Locke's moral philosophy are distinctly separated by most of his followers. His utilitarianism resting upon the basis of a sensationalistic psychology of pleasure and pain is

---

[1] *Essay*, Book IV, chap. III, § 18.
[2] See above earlier comments upon Locke's idea of self and of God, p. 51.
[3] *Essay*, Book II, chap. XXVIII, § 8. Added to the text in the second edition.

adopted; his idea of a body of moral principles mathematically demonstrable is ignored; and his theological account of our supreme moral incentives is rejected. Whether it be possible to harmonise the various phases of his ethical system or not, it at least must be conceded by the most valiant champion of Locke that the utilitarian aspect of his theory of morals is the one which profoundly affected the various currents of thought in the eighteenth century.

Locke's ideas are rendered consistent by Hume. He sees, as Locke did not see, the inevitable consequences of his original position from which he attempts to develop a consistent body of knowledge. Hume's moral philosophy is the logic of Locke's psychology. He accepts the full rigour of Locke's assumption that thought has no originating power, but receives the elements upon which its activity operates from the feelings, and that the morally good as an object of desire is a feeling which must possess an essential pleasure tone. He has no patience with the efforts to justify a rational evolution of our moral ideas, but rigorously "attempts to introduce the experimental method of reasoning into moral subjects," as the sub-title of the second part of his *Treatise of Human Nature* runs. He holds that there are two fundamental principles of interpretation in reference to our moral life: (1) That reason alone can never be a motive to any action of the will; (2) that it can never oppose passion in the direction of the will.[1]

He declares that "a passion is an original existence, or, if you will, modification of existence, and contains not any representative quality which renders it a copy of any other existence or modification. When I am

---

[1] *A Treatise of Human Nature*, Green and Grose edition, vol. II, p. 193.

angry, I am actually possest with the passion, and in that emotion have no more a reference to any other object than when I am thirsty or sick, or more than five foot high 'Tis impossible, therefore, that this passion can be oppos'd by, or be contradictory to, truth and reason; since this contradiction consists in the disagreement of ideas, consider'd as copies, with those objects, which they represent.

"What may at first occur, on this head, is, that as nothing can be contrary to truth or reason, except what has a reference to it, and as the judgments of our understanding only have this reference, it must follow that passions can be contrary to reason only so far as they are *accompany'd* with some judgment or opinion. According to this principle, which is so obvious and natural, 'tis only in two senses that any affection can be call'd unreasonable. First, when a passion, such as hope or fear, grief or joy, despair or security, is founded on the supposition of the existence of objects, which really do not exist. Secondly, when in exerting any passion in action, we chuse means insufficient for the design'd end, and deceive ourselves in our judgments of causes and effects." [1]

In this play of the passions, therefore, moral distinctions cannot be derived from the reason, but from our moral sense. And the moral sense is very definitely defined by Hume. He says: "Virtue is distinguished by the pleasure, and vice by the pain that any action, sentiment or character gives us by the mere view and contemplation. This decision is very commodious, because it reduces us to this simple question, *Why any action or sentiment upon the general view or survey, gives a certain satisfaction or uneasiness*, in order to show the origin of its moral

[1] *A Treatise of Human Nature*, vol. II, p. 195.

rectitude or depravity, without looking for any incomprehensible relations, and qualities, which never did exist in nature, nor even in our imagination, by any clear and distinct conception." [1]

The virtue which Hume defines in terms of pleasure is not confined solely to those interests in life which are exclusively selfish. There is a genuine pleasure, which is not a disguised form of selfishness, in the pleasure of others, and a feeling of uneasiness and often pain at their distress. Thus, not only self-interest, but also *sympathy* Hume regards as one of the springs of our action. The progress of utilitarianism in its historical development has been from an egoistic to an altruistic interpretation of the utility of conduct—from the happiness of the individual to the consideration of "greatest good of the greatest number." The idea of *sympathy* with Hume accounts for the transition from the self-regarding virtues to those which arise in the thought and in the service of others. Sympathy is the art of projecting ourselves into the condition or estate of another. It is the product of the imagination which holds up an idea of another's joy or sorrow, pain or pleasure, until it seems to be our own and takes on all the emotional colouring of an original impression actually experienced by us. It is in this sense that Hume defines sympathy as a process of "converting an idea into an impression."

He says: "Sympathy being nothing but a lively idea converted into an impression, 'tis evident that, in considering the future possible or probable condition of any person, we may enter into it with so vivid a conception as to make it our own concern; and by that means be sensible of pains and pleasures which

---

[1] *A Treatise of Human Nature*, vol. II, p. 251.

neither belong to ourselves, nor at the present instant have any real existence." [1]

The social postulates of Hume, namely, that the interests of the individual are both directly and indirectly identified with the welfare of society, and, also, that sympathy is a natural instinct of man as a member of society, certainly go beyond the premisses in which he would trace all knowledge to original impressions received through the channels of the senses, and the corresponding ideas which are the memory images of them. His contribution, however, to the utilitarian ethics has been an exceedingly significant one, in establishing sympathy as an elemental motive in our moral life which cannot be reduced to a form of mere selfishness in disguise. True sympathy, while a pleasure or pain to the individual, is, nevertheless, disinterested. With him *interest* and *sympathy* account for all obligation both civil and moral. He recognises no other law of obligation than a general sense of common interest. He has no conception of right for right's sake; and the idea of *oughtness* with him is that of civil or social authority which the individual is bound to respect if he would escape censure or punishment, but the idea of oughtness as an inner compulsion is quite foreign to his treatment of the subject. Indeed, he explicitly states that "no action can be virtuous or morally good unless there be in human nature some motive to produce it, distinct from the sense of its morality." [2]

Hume's idea of sympathy was developed at length by his friend and countryman, Adam Smith (1723–90), in his *Theory of the Moral Sentiments*. He suggests that, while through sympathy one projects him-

[1] *A Treatise of Human Nature*, vol. II, p. 170.
[2] *A Treatise of Human Nature*, vol. II, p. 253.

self into the station and circumstance of others with a fellow-feeling of their joys and sorrows as the case may be, there is also the possibility of projecting one's self into another's *point of view* as well, and from that point of view of looking in an external fashion, as it were, upon our moral motives and purpose. This power of externalising the self in judging of one's own conduct Adam Smith regards as the peculiar function of conscience. For in the workings of the conscience one divides himself into two persons: the one is actor and the other spectator in the moral life. A man may thus assume the rôle of an impartial critic of his own conduct. "This is the only looking-glass by which we can in some measure with the eyes of other people scrutinise the propriety of our own behaviour."[1] This disinterested spectator of the motives and purposes of our moral life, Adam Smith refers to always as "the man within the breast." While an inner judge, his judgment is, nevertheless, based upon an external point of view, and this enables us to see ourselves as others see us. And yet the inner spectator is not merely the interpreter of public opinion and a representative of what other men may think. Because of his more intimate knowledge of the inner play of motive and desire, his judgment is superior to that of the passing judgment of "the man without"; for there is a finality about the decisions of "the man within the breast." He combines the inner knowledge with the external and disinterested point of view, which is essentially the stand-point of reason.

One of the problems which confronts the utilitarian philosophy of our moral life is to explain the total absence of any suggestion of utility about certain moral sentiments and conduct. According to the theory of

[1] *Theory of Moral Sentiments*, I, Part III, chap. I.

Locke and of Hume ideas, however complex, should show, through a proper process of analysis, their ultimate nature as revealed in the elements out of which they are combined. If utility is at the basis of all our moral judgments and sentiments, then every moral concept, however complex, should disclose its underlying utility when subjected to a sufficiently rigorous investigation. Hume draws attention to the fact that the association of ideas is so exceedingly subtle at times, and so indefinitely complicated by the mingling of artificial and conventional notions that the original utility is hopelessly obscured. David Hartley, however, takes up this problem more systematically, and endeavours to show in detail how the association of ideas is the universal solvent of all our concepts, however complex they may be. He declares that all of our moral ideas are reducible in this way to the elementary pains and pleasures of sensation, and he contributes to the doctrine of association the significant suggestion, as we have already seen, that the character of the original elements is lost sight of when associated together in certain highly complex ideas, in much the same way as the properties of chemical elements are transmuted and blended in their various compounds. Despite Hartley's theological interpretation of the ground and goal of moral progress, his physiological explanation of our mental states indicates a materialistic conception of our moral as well as intellectual life. His position in the development of the ethical thought of his age is an exceedingly important one, because his discussion of the association of ideas was the first systematic attempt of its kind; and his pioneer studies in this field mark the beginnings of the philosophy of associationism which has proved such a conspicuous and significant factor in history of the utilitarian doctrines. The ideas of Hartley were developed at length by James Mill in his *Analysis of the Human Mind*, and most skilfully and subtly treated in the masterly discussion of John Stuart Mill in his *Utilitarianism*.

The ethic of selfishness was also developed and emphasised by certain exponents of a purely sensationalistic philosophy during this period—notably in the writings of Bernard de Mandeville (1670-1722), who was of French extraction, was born in Holland and settled later as a physician in London. In his ethical work, *The Fable of the Bees, or Private Vices Publick Benefits*, the title indicates his point of view. The ceaseless activity of a colony of bees is depicted as an appropriate allegory of a community of human beings; the selfish instincts, appetite and passion, discontent, deceit, striving and competing, each seeking his own, and asserting his desire and will in disregard of the interests or claims of others—all this, nevertheless, works out the weal of the whole and satisfies the common needs. The ministration to the luxurious vices of a people gives occupation and employment to a vast army of artisans and labourers. The self-indulgence of the rich is the bread of the poor. If all persons were virtuous, all considerate and all content, ambition would fail, effort would cease and the stagnation of society would prevail. Such is Mandeville's paradoxical and whimsical satire on virtue. It provoked the criticism and scorn of Berkeley in his second dialogue of the *Alciphron*, wherein the ideas of Mandeville are defended by one of the interlocutors, Lysicles. Lysicles expounds the doctrine of Mandeville as follows: "I love to speak frankly what I think. Know then that *private* interest is the first and principal consideration with philosophers of our sect. Now of all interests pleasure is that which hath the strongest charms, and no pleasures like those which are heightened and enlivened by licence. Herein consists the peculiar excellency of our principles, that they show people how to serve their country by diverting themselves, causing the two streams of public spirit and self-love to unite and run in the same channel. I have told you already that I admit a nation might subsist by the rules of virtue. But give me leave to say, it will barely subsist, in a dull joyless insipid state; whereas the sprightly excesses of vice inspire men with joy. And where particulars rejoice, the public, which is made up of particulars, must do so too; that is, the public must be happy. This I take to be an irrefragable argument. But to give you its full force and make it as plain as possible, I will trace things from their original. Happiness is the end to which created beings naturally tend; but we find that all animals, whether men or brutes, do naturally and principally pursue real pleasure of sense; which is, therefore, to be thought their supreme good, their true end and happiness. It is for this men live; and whoever understands life must allow that man to enjoy the top and flower of it who hath a quick sense of pleasure, and withal spirit, skill and fortune sufficient to gratify every appetite and every taste. Niggards and fools will envy or traduce such a one because they cannot equal him. Hence all that sober trifling in disparagement of what every one would be master of if he could—a full freedom and unlimited scope of pleasure." [1]

Berkeley, through the mouth of Euphranor, very pointedly replies to a question of Lysicles, which he

[1] *Berkeley's Works*, Fraser, vol. II, p. 89 *f.*

asks in the same vein as in the paragraph just quoted, namely, whether sense is not as natural to man as to the brutes: "It is, but with this difference: it maketh the whole of a brute, but is the lowest part or faculty of a human soul. The nature of anything is peculiarly that which doth distinguish it from other things, not what it hath in common with them."[1]

Again, the materialistic development of the sensationalistic philosophy which occurred in France showed also an extreme expression of the ethic of self-interest, and it may be appropriately associated in our minds with the grossly conceived and baldly expressed doctrines of Mandeville. I refer to the ethical views of Lamettrie. He draws a distinction between *débauche*, that kind of pleasure which is injurious to society, and *volupté*, that pleasure which involves no harm to others. In his *L'art de jouir* he represents the indulgence of appetite and passion as a fine art, and certainly forms a sufficient ground, despite Lange's spirited defense of him, for the remark of Hettner that he was a "licentious profligate, who sees in materialism only the justification of his own debauchery."[2]

It must not be inferred, however, that all of the writers of the French school of materialism subscribed to a low code of morals, either theoretically or practically. There was another influence at work in France which affected many of the writers of this period, and gave to their ethical doctrines a distinctly higher tone and standard. This ethical influence, which was strongly marked not only in France, but also in Germany among the philosophical writers of this period, emanated from England,

---

[1] *Berkeley's Works*, Fraser, vol. II, p. 93.
[2] Hettner, *Litteraturgeschichte des achtzehnten Jahrhunderts*, II, p. 388.

and had its beginnings in the doctrines of Anthony Ashley Cooper, the third Earl of Shaftesbury (1671–1713). Shaftesbury's education was conducted under the direction of Locke, and he was early impressed and influenced by his master's philosophical interests and tastes, although he never shared his point of view. He develops a theory of ethics which is in no sense the outcome of the teachings of Locke's *Essay*. He does not seek to analyse our ethical concepts after the manner of Locke, but accepts them as given in consciousness and as possessing an essential and elementary significance which the power of analysis is capable of discovering. Shaftesbury's writings were collected under the general title of *Characteristics of Men, Manners, Opinions and Times*. His especial ethical treatise is his *Inquiry Concerning Virtue and Merit*, in which he attacks most vigorously the egoistic morality of Hobbes, and insists that the true happiness of the individual consists in the proper co-ordination of his egoistic and altruistic impulses. The latter also are quite as primitive and natural as the former. Moreover, there is a moral sense in man which reports an action or desire as good or bad. This moral sense is akin to the æsthetical sense. As beauty discloses itself immediately to our admiring taste, so also a moral action attracts or repels us, and commands our approval or disapproval in a similar manner. It is not necessary to go beyond the action or disposition for a higher sanction. Whatever its consequences may be, or whatever the elements which enter into its composition, the good act or good character is pleasing in itself, the evil act is displeasing. Vice is repulsive, as an unwholesome sight or a nauseous taste or smell is repulsive. Morality, therefore, is a matter

INFLUENCES OF ENLIGHTENMENT 269

of taste. There is, moreover, no code of taste, no stereotyped principles, no formal law. Every man is a law unto himself, or rather upon every one there rests the supreme obligation to develop his inner nature to the fullest possible extent. This presents an ethic of perfectionism or self-realisation.

While there is no body of principles, there is one general concept which should be the guide of every man's effort and the standard of character and of conduct. That is the idea of harmony. Man must so develop that all his powers will be harmoniously co-ordinated; that the love of self and the love of others will be harmoniously adjusted; that he will be in harmony with nature, of which he is a part, properly subjecting the lower desires and dispositions to the rule of the higher; and that he will adapt himself harmoniously to the needs and welfare of the society of which he is a member. Thus the conduct of life becomes a work of art, and he who is adequately perfecting his own nature and realising the full measure of his potential powers is indeed a *virtuoso*, as Shaftesbury styles him, in that architectural venture of constructing character in true line and proper proportion.

Berkeley criticises the one-sidedness of Shaftesbury's theory of the *virtuosoship* of the moral life in the third dialogue of his *Alciphron*, on the ground that a mere recognition of goodness as beautiful is not sufficient to make men good, and that all natures are not sufficiently tempered to follow the lead of their native tastes and inclinations.

In this dialogue Berkeley gives an excellent and fair statement of the Shaftesbury view of the moral life, which is put into the mouth of Alciphron: "To go to the bottom of things, to analyse virtue into its first principles, and fix a scheme of duty on its true basis, you must understand that there is an Idea of Beauty natural to the mind of man. This all men desire, this they are pleased and delighted with *for its own sake*, purely from an instinct of nature. A man needs no arguments to make him discern and approve what is beautiful; it strikes at first sight and attracts without a reason. And as this beauty is found in the shape and form of corporeal things; so also is there analogous to it a beauty of another kind —an order, a symmetry and comeliness, in the moral world. And as the eye perceiveth the one, so the mind doth, by a certain interior sense, perceive the other; which sense, talent or faculty is ever quickest and purest in the noblest minds. Thus, as by sight I discern the beauty of a plant or an animal, even so the mind apprehends the moral excellence, the beauty and decorum of justice and temperance. And as we readily pronounce a dress becoming, or an attitude graceful, we can, with the same free untutored judgment, at once declare whether this or that conduct or action be comely and beautiful. To relish this kind of beauty, there must be a delicate and fine taste; but where there is this natural taste, nothing further is wanting, either as a principle to convince, or as a motive to induce men to the love of virtue. And more or less there is of this taste or sense in every creature that hath reason." [1]

In the course of this dialogue Berkeley criticises the position of Shaftesbury because it seemed to him that it made morality independent of religion, and also that it deprived man of those strong motives to upright conduct, namely, the fear of punishment and the expectation of reward. Shaftesbury had

[1] *Berkeley's Works*, vol. II, p. 125.

already met this objection in his own discussion of the subject, wherein he most emphatically declares that "a true love of God for His own sake should diminish the over-solicitous regard to private good expected from Him." [1]

There were two ideas peculiarly characteristic of Shaftesbury's ethic—that to be virtuous there must be a love of virtue, and that the man of good taste cannot go far wrong—which exerted a profound influence upon a large following, both in his day and in the generations after him. All who were repelled by the calculating morality of the utilitarians, or, on the other hand, by the stern rigour of the moral law of Kant, found in his doctrines a convenient and satisfying expression of their ethical need. Not only in England but also on the Continent, the influence of Shaftesbury was widely extended. LeClerc and Leibniz were deeply impressed with the moral teachings of the *Characteristics*. Shaftesbury's doctrine that the supreme duty of man consists in perfecting his own powers in every possible way, found an intimate affinity with Leibniz's theory of the self-developing function of the monad. In 1745 Diderot reproduced the *Inquiry Concerning Virtue* under the title, *Essai sur le mérite et la vertu*. In 1769 a French translation of Shaftesbury's works was published in Geneva. And between 1776 and 1779 there appeared in Germany a complete translation of the *Characteristics*. Lessing, Mendelssohn and Herder fell under the charm of this high-minded philosophy of life. And later his ideal of virtue is represented in Schiller's *Schöne Seele*, one who acts nobly because he himself is noble. Hettner says of Shaftesbury that "all the moral forces of this period are

[1] *Characteristics*, vol. II, p. 58 *f*.

traceable to his writings, and, indeed, from him it is possible to gain not only the truth but at the same time the beauty of philosophy."[1]

Such then are the ethical influences of the *Enlightenment*—utilitarianism appears both in its altruistic and also in its egoistic phases; and parallel to its course of development, there appears also this philosophy of the "moral sense" which establishes its cardinal doctrine in the beauty of virtue. Utilitarianism is at times modified by the enthusiastic morality of Shaftesbury, and again is brought into actual conflict with it.

In addition to the moral forces of the *Enlightenment* there is also a significant religious tendency with marked characteristic features. The belief of this age was predominantly deistical. The deist acknowledges the being of God, but regards him as transcendent, that is, above his creatures and wholly unconcerned as regards their interests and activities, leaving them completely free to order the conduct of their own lives. In the eighteenth century the deist opposed the dogmatism of the theologians and the authority of the ecclesiastical system. Revelation was regarded either as incredible or as superfluous. While there were certain writers who were willing to admit the possibility of revelation, nevertheless, they were insistent upon the necessity of submitting revelation to the supreme test of the reason, and of discarding any alleged truth of revelation which could not be thus reasonably defended. The deist believed, moreover, in the possibility of a natural religion, evidenced by experience and grounded in the incontrovertible implications which reason is able to read in the phenomena of

---

[1] Hettner, *Litteraturgeschichte des achtzehnten Jahrhunderts*, I, 205 *f.*

nature and the events of life. It was urged also that Christianity, in the simplicity of its primitive teachings, particularly in the life and words of Christ, conforms most exactly to and expresses most adequately the truths of natural religion. Through the growth of dogma and the development of ecclesiastical power the truths of nature which revealed religion voices in the Bible have become distorted and obscured. The central idea of the deistical movement is the self-sufficiency of man. The supreme emphasis is laid upon this idea that man is capable of evolving the truths of religion out of his own experience, and that human wisdom and power are abundantly equal to the tasks of life and the problems of conduct, needing no divine guidance, and above all no divine intervention. Not only is morality considered to be the essence of religion, but in many quarters during this age morality is regarded also as a natural substitute for religion, and enthusiasm for the beauty of the noble life takes the place of religious fervour and devotion.

Locke marks the beginnings of the deistical doctrines of the *Enlightenment*. In his *Letters on Toleration* he enters a vigorous plea for religious toleration, and thus sets the key-note for the spirit of the age, which declared its independence, alike of theological dogma and of ecclesiastical authority. While Locke was still a student at Oxford his free disposition and inquiring mind protested against the lack of open-mindedness, the indifference to truth and the sense of security in traditional belief which characterised the Oxford scholarship of his day. Indeed, in an early essay written soon after the completion of his university career, in the year 1666, entitled *An Essay on Toleration*, he forcibly expresses the convictions which many years later became embodied in the famous *Letters on Toleration*. Moreover, Locke's philosophical point of view is such that it accords naturally with a deistical conception of religion. His idea of God is that of a being who exists outside of his works and operates upon them in an external manner. As the activities of the reason fashion the elements of knowledge by working upon them in a manner external to these elements themselves, so also, in a similar way, the architect of the universe constructs the great world machine.[1] For Locke himself says that "even the most advanced notion we have of God is but attributing to Him the same simple ideas which we have got from reflection on what we find in ourselves."[2]

Not only in the general implications of his philosophical point of view, but more specifically in his religious treatise, *The Reasonableness of Christianity*, published in 1695, Locke gives expression to the doctrines of deism. As the title of this work indicates, the author attempts to show that the religion which was taught and illustrated by the founder of Christianity corresponds completely with the essential features of natural religion. He draws the distinction between that which is contrary to reason and that which is above reason, insisting that revelation may contain a certain body of truth which the reason unaided could never have discovered, but which is nevertheless not in any sense necessarily opposed to reason. After Locke, John Toland (1670–1722) published a volume entitled *Christianity not Mysterious*, wherein he wipes out Locke's distinction between that which is contrary to reason and

---

[1] See above, p. 54.
[2] *Essay*, Book III, chap. VI, § 11.

INFLUENCES OF ENLIGHTENMENT

that which is above reason. He insists that we must allow as true only that which reason certifies. The seat of authority, therefore, is not in revelation at all, but in the reason which is the supreme judge as to the credibility of the content of revelation. He maintains that miracles are merely extraordinary manifestations of natural law under peculiar circumstances, and that the Bible must be rationalised in order to free it from the accretions of superstition and tradition, and to discover its true message to mankind, namely, its consummate moral ideal.

Anthony Collins (1676–1729), in his work, the *Discourse of Free-thinking*, contributes to the literature of deism by insisting upon the right of free untrammelled opinion in thought, and particularly in reference to a man's religious convictions. He declares, moreover, that the result of a full and free inquiry must inevitably lead an unprejudiced mind to deny the possibility of any supernatural element whatsoever in religion. Collins exposed himself to a bitter attack from Dean Swift, who by his keen satire gave a sharp edge to his searching criticism of deism.

In the line of the deistical writers there followed Matthew Tindal (1657–1733) with his work, *Christianity as Old as the Creation*. In his argument he takes the position that the truth of Christianity is contained in natural religion, and the truth of natural religion expresses the universal needs and desires of mankind, which can experience no restriction of time or place. This is the truth which has been from the beginning. God must deal equally with all men. There can be no chosen people to whom is given a special revelation. The sole revelation of God to man is through the channels of reason. The deistic succession was carried on in the writings of

Thomas Chubb (1679–1747), a man of the people, who gave homely expression and popular form to the prevailing ideas of natural religion; associated with him also are the names of his contemporaries, Thomas Morgan (d. 1751) and Lord Bolingbroke (1672–1751).

Through all the argument of the deistical writers there is the assumption that natural religion is justifiable in reason, and as such can be regarded as scientifically grounded. Hume, however, examines this claim of natural religion, subjecting it to his searching analysis, wherein he reaches the conclusion that no such basis in reason can be established. In his *Dialogues Concerning Natural Religion*, and in his essay on the *Natural History of Religion*, Hume takes the point of view that while reason in a general and indefinite manner testifies as to the being of God, man cannot "by reason find out the Almighty unto perfection," nor come to any satisfactory knowledge of His nature, His attributes and purposes. In the traditional argument based upon design he finds evidence of a finite being or beings, rather than an infinite God, and in the evil of the world and the disharmony of the universe, doubt is thrown upon the goodness or the wisdom and power of God. In the introduction to the *Dialogues Concerning Natural Religion* Hume says in point: "What truth so obvious, so certain as the BEING of a God, which the most ignorant ages have acknowledged, for which the most refined geniuses have ambitiously striven to produce new proofs and arguments? What truth so important as this, which is the ground of all our hopes, the surest foundation of morality, the firmest support of society and the only principle which ought never to be a moment absent from our thoughts and medita-

INFLUENCES OF ENLIGHTENMENT

tions? But in treating of this obvious and important truth, what obscure questions occur, concerning the NATURE of that divine being; his attributes, his decrees, his plan of providence! These have been always subjected to the disputations of men: Concerning these, human reason has not reached any certain determination: But these topics are so interesting that we cannot restrain our restless enquiry with regard to them; though nothing but doubt, uncertainty and contradiction have, as yet, been the result of our most accurate researches." [1]

Through the course of these dialogues Hume follows the argument for and against the possibility of an adequate natural religion. In his summing up of the case, unfortunately, he does not clearly indicate his own judicial opinion concerning the issue of the discussion. He, however, may be considered fairly in sympathy with the closing paragraph of the last dialogue, where Philo, who has taken throughout the position of a reverent sceptic as regards the rational justification of natural religion, concludes the controversy with the following significant passage: "If the whole of Natural Theology, as some people seem to maintain, resolves itself into one simple, though somewhat ambiguous, at least undefined, proposition, *That the cause or causes of order in the universe probably bear some remote analogy to human intelligence:* If this proposition be not capable of extension, variation or more particular explication: If it affords no inference that affects human life, or can be the source of any action or forbearance: And if the analogy, imperfect as it is, can be carried no farther than to the human intelligence; and cannot

[1] *Dialogues Concerning Natural Religion*, Green and Grose edition, p. 378.

be transferred, with any appearance of probability, to the qualities of the mind: If this really be the case, what can the most inquisitive, contemplative and religious man do more than give a plain, philosophical assent to the proposition, as often as it occurs, and believe that the arguments, on which it is established, exceed the objections which lie against it? Some astonishment, indeed, will naturally arise from the greatness of the object: Some melancholy from its obscurity: Some contempt of human reason that it can give no solution more satisfactory with regard to so extraordinary and magnificent a question. But believe me, Cleanthes, the most natural sentiment, which a well-disposed mind will feel on this occasion, is a longing desire and expectation that heaven would be pleased to dissipate, at least alleviate, this profound ignorance by affording some particular revelation to mankind, and making discoveries of the nature, attributes and operations of the divine object of our faith. A person, seasoned with a just sense of the imperfections of natural reason, will fly to revealed truth with the greatest avidity: While the haughty Dogmatist, persuaded that he can erect a complete system of Theology by the mere help of philosophy, disdains any farther aid, and rejects this adventitious instructor. To be a philosophical Sceptic is, in a man of letters, the first and most essential step toward being a sound believing Christian." [1]

If Hume would not fully indorse the appeal of Philo from the insecurity of reason to the certitude of revelation, he does at least allow in this passage the possibility of revelation. Later, however, in Hume's chapter on *Miracles* in the *Enquiry Concern-*

[1] *Dialogues Concerning Natural Religion*, p. 467.

ing Human Understanding, he denies the possibility of any revelation whatsoever on the ground of the assumptions concerning miracles which it involves.

The negative assertions of Hume carried more weight, however, than his speculative queries. His argument against natural religion tended to undermine the very foundations of deism, and to accelerate the tendency of deistical opinion to drift into atheism. This was particularly true of the development of religious thought in France during this period, where the writings of Hume exerted no inconsiderable influence. A hatred of the priests, a protest against ecclesiastical authority and a sensationalistic psychology all combined in France to produce a philosophy of atheism. This was resisted from the standpoint of the traditional deism by Voltaire and by Rousseau. Diderot for a while strove against the inner drift of his own thought, to which, however, he finally yielded; and he also was carried into the abysmal depths of Holbach's materialistic and atheistic *Système de la nature.*

With a practical suggestion as to the proper frame of mind to cultivate in reference to so serious and so difficult a question, Rousseau puts into the mouth of the Savoyard Vicar the sage advice: "Keep thy soul in such a condition that thy *wish* is always that God exists; then wilt thou never doubt it." Rousseau always declared that he was the only man of his age who believed in God.

In Germany the deistical influences were wide-reaching. Reimarus represents the critical point of view in reference to the truth of revelation both in his *Schutzschrift,* and in the *Wolfenbüttler Fragmente,* which Lessing edited. With Lessing, however, and with Herder there was a recognition of a more intimate relation between man and God which was revealed to their deeper poetic insight. This relation brought the far-off God of deism, speculatively discerned, to his place in the centre of the world's history and of the life of the individual. It was essentially the conception of Leibniz, who regarded God as the supreme Monad, in whom each separate monad of the universe lived and moved and had its being. Lessing and Herder, as we have seen, also leaned somewhat toward a pantheistic interpretation of God's relation to the world—a tendency, no doubt, due in a large measure to Spinoza.

The movement of thought which has been the subject of our inquiry has also its practical outcome in the political philosophy of this period. Locke again marks the beginnings of the political tendencies of the *Enlightenment*. In his *Treatise of Government*, published in 1690, the same year as the *Essay*, he defends the Revolution of 1688, and endeavours to "establish William's throne and make good his title in the consent of the people." The first treatise is a scathing criticism of the royalist Sir R. Filmer, who in his *Patriarcha* had attempted to prove the claims of absolute monarchy by deriving the power of kings from the native authority exercised by Adam, and transmitted through inheritance to his royal successors. He was hardly a worthy foeman for Locke, and his contention was one in which that age was fast losing both its interest and its belief. The second treatise contains the really significant material. In it Locke explains the nature of civil society by a reference to its primitive origin, wherein a law of nature prevailed which recognised the common needs and obligations of men, as also their equal rights. This state of nature was one of peace, unlike the original state of warfare which the theory of Hobbes presupposed. It was, however, unsatisfactory, because indefinite and ineffectual, particularly with the increasing complexity of expanding social relations. The state of nature lacks a clear definition of the laws of nature, and an impartial application and an effective enforcement of them. It is a state in which "a random right redresses a random wrong." Consequently, by common consent, men entered into a compact whereby a governing body was constituted which was to bear rule according to the will and the sufferance of the majority. This government may be a monarchy in form, but it must be democratic in principle, and the supreme standard by which rulers stand or fall is essentially utilitarian—the good of the people. Therefore, to secure this end, it is the inalienable right of the people to make "an appeal to Heaven," to depose magistrates and reconstruct governments.

Locke's theory of government is in accord with his theory of mind, at least as regards the ground motive of each, which is essentially the mechanical rather than the organic point of view. As all the separate elements of knowledge are brought together, and variously modified and compounded by the activity of the mind working upon them from without, so also the separate and distinct units of society are held together by external and artificial bonds, in which there is no naturally cohesive power, no organic development, and as a result no social organism.

The influence of Locke's political ideas reaches far into the eighteenth century. The revolutionary element which is contained in his doctrines, but not conspicuously exploited, was brought more into the foreground in Priestley's *Treatise on Civil Govern-*

ment, and Price's *Observations on Civil History*. Both of these works show marks of the influence of Lockian principles of government. In France also the same influence is evident in Montesquieu's *Esprit des lois*, and in Rousseau's *Contrat Social*.

While Locke derives government from a state of nature, Rousseau would have government re-establish a new state of nature, not, indeed, the *véritable état de la nature*, but at least a new social order. To this end it would be necessary to destroy all the existing conventions and institutions which interfere with the native rights, and which destroy the natural spirit of man. In Locke's theory, the equal rights of man are restricted by a common surrender of privilege to the governing body for the good of the whole; in Rousseau, however, it is the essential purpose of government to conserve and guarantee these rights to all equally and in perpetuity.

The French Revolutionists were not slow to draw the conclusions to which the doctrines of Rousseau formed the appropriate premisses. Locke would hardly have recognised, much less have accepted, the extreme and exaggerated form which his doctrines assumed in the course of a century's development. While defending the English Revolution of 1688, the French Revolution of 1789 could scarcely have claimed him as an advocate. It would be manifestly unfair to ascribe to Locke the extreme views entertained by the various writers who were, nevertheless, deeply influenced by him. It is a long way which one travels in the course of a century from the empiricism of Locke to the materialism of Holbach, from the reverent deistical convictions of the *Essay* to the unmitigated atheism of the *Système de la nature*. So also the influence which Locke's political philosophy exerted upon that distant age ran far beyond the most remote implications of his fundamental principles. The American Revolution more adequately embodies these principles, and Alexander Hamilton may be cited as one who profited by the political philosophy of Locke without perverting it. The contract theory, which grounds all social relations ultimately upon the conscience and consent of the individual, was not able to maintain its cause through this century wholly free from challenge. Hume was not deceived by the plausible arguments which were urged in its defence, and which were accepted as a popular gospel. He draws attention to the logical inconsistency in an idea which essentially bases allegiance upon a promise. Edmund Burke also subjects the idea of a *Contrat Social* to a running fire of criticism, and suggests in its stead the idea of the organic growth of all government.

The contract theory, however, "lived long after the brains were out," as Leslie Stephen characterises it.[1]

It lived both because it was convenient to believe it, and because it was closely associated in the popular thought of the day with certain convictions concerning the rights and privileges of man, which, in spite of their exaggerated expression and application, nevertheless contained essential elements of the truth.

The practical influences of this century which we have hastily surveyed, moral, religious and political, can be more adequately estimated in the light of Kant's criticism of them. Practically as well as theoretically we look to him for the last word upon the problems of the *Enlightenment*. The Kantian ethic, on the one hand, opposes utilitarianism, and on the other introduces a stern rigourism into the

[1] *History of English Thought*, vol. II, p. 180.

philosophy of conduct which the enthusiastic morality of Shaftesbury wholly lacks.

The moral centre of gravity, he insists, lies not in the consequences of an act, but in the disposition of the actor. From a moral point of view the only good is the good-will. It is character, primarily, and not conduct which is the object of our moral judgment. The utilitarian view of conduct, whether it be interpreted in terms of selfish pleasure, or of altruistic consideration of the highest order, must necessarily express the moral command in terms of an hypothetical imperative: Do this if you would be happy. Do this if you would give happiness to others. Give happiness to others if you would be happy yourself. Excellent maxims, all of them, but merely maxims. They do not express the fundamental law of morality. They do not go to the heart of the matter. For the true ethical concept confronts us always with a *categorical imperative*. Do the right, with reverence for the law which commands it and in scorn of consequence. Kant's question, which he puts in his metaphysic of morals as well as in his philosophy of the pure reason, is whether it is possible to attain any truth possessing an *a priori* validity. This he discovers in the moral law, which bears the same relation to the will that the categories of the understanding do to the intellect. By the moral law our concrete experiences, whatever may be the variable element they furnish, are organised and directed according to a constant standard. This moral law Kant expresses as follows: "Act as if the maxim from which you act were to become, through your will, the universal law of nature." The maxims must have, of course, empirical content. They may, and in many cases are, the result of utilitarian con-

INFLUENCES OF ENLIGHTENMENT

siderations. But the law of reason demands that, whatever the considerations may be which experience suggests, nevertheless they must be capable of becoming universalised in this sense. Demands which spring from the senses, from inclination, appetite, or passion must thus be brought into harmony with the coldly judicial decisions of the will. The moral law, because it is the supreme expression of one's reason, is, therefore, self-imposed. Man's will is autonomous. The command is from within, and therefore man is free, because the kind of determination to which his activities are subjected is a self-determination.

Kant maintains, moreover, that there is an absolute distinction between conduct which is performed from a sense of duty and conduct which arises from inclination, no matter how wisely and how beneficently that inclination may be directed; that is, morality is essentially a question of one's attitude. In the conduct of a man's life, does the sense of obligation count as a determining factor, or is it rather the pressure of desire or possibly the suggestion of a shrewd calculating wisdom? This is the issue which Kant draws, and to which he gives clear answer and uncompromising argument. While early in his philosophical thinking he experienced the fascination of Shaftesbury and his doctrine of the beauty of the moral life, nevertheless he broke with him completely in the *Dissertation* of 1770, and characterised his philosophy as a form of Epicureanism. He regarded it as at best an attempt to formulate the various experiences of life so as to indicate the path in which noble natures walk. It is morality for a special class. There is in Shaftesbury's moral ideal no law of common obligation for the noble and ignoble alike; no universal command of duty; and no superior court of last appeal in universal reason.

Kant's ethics are naturally exposed to the criticism that he gives us a formal law of obligation only, without presenting at the same time a practical criterion as to what actual lines of conduct in any given case such a law prescribes. The categorical imperative commands me to do what is right, and I may very properly reply, But what precisely is the nature of the right which I must do? In the concrete case, what differentiates exactly the right from the wrong? Here Kant maintains that the thought of our own happiness, or even of the happiness of others, must be still subordinated to a feeling of respect for a law of obligation; and that this law, moreover, admits of a more concrete expression in the following practical principle of conduct: "So act as to treat humanity, whether in thine own person or in that of any other, in every case, as an end, never as a means only." [1]

In this principle there is a possibility of subordinating the lower to the higher claims of our nature on the one hand; and on the other, of harmonising the egoistic and altruistic motives of conduct. Thus a synthesis of the conflicting elements in the moral influences of this century is rendered possible.

The religious tendencies of this period also meet in Kant, and meet in him in the same sense as the moral tendencies found in his doctrines a natural corrective and supplementation. The general drift of deism is toward a separation of God from his works; toward a substitution of morality for religion; and in its extreme expression toward some form of materialistic philosophy. Kant does not rest his conviction as to the being of God upon the observation

[1] *Kritik der praktischen Vernunft*, i. I, 3.

of his works. He does not rise in his thoughts from nature to God. He finds God primarily within. In the compulsion of the moral law, inevitable, irresistible; in the inner command which admits of no compromise, and offers no bribe; in the high ideal which as the author of his own destiny man is constrained to set for himself; in the moral order which such an ideal necessitates, and in the progress which it promises and guarantees; in all this there is the profound intimation of God as the necessary postulate of our moral life. While many of the deists were content to subscribe to a code of morals with no reference whatsoever to religion, and, on the other hand, formal ecclesiasticism had grown strangely indifferent to the commands of a rigorous morality, Kant, on the contrary, endeavoured to restore the naturally inseparable relations of religious conviction and the sense of moral obligation, and to prove that the moral consciousness is the sole ground and source of religious feeling. A man who is conscious of the worth and dignity of his own personality, and of the possible nobility within which awaits an actual realisation in his outer life, who also orders his conduct upon a plane above the dictates of inclination or the maxims of prudence, that man belongs naturally to the intelligible rather than the merely sensible world—the world of freedom; and so far forth is a citizen of the Kingdom of God.

The argument which Kant advances for the necessity of regarding the idea of God as a postulate of our moral convictions enables us to appreciate the true significance of his contribution to the religious phase of philosophical thought in this century. I therefore venture to quote it somewhat at length:

"Happiness is the state of a rational being existing in the world who experiences through the whole of his life whatever he desires and wills. It therefore presupposes that nature is in harmony with his whole end, as well as with the essential principles by which his will is determined. Now, the moral law, being a law of free beings, commands us to act from motives that are entirely independent of nature and of the harmony of nature with our desires. But a rational agent in the world is not the cause of the world, and of nature itself. There is no reason, whatever, in the case of a being who is a part of the world and is dependent upon it, why the moral law should imply a necessary connection between happiness and morality proportionate to happiness. For the will of such a being is not the cause of nature, and therefore he has no power to bring nature into complete harmony with his principles of action. At the same time, in the practical problem of pure reason, that is, in the necessary pursuit of the highest good, such a connection is postulated as necessary. He *ought* to seek to promote the highest good, and therefore the highest good must be possible. He must therefore *postulate* the existence of a cause of nature as a whole, which is distinct from nature, and which is able to connect happiness and morality in exact harmony with each other. Now, this supreme cause must be the ground of the harmony of nature, not simply with a law of the will of a rational being, but also with the consciousness of this law in so far as it is made the supreme principle of the agent's will. That cause must therefore be in harmony, not merely with the form of morality, but with morality as willed by a rational being, that is, with his moral character. The highest good is thus capable of being realised in the world only if there exists a supreme cause of nature whose causality is in harmony with the moral character of the agent. Now, a being that is capable of acting from the consciousness of a law is a rational being, an *intelligence*, and the causality of that being, proceeding as it does from the consciousness of law, is a *will*. There is therefore implied, in the idea of the highest good, a being who is the supreme cause of nature; and who is the cause or author of nature through his intelligence and will, that is God. If, therefore, we are entitled to postulate the *highest derivative good*, or the best world, we must also postulate the actual existence of the highest original good, that is, the existence of God. Now, it is our duty to promote the highest good, and hence it is not only allowable but it is necessarily bound up with the very idea of duty that we should presuppose the possibility of this highest good. And as this possibility can be established only under condition that God exists, the presupposition of the highest good is inseparably connected with duty, or, in other words, it is morally necessary to hold that God exists." [1]

Kant would thus ground religion in the necessities of the moral concept. No one has more thoroughly or more emphatically defended the inseparable connection of morality and religion than he. All of the influences of the deistic movement had tended to force them asunder. Kant, however, seeks to establish their true relation upon a sure foundation; and in this attempt he stands as an uncompromising opponent of those who in his age would glorify morality at the expense of religion, or who on the other hand would profess a religion which had little or no concern for morality.

[1] *Kritik der praktischen Vernunft*, ii, II, V.

In Kant's philosophy of the state he endeavours to rationalise the doctrines of Rousseau in reference to the social contract and the rights of man. It is true that in a certain sense Kant follows Rousseau's account of the origin of government; however, he claims that the social contract is not to be conceived at all as an historical event, but is merely a point of view from which to regard the nature of social relations as determined by the reason. It is the way, the necessary way, in fact, of adjusting the free-will of the individual to the free activities of all who are associated with him in society. The compact into which he enters is one compelled by reason, and not suggested merely by convenience or the necessities of circumstance. Every acquired right is derived from the native right of freedom. Kant holds that the very idea of freedom itself implies equality. For no obligation can be laid upon an individual without that individual, in turn, being privileged to lay a similar obligation upon all who may be like circumstanced. The native right, therefore, of every individual to the free play of his activities must of itself necessitate its own limitation so as to allow a similar privilege to all. In this sense the individual is always regarded from a universal point of view, that is, wholly irrespective of the particular elements of his setting or the adventitious circumstances of birth, position, wealth, or distinction. And this is essentially the procedure which reason follows, namely, to estimate every particular instance in the light of its universal significance. The will, therefore, which exercises control in society, the *volonté générale*, is not the collective will of a number of individuals; it is not the combined wisdom of the majority; it is rather the will which represents in a typical way the stand-point of reason. The individual thus universalised is already conceived as a member of society and of an established order of things. Here again the relation is an organic one; it cannot be artificially created or mechanically maintained.

Kant's most significant service, however, in the development of political principles is his insistence upon the guiding maxim of conduct that man must always be regarded as an end and never as a means to an end. In this dictum the rights of the individual are safeguarded against their undue limitation in behalf of the public welfare; and the public welfare, in turn, is conserved by assuring the full and free play of the activities of all the individual members composing the social organism. From this point of view that crude and extreme individualism which exercises a disintegrating influence in national life, destroying its unity and undermining its solidity, undergoes a certain process of transmutation whereby the idea of individuality is enriched and deepened, and its universal significance revealed in its essential setting of reciprocal rights and duties.

Kant's religious, ethical, and political views may be open, no doubt, to serious criticism. He is not always consistent, nor always clear. The formal elements are at times unduly emphasised at the expense of the material content. But whatever may be the strictures which we may be inclined to place upon his philosophical creed in respect to these most momentous problems of life, we will, nevertheless, be constrained to confess that through Kant's words of challenge the practical ideals of the *Enlightenment* as well as its speculative thought were raised to a higher plane, which to the philosophers of subsequent generations has proved a vantage-ground of wider prospect and clearer vision.

THE ENLIGHTENMENT

REFERENCES.—Ernest Albee: *A History of English Utilitarianism.* London and New York, 1902.
S. Alexander: *Locke.* London, 1908.
Ch. Bastide: *John Locke. Les Theories Politiques.* Paris, 1906.
Cairns: *Unbelief in the Eighteenth Century.* London, 1881.
Curtis: *Outlines of Locke's Ethical Philosophy.* Leipzig, 1890.
Graham: *English Political Philosophy from Hobbes to Maine.* London, 1899.
T. H. Green: *Principles of Political Obligation. Phil. Works,* vol. II. London and New York, 1885–88.
Hunt: *History of Religious Thought in England.* London, 1873.
Kent: *The English Radicals.* London and New York, 1899.
V. Lechler: *Geschichte des Englischen Deismus.* Stuttgart, 1841.
F. Pollock: *Locke's Theory of the State.* Proceedings of British Academy, 1903–04.
F. Pollock: *History of the Science of Politics.* London, 1893.
H. Sidgwick: *History of Ethics.* London, 1886.
H. Sidgwick: *The Development of European Polity.* London, 1903.
Leslie Stephen: *History of English Thought in the Eighteenth Century.* London, 1876.
Leslie Stephen: *The English Utilitarians.* London, 1900.
Leslie Stephen: *Essays on Freethinking and Plainspeaking.* London, 1874.

CHRONOLOGICAL TABLE OF PHILOSOPHICAL WORKS IN THE AGE OF THE ENLIGHTENMENT

CHRONOLOGICAL TABLE OF PHILOSOPHICAL WORKS IN THE AGE OF THE ENLIGHTENMENT[1]

ENGLAND	FRANCE, HOLLAND, ITALY, SWITZERLAND	GERMANY
1689. John **Locke**, Epistola de tolerantia.	1689. Pierre Daniel **Huet**, Censura philosophiae Cartesianae.	
——, Two treatises on government.		
1690. ——, An essay concerning human understanding. Translated into French, 1700; into German, 1757.	1692. **Huet**, Nouveaux mémoires pour servir a l'histoire du Cartésianisme.	
1693. **Locke**, Some thoughts on education. In French, 1705; German, 1788.		1695. **Leibniz**, Système nouveau de la nature et de la communication des substances.
1695. ——, The reasonableness of christianity.	1697. Pierre **Bayle**, Dictionnaire historique et critique. In German, 1741–4.	
1696. John **Toland**, Christianity not mysterious.		1698. ——, De ipsa natura.

1705-6. Samuel **Clarke,** Demonstration of the being and attributes of God. In German, 1756.

1708. **Clarke,** Discourse concerning the unchangeable obligation of natural religion.

1709. George **Berkeley,** Essay towards a new theory of vision.

1710. **Berkeley,** Treatise concerning the principles of human knowledge.

1711. Anthony Earl of **Shaftesbury,** Characteristics of men, manners, opinions, times. In German, partly in 1745 and 1747; wholly in 1776-79.

1713. **Berkeley,** Three dialogues between Hylas and Philonous. In German, 1756.

1701. **Descartes,** Opera posthuma mathematica et physica.

1713. Jacob **Bernoulli,** Ars conjectandi. (Posthum.)

1705. Christian **Thomasius,** Fundamenta juris naturæ.

1708. **Leibniz,** Réflexions sur l'essai de l'entendement humain de Mr. Locke. Verfasst und an Locke gesandt 1696.

1710. ———, Essais de Théodicée sur la bonté de Dieu, la liberté de l'homme et l'origine du mal. In Latin, 1716; in German, 1720.

1712-25. Christian **Wolff,** Deutsche Schriften:
1712. Vernünftige Gedanken von den Kräften der menschlichen Verstandes.

---

[1] Adapted from *Litteratur zur Geschichte der Philosophie*, von C. Stumpf, Berlin, 1900.

ENGLAND	FRANCE, HOLLAND, ITALY, SWITZERLAND	GERMANY
Arthur **Collier**, Clavis universalis (Engl.). In German, 1756. Anthony **Collins**, Discourse of free-thinking.		
1714. Bernard de **Mandeville**, The fable of the bees, or private vices public benefits. II. Part, 1729.		
1715. **Collins**, Philosophical inquiry concerning human liberty.		
1717. **Clarke**, A collection of papers, which passed between Dr. Clarke and Mr. Leibnitz. In German, 1720.		1718. **Leibniz**, Principes de la nature et de la grâce fondés en raison.
	1719. Jean Baptiste **Dubos**, Réflexions critiques sur la poésie et la peinture.	
1720. **Toland**, Pantheisticon (Latin). In English, 1751.		1720. ——, Monadologie. 1840, in French (original). **Wolff**, Vernünftige Gedanken von Gott, der Welt und der Seele des Menschen.

——, Vernünftige Gedanken von der Menschen Thun und Lassen.
1721. ——, Vernünftige Gedanken von dem gesellschaftlichen Leben der Menschen.
1723. **Wolff,** Vernünftige Gedanken von den Wirkungen der Natur.
1728–53. **Wolff,** Lateinische Schriften: Philosophia rationalis sive logica.
1730. ——, Philosophia prima sive ontologia.
1731. ——, Cosmologia generalis.
1732. ——, Psychologia empirica.
1734. ——, Psychologia rationalis.

1723. **Huet,** Traité philosophique de la faiblesse de l'esprit humain. (Posthum.)
1725. Giovanni Battista **Vico,** Principj di una scienza nuova intorno alla commune natura delle nazioni.
1731. François Marie **Voltaire** (Arouet l. j.), Lettres philosophiques.

1722. William **Wollaston,** The religion of nature delineated. In French, 1726.
1725. Francis **Hutcheson,** An inquiry into the original of our ideas of beauty and virtue. In German, 1762.
1728. **Hutcheson,** Essay on the nature and conduct of the passions and affections. In German, 1760.
1732. **Berkeley,** Alciphron or the minute philosopher. In French, 1734; in German, 1737.

ENGLAND	FRANCE, HOLLAND, ITALY, SWITZERLAND	GERMANY
1736. Joseph **Butler,** The analogy of religion natural and revealed. In German, 1756.	**1736.** **Voltaire,** Examen important de Mylord Bolingbroke.	**1736-7.** ——, Theologia naturalis.
1738-40. David **Hume,** A treatise on human nature. In German, 1790-1.	**1738.** ——, Eléments de la philosophie de Newton.	**1738-9.** ——, Philosophia practica universalis.
		1739. Alex. Gottlieb **Baumgarten,** Metaphysica.
		1740-48. Wolff, Ius naturae.
1741-2. Hume, Essays moral and political. In French, 1764.	**1743.** Antonio **Genovesi,** Elementi di scienze metafisichi.	
	1745. Julien Offroy de **Lamettrie,** Histoire naturelle de l'âme.	**1745.** Christian August **Crusius,** Entwurf der nothwendigen Vernunftwahrheiten.
	1746. Charles **Batteux,** Les beaux arts réduits à un même principe.	
	Etienne Bonnot de **Condillac,** Essai sur l'origine des connaissances humaines.	

Denis **Diderot,** Pensées philosophiques. In German, 1747.	1747. **Crusius,** Weg zur Gewissheit und Zuverlässigkeit der menschlichen Erkenntniss.
1748. **Lamettrie,** L'homme machine. Charles de Secondat de **Montesquieu,** De l'esprit des lois. In German, 1753.	
1749. **Condillac,** Traité des systèmes. **Diderot,** Lettre sur les aveugles à l'usage de ceux qui voient. 1749-88. George Louis Leclerc de **Buffon,** Histoire naturelle générale et particulière.	1749. Immanuel **Kant,** Gedanken von der wahren Schätzung der lebendigen Kräfte. Gedruckt, 1746-49. **Wolff,** Ius gentium.
1750. Jean Jacques **Rousseau,** Discours sur les sciences et les arts. 1751-72. **Diderot** und Jean le Rond d'**Alembert,** Encyclopédie ou dictionnaire raisonné des sciences, des arts et des métiers (Discours préliminaire von d'Alembert).	1750-53. ———, Philosophia moralis. 1750-8. **Baumgarten,** Æsthetica.

1748. **Hume,** Philosophical essays concerning human understanding (Later title: Enquiry concerning human understanding). In German, 1755. 1749. David **Hartley,** Observations on man, his frame, his duty and his expectations. In German, 1772-3.	
1751. Henry **Home,** Essays on the principles of morality and natural religion. In German, 1768. **Hume,** Inquiry concerning the principles of morals. 1752. ———, Political discourses.	

ENGLAND	FRANCE, HOLLAND, ITALY, SWITZERLAND	GERMANY
1753-4. ——, Essays and treatises on general subjects. 1755. **Hutcheson**, System of moral philosophy. In German, 1756. 1756. Edmund **Burke**, Philosophical inquiry into the origin of our ideas of the sublime and the beautiful. In French, 1763; in German, 1773.	1754. **Condillac**, Traité des sensations. **Diderot**, Pensées sur l'interprétation de la nature. 1755. Charles **Bonnet**, Essai de psychologie (anonym). In German, 1773. **Condillac**, Traité des animaux. **Rousseau**, Discours sur l'origine et les fondements de l'inégalité parmi les hommes, 1756. 1756. **Voltaire**, Essai sur l'histoire générale et sur les mœurs et l'esprit des nations.	1755. **Kant**, Allgemeine Naturgeschichte und Theorie des Himmels (anonym). Moses **Mendelssohn**, Briefe über die Empfindungen. Herrmann Samuel **Reimarus**, Abhandlungen von den vornehmsten Wahrheiten der natürlichen Religion. 1756. **Reimarus**, Vernunftlehre.

LITERATURE

1757. **Hume,** Four dissertations: The natural history of religion; Of the passions; Of tragedy; Of the standard of taste.	1758. Claude Adrien **Helvetius,** De l'esprit. In German, 1758–59.	1759. Johann Georg **Hamann,** Sokratische Denkwürdigkeiten (anonym).
1759. Adam **Smith,** The theory of moral sentiments. In German, 1770.	1759. **d'Alembert,** Eléments de philosophie. **Voltaire,** Candide ou l'optimiste. In German, 1778.	1761. Johann Heinrich **Lambert,** Kosmologische Briefe. **Mendelssohn,** Philosophische Schriften.
	1761. Jean Baptiste **Robinet,** De la nature (anonym). In German, 1764.	1762. **Kant,** Die falsche Spitzfindigkeit der vier syllogistischen Figuren.
1762. **Home,** Elements of criticism. In German, 1763–66.	1762. **Rousseau,** Du contrat social ou principes du droit politique. In German, 1763. ———, Emile ou de l'éducation. In German, 1763.	1763. ———, Versuch, den Begriff der negativen Grössen in die Weltweisheit einzuführen. ———, Der einzig mögliche Beweisgrund zu einer Demonstration des Daseins Gottes.

ENGLAND	FRANCE, HOLLAND, ITALY, SWITZERLAND	GERMANY
1764. Thomas **Reid**, An inquiry into the human mind on the principles of common sense. In French, 1768; in German, 1782.	1764. Cesare **Beccaria**, Trattato dei delitti e delle pene. **Voltaire**, Dictionnaire philosophique.	1764. ——, Untersuchung über die Deutlichkeit der Grundsätze der natürlichen Theologie und Moral. ——, Beobachtungen über das Gefühl des Schönen und Erhabenen. **Lambert**, Neues Organon. **Mendelssohn**, Ueber die Evidenz in den metaphysischen Wissenschaften.
	1765. **Voltaire**, La philosophie de l'histoire.	1765. **Leibniz**, Nouveaux essais sur l'entendement humain (Posthum. Verfasst 1704).
		1766. **Kant**, Träume eines Geistersehers, erläutert durch Träume der Metaphysik. Gotthold Ephraim **Lessing**, Laokoon.

	1767.	Mendelssohn, Phaedon oder über die Unsterblichkeit der Seele.
	1767–69.	Lessing, Hamburgische Dramaturgie.
	1768.	Kant, Von dem ersten Grunde des Unterschiedes der Gegenden im Raume.
	1770.	——, De mundi sensibilis atque intelligibilis forma et principiis.
	1771–4.	Johann Georg Sulzer, Allgemeine Theorie der schönen Künste.
	1772.	Johann Gottfried Herder, Ueber den Ursprung der Sprache (anonym).
	1774–77.	Lessing, Wolfenbüttler Fragmente (Reimarus, Apologie oder Schutzschrift für die vernünftigen Verehrer Gottes. Posthum).

1767.	Robinet, Considérations philosophiques de la gradation naturelle des formes de l'être.	
1770.	Paul Heinrich Dietrich v. Holbach (Pseud. Mirabaud), Système de la nature. In German, 1783.	
1772.	Helvetius, De l'homme, de ses facultés et de son éducation. (Posthum.) In German, 1774.	
	Franz Hemsterhuis, Lettre sur l'homme et ses rapports.	

1769.	Adam Ferguson, Institutes of moral philosophy. In German, 1772.	
1770.	James Beattie, An essay on the nature and immutability of truth. In German, 1772.	
1775.	Joseph Priestley, Hartley's theory of human mind.	

ENGLAND	FRANCE, HOLLAND, ITALY, SWITZERLAND	GERMANY
1776. **Smith**, Inquiry into the nature and causes of the wealth of nations. In German, 1776.		1776–7. Johann Nicolaus **Tetens**, Philosophische Versuche über die menschliche Natur.
1777. **Priestley**, Disquisitions relating to matter and spirit.		
——, The doctrine of philosophical necessity.		
1778. ——, A free discussion of the doctrine of materialism and philosophical necessity.	1778. **Buffon**, Les époques de la nature.	
1779. **Hume**, Dialogues concerning natural religion. (Posthum.) In German, 1781.	1780. **Condillac**, La logique.	1780. **Lessing**, Die Erziehung des Menschengeschlechts.
		1781. **Kant**, Kritik der reinen Vernunft.
		1783. ——, Prolegomena zu einer jeden künftigen Metaphysik.

1784. ——, Idee zu einer allgemeinen Geschichte in weltbürgerlicher Absicht.

1784-91. **Herder,** Ideen zur Philosophie der Geschichet der Menschheit.

1785. Friedrich Heinrich **Jacobi,** Ueber die Lehre des Spinoza.

Kant, Grundlegung zur Metaphysik d. Sitten.

Mendelssohn, Morgenstunden oder Vorlesungen über das Dasein Gottes.

1786. **Kant,** Metaphysische Anfangsgründe der Naturwissenschaft.

1786f. Karl Leonhard **Reinhold,** Briefe über die Kantische Philosophie.

1787. **Jacobi,** David Hume über den Glauben oder Idealismus und Realismus.

Kant, Kritik der reinen Vernunft. 2. Auflage.

1785. William **Paley,** Principles of moral and political philosophy. In German, 1787. **Reid,** Essays on the intellectual powers of man.

ENGLAND	FRANCE, HOLLAND, ITALY, SWITZERLAND	GERMANY
1788. **Reid,** Essays on the active powers of man.		1788. ——, Kritik der praktischen Vernunft. 1788–90. Gottlob Ernst **Schulze,** Grundriss der philosophischen Wissenschaften. 1789. **Reinhold,** Versuch, einer neuen Theorie des menschlichen Vorstellungsvermögens. 1790. **Kant,** Kritik der Urtheilskraft.

INDEX

Abstract ideas, 59, 99.
Adamson, R., 55, 84, 110, 193, 251.
Albee, Ernest, 292.
d'Alembert, 126 f, 136.
Antinomies, Kantian, 244 f; mathematical, 245; dynamical, 245.
Alexander, S., 56, 292.
Appetition, 172.
A priori, 221 f, 224 ff, 229, 236.
d'Argenson, 140.
Aristotle, 169 f. n. 2.
Arnobius, 121.
Association of ideas, 114.
Associationism, 264.
Atheism, 19, 282.
Aufklärung, defined and described, 3 ff. See *Enlightenment*.

Bastide, Ch., 292.
Bayle, Pierre, 118.
Berkeley, 9 ff; idealism, chapter III; criticism of Locke, 59 ff; theory of perception, 62 ff; idea of existence, 65; idea of God, 66 f; idea of substance as spiritual, 68 f; idea of causation, 69 f; idea of the symbolic language of nature, 70 f; idea of the laws of nature, 70 f; idea of substance as spiritual, 72 f; distinction between *idea* and *notion*, 73 ff; later idealism in the *Siris*, 75 ff; relation to Kant, 81 f.
Berkeley in America, 83 f; his criticism of Mandeville, 265 f; criticism of Shaftesbury, 269.
Bolingbroke, Lord, 276.
Bordeu, 128.
Bourne, Fox, H. R., 55.
Bruno, Giordano, 170 f. n.
Burke, Edmund, 283.
Burton, J. H., 110, 139.

Cabanis, 134.
Caird, 151 f. n. 2, 160, 251.
Cairns, 292.
Canon of philosophical criticism 40 f.
Cassirer, Ernst, 193.
Categorical imperative, 284.
Categories of Kant, 236.
Causation, 90 f, 102 f, 176, 183 f.
Chubb, Thomas, 276.
Collins, Anthony, 41, 275.
Condillac, 120 f, 138.
Contrat Social, 148, 282 f.
Copernican method of Kant, 239.
Coste, Pierre, 119.
Cousin, 56.
Couturat, Louis, 165 f. n. 2, 193.
Critical method, 222.
Curtis, 292.

Darwin, Erasmus, 10.
Deism, 19, 254, 272 ff.
Descartes, 7, 13, 166, 216.
Dewey, John, 193.
Diderot, Denis, 10, 124 ff, 138, 146, 271, 279.
Dillmann, E., 193.
Ding-an-Sich, 239.
Dissertation, Kant's, 219 ff, 285.
Duncan, Geo. M., 193.

Edwards, Jonathan, 83.
Empiricism, 15 f, 161, 184, 213, 215, 217, 223, 236.
Encyclopædists, 10, 136, 138.
Engel, 210.
Enlightenment, defined and described, 3 ff; Kant on, 24; in England, 25 ff; in France, 111 ff; in Germany, 194 ff; practical influences of, 253.
Entelechy, 169.

INDEX

Epistola de Tolerantia, Locke, 27.
de L'Espinasse, Mademoiselle, 128.
Evolution, 190 f, 202, 208.

Fatalism, 247.
Ferrier, James F., 84.
Filmer, Sir R., 280.
Fischer, Kuno, 24, 193, 252.
Fowler, T., 56.
Francke, 195.
Fraser, A. C., 56, 84.
Frederick the Great, 201.

Galiani, 133.
Germany, *Aufklärung* in, chapter VIII.
Gerardin, Saint Marc, 160.
Gervinus, G. G., 214.
God, Kantian *Idea* of, 246–249; Locke's idea of, 51 f; Berkeley's idea of, 66 f; Locke's idea of God as ground of morality, 258.
Goethe, 133, 203.
Graham, 292.
Green, T. H., 56, 84, 108, 110, 160, 292.
Green and Grose, 89 f. n., 110.

Hamilton, Alexander, 283.
Hartley, 10, 112 f, 264 f.
Haym, R., 207 f, 214.
Hegelian movement of thought in eighteenth century, 8 f.
Hegel, 24, 37.
van Helmont, F. M., 170 f. n.
Helvetius, 10, 122, 138.
Herder, 197, 200, 206 ff, 271, 280.
Herz, Marcus, 220.
Hettner, H., 24, 135, 214, 271.
Hobbes, 281.
Höffding, 160.
Holbach, 10 f, 117, 131 ff, 138, 279, 282.
Hume, David, relation to the *Enlightenment*, 11 f; on Locke's theistic proof, 53; on abstract ideas, 60; his scepticism, chapter IV; his argument a *reductio ad absurdum* of Locke's position, 86 f; relation to Kant, 88; beginnings of knowledge in impressions and ideas, 88 f; fundamental canon of criticism, 89 f; causation, 90 ff; substance, 93 ff; criticism of Berkeley, 95; doctrine of self, 95 ff; scepticism as a transition stage in knowledge, 98; criticism of, 99 ff; function of imagination, 100; sceptical of his own position, 102 ff; theory of perception, 104; relation to Kant, 105 f; Green's estimate of, 108; Reid concerning, 108 f; on Rousseau, 139; his moral philosophy, 259 f; on sympathy, 261 f; on association of ideas as basis of our moral concepts, 264; on natural religion, 276 f; on miracles, 278; Kant on his view of causation, 226 f; on *Contrat Social*, 283.
Hunt, 292.
Huxley, 84, 87, 110.

Ideas as *archetypes*, 50; as *ectypes*, 50; abstract ideas, 59, 99; Berkeley's distinction between *idea* and *notion*, 73 ff; relation to impressions 88 f; Kantian *Ideas* of Reason, 241 f;
Identity of indiscernibles, 171.
Imagination and knowledge, 100 f.
Immanence of God, 21 f.
Individualism, 19 f, 254.
Intellectualism. See Rationalism.
Intellectualism of Locke, 39 f.

Jacobi, 200.
Johnson, Samuel, 83.
Judgment, analytic, 225, 234; the Kantian types, 236; synthetic, 225, 234.

Kant, *Critique of Pure Reason*, 3; his contribution to the philosophy of the *Enlightenment*, 14 ff; on *Was ist Aufklärung?*, 24; relation of Berkeley to, 75, 81; relation to Hume, 88, 104 ff; indebtedness to Rousseau, 159; completed work of Leibniz, 188; on the *Enlightenment*, 194; relation to Martin Knutzen, 196; the preparation for his critical philosophy, 213; the philosophy

of, chapter IX; his preparation for his task, 216; his mediating tendency, 216; periods of his philosophical progress, 217; the various publications of these periods, 218; his break with Leibniz, 219; inaugural dissertation, 219; differs from Leibniz regarding the sensible and intelligible worlds, 219; letter to Marcus Herz, 220; the intellect in sense-perception, 221; philosophy as "critical," 222; the logic of limits, 222; "transcendental" logic, 222 *f;* the critical method, 222; *a priori*, 222; transcendental method, 223 *f;* analytic and synthetic judgments, 225; possibility of synthetic judgments *a priori?*, 226; Hume's view of causation, 226 *f;* the metaphysic of induction, 227 *f;* synthetic character of the causal idea, 229; function of thought in acquiring knowledge, 230; differs from Locke, 230; divisions of the *Critique*, 231; space and time, 233 *ff;* the truths of geometry, 234; reality of space and time, 235; the categories, 236 *ff;* empiricism and rationalism complementary, 237 *f;* phenomena and noumena, 238 *f; Ding-an-sich*, 239; Copernican method, 239; possibility of a metaphysic, 240; *Verstand* and *Vernunft*, 240; the *Ideas* of Reason, 241; relation to syllogistic process, 241; follows Leibniz's idea of substance, 242; *Idea* of self, 243; *Idea* of world, 244; antinomies, 244 *ff; Idea* of God, 246 *f;* regulative use of the *Ideas*, 246; relation of *Ideas* to materialism, naturalism, fatalism, 247; *Critique of the Practical Reason*, 248 *f;* noumenal aspect of our moral nature, 248; postulates of the practical reason, 249 *f;* the *Critique of Judgment*, 249 *f;* teleology, 250; teleology, *Critique of Judgment*, 250; synthesis of theoretical and practical reason, 250; summary, 251; on practical influences of the *Enlightenment*, 283 *ff.*
Kent, 292.
King, Lord, 55.
Knight, William, 110.
Knowledge of reality, 44 *f.*
Knowledge and imagination, 100 *f.*
Knutzen, Martin, 196.

Lagrange, 131.
Lamettrie, 121, 123 *f*, 131, 132, 267.
Lange, 121, 135.
Latta, R., 169 *f. n.* 2, 193.
LeClerc, 118 *f*, 271.
Lechler, V., 292.
Leibniz, Gottfried Wilhelm, relation to the *Enlightenment*, 13 *f;* criticism of Locke, 38 *f;* the *Nouveaux Essais*, 56; differs from Kant regarding sensible and intelligible worlds, 119; his philosophical system, chapter VIII; relation to Locke, 161 *ff;* ideas born of reason, 163; deduction of truth, 164; symbolic logic, 164 *f;* doctrine of substance, 166; departure from Descartes, 166; substance as a force centre, 167; logical deduction of nature of substance, 168; self as substance, 168 *f;* entelechy, 169; monadology, 170 *ff;* identity of indiscernibles, 171; appetition, 172; independence of monads, 172 *f;* representative function of the monads, 173; perception, 174; mathematical concept of function, 175; idea of causation, 176; pre-established harmony, 177 *ff;* mind and body, 181 *ff;* parallelism, 183; efficient and final causes, 183 *f;* world of nature and world of divine purpose, 184; empiricism and rationalism, 184 *f;* the external world, 186; innate ideas, 186; suprasensible element in perception, 187; divine concurrence, 187; relation to Kant, 188; individualism of the monad, 188; com-

bination of monads, 189; idea of evolution, 190; harmony of universe, 192; synthesis of empirical and rationalistic elements, 192; influence upon philosophical thought, 193; influence in Germany, 194; relation to Wolff, 198 *ff*; Kant on Leibniz and Descartes, 216; relation to Kant, 219; idea of substance as used by Kant, 242; relation to Shaftesbury, 271; his idea of God, 280 *f*.
Lessing, 200 *ff*, 271, 280.
Levy-Bruhl, 135, 160.
Locke, John, the *Essay*, 3 *ff*; beginnings of the *Enlightenment*, 6 *f*; influence of, 9; relation to Hume, 11; relation to Leibniz, 13; relation to Kant, 16; practical results, 19 *f*; his inner and outer world, chapter II; origin of the essay, 26; the method of, 27; on sensation and reflection, 29; regards mind as passive in sensation, 31; its activity later is mechanical, 34; idea of infinity, 37; Leibniz's criticism of, 38; intellectualism of, 39; idea of the self, 42 *f*; his outer world, 44; his idea of reality of knowledge, 44; primary and secondary qualities of matter, 46; on substance, 48; proof of being of God, 51 *ff*; view of causal relation, 53; influence of, 55; influence on Berkeley, 58 *f*; Berkeley's criticism of Locke's distinction between primary and secondary qualities, 60; relation to Hume, 85 *ff*; Reid's criticism, 109; influence on the materialistic philosophy, chapter V; relation to Leibniz, 161 *ff*; influence in Germany, 195; influence on Kant, 219; how his theory of knowledge differs from that of Kant, 230; ethics of, 254 *f*; his utilitarianism, 254 *f*, 259; relation to Hume as regards system of ethics, 259; relation to Shaftesbury, 270; the deism of, 273 *f*; on government, 280 *f*.

Lowell, J. R., 160.
Luther, 196.

Macdonald, Frederika, 160.
McCosh, J., 56, 84, 110.
Mackintosh, J., 24.
de Malesherbes, 146.
Mandeville, 265, 267.
Materialism, 10, 247, 267, chapter V.
Mendelssohn, Moses, 210, 211, 271.
Merz, J. T., 193, 214.
Metaphysics, *in the Enlightenment*, 4, 17; in Locke's philosophy, 43, 46, 54; in Berkeley, 81 *f*; in Hume, 105 *f*; in Leibniz, 166 *ff*; according to Kant, 240 *ff*.
Mill, James, 265.
Mill, John Stuart, 84, 265.
Mind and body, 181 *ff*.
Molyneux, William, 57, 256.
Montesquieu, 282.
Moore, A. W., 56.
Morgan, Thomas, 276.
Morley, John, 119, 135, 142, 158, 160.
Morris, George S., 252.

Naigeon, 131.
Naturalism, 247.
Newton, 113.
Nicolai, 210, 212.

Osborn, H. F., 191.

Paley, 258.
Parallelism, 183 *f*.
Parmenides, 79.
Paulsen, F., 252.
Perception, 174.
Pfleiderer, E., 110.
Pietism, 195 *ff*.
Plato, 219.
Platonic idealism, 78 *f*.
Pollock, Frederick, 292.
Pope, 5, 211.
Pre-established harmony, 177 *ff*.
Price, 282.
Priestley, Joseph, 10, 116 *f*, 132, 282.

INDEX 311

Primary qualities of matter, 46 ff, 60 ff.
Pringle-Pattison, A. S., 110.

Raison commune, 151.
Rationalism, 14 f, 161 f, 184, 213, 215, 217, 223, 236.
Reason, pure, 3, 16, 81, 88, 222 ff; 232; practical, 16 f, 248, 289.
Reid, Thomas, 56, 108.
Reimarus, 203, 279.
Reflection, as source of knowledge, 30 f.
Remond, 184.
Riehl, A., 24, 25.
Rosenkranz, 124, 125, 129, 130, 135.
Rousseau, Jean Jacques, influence upon Kant, 16 f; relation to the *Enlightenment*, 20; opinion of Holbach, 134; chapter VI, early materialism, 136; reaction from materialistic tendencies, 138; philosophy of feeling, 139 ff; his mysticism, 143 f; man not a mere machine, 144; the *Discourses*, 145 ff; *Contrat Social* 148 f; feeling and intellect, 150 f; *Raison commune*, 151; *volonté générale*, 152; individualism, 152 ff; *Confessions*, 153 f; feeling and action, 154 f; pragmatism, 157; influence upon Kant, 158 ff; influence in Germany, 195; on deism, 279; *Contrat Social*, 282; Kant's interpretation of *Contrat Social*, 290 f.
Royce, Josiah, 252.
Russell, Bertrand, 193.

Sainte Beuve, 160.
Savoyard, Vicar, 141 f, 150, 279.
Scepticism, 14, chapter IV.
Schiller, 271.
Schinz, A., 157 f. n. 1.
Secondary qualities of matter, 46 ff, 60 ff.
Sensation as source of knowledge, 29 f.
Sensationalism, 120, 138.

Shaftesbury, 268 ff.
Sidgwick, H., 292.
Sime, J., 214.
Smith, Adam, theory of morals, 262 f.
Space, Kant's view of, 233.
Spener, 195.
Spinoza, 13, 280.
Stirling, J. H., 252.
Stephen, L., 24, 283, 292.
Stern, L., 170 f. n.
Stewart, Dugald, 56, 84.
Stillingfleet, 42, 50, 54.
Streckeisen-Moultou, 160.
Substance, Locke's idea of, 48 f; Berkeley's idea of, 59 ff; Hume's idea of, 93 ff; 102 f; Leibniz's idea of, 166 f, 237, 242.
Swift, Dean, 275.
Syllogistic process in the Kantian *Ideas* of reason, 241.

Tetens, J. N., 212.
Texte, Joseph, 160.
Thomasius, 210.
Timæus, 79.
Time, Kant's view of, 233.
Tindal, Matthew, 275.
Toland, J., 274.
Transcendence of God, 21.
Transcendental method, 223 f.
Treatises on government, Locke, 27.

Utilitarianism, 19, 254 f, 258, 265.

Vernunft, 240.
Verstand, 240.
Vibrations of brain molecules, 115 f.
Volonté générale, 290.
Voltaire, 36, 119, 132, 252, 279.

Wallace, W., 252.
Watson, J., 252.
Webb, T. E., 39 f, 56.
Windelband, W., 24.
Wolff, Christian, 13, 14, 194, 197 ff, 218.